Get Along!

WITH

ANYONE
ANYTIME
ANYWHERE

8 Keys to Creating Enduring Connections

with Customers, Co-workers... *even Kids!*

www.GetAlongWithAnyone.com

New York

Arnold Sanow and Sandra Strauss

Library of Congress Cataloging-in-Publication Data
Sanow, Arnold.
  Get along with anyone, anytime, anywhere! : 8 keys to creating enduring connections with customers,
co-workers ... even kids! / Arnold Sanow and Sandra Strauss.-- 1st ed.
  p. cm.
Includes bibliographical references.
  ISBN 978-1-60037-219-3
  1. Interpersonal relations--Handbooks, manuals, etc. 2. Social psychology--Handbooks, manuals, etc.
I. Strauss, Sandra. II. Title.
  HM1111.S26 2004
  302--dc22
                                    2003018022

Published by:

MORGAN · JAMES
THE ENTREPRENEURIAL PUBLISHER ™
www.morganjamespublishing.com

Morgan James Publishing, LLC
1225 Franklin Ave. Ste 325
Garden City, NY 11530-1693
Toll Free 800-485-4943
www.MorganJamesPublishing.com

**Habitat
for Humanity®**
Peninsula
Building Partner

First edition, 2004
Book and cover design by Syzygy Media (Silver Spring, Maryland)
Cover photos by Philip Kent (Vienna, Virginia)

Disclaimer

Note to readers: This book contains information, suggestions, and opinions from the authors. It is
intended to provide helpful and informative material on the subject matter covered. The use, misuse or
interpretation of the material, in whole or part, is the sole responsibility of the reader.

The publisher and authors assume no responsibility for errors or omissions. Neither is any liability
assumed for any emotional or material loss, damage or injury caused, or alleged to be caused, directly
or indirectly from the use and application of information contained in this book.

If a reader requires personal assistance or advice, professional counseling and/or legal services should
be consulted.

Acknowledgements and Dedication

One of the fundamental concepts of creating enduring connections is acknowledging the valuable contributions that people provide in support of our goals. Both of us always try to "walk our talk" and "practice what we preach." With that connecting spirit in mind, it gives us immense pleasure to thank some of our very special "connections" who have shared their wisdom, time, talent and enthusiasm to bring this book to life.

In Dedication

To Nancy Burke Sanow, my wife, who provided encouragement, insight and valuable suggestions and to my son, Stephen Sanow, who teaches me great lessons on some of the best ways of how to "get along." I would like to acknowledge all members of my mastermind group: Ron Culberson, Lynn Waymon, Mariah Burton Nelson and Rick Mauer who were instrumental in providing me with guidance and keeping me focused.

Arnold Sanow

To Rick, Stephanie and Stacy Strauss, for getting in the "get along" groove and the enduring connections we've forged. Your love is always an adventure, an inspiration and an abundant source of joy and wonder ("I wonder how best to handle this situation!");

To my brother and sister, Art and Connie, for sensational sibling "revelry;"

To my "forever friends" whose gifts of friendship provide pure bliss;

To Mom, the most perfect teacher of the art of getting along.

Sandra Conrad Strauss

Acknowledgements

Both of us would like to thank the circle of talented professionals who were instrumental to the creation of this book (all of whom "got along" great in all phases of production):

Katherine Hutt, of Nautilus Communications, for your vision, genius, and support;

Sandi Holt for your editing expertise and sharing your words of wisdom in the most skillful ways;

Wardell and Rosi Parker, the dynamic duo of SYZYGY Media, artists and designers who literally brought the art of getting along to life;

Sam Horn whose brilliance brought the title to life.

We dedicate this book to all who wish to enjoy positive and productive connections at work, at home, and everywhere!

Foreword

Getting along with people is a life-long endeavor. While it can be exceptionally challenging at times, the rewards for success are great. Good relationships are vital to our well being and make a big difference in our effectiveness—at work, with family, with friends—in all our connections.

As President of the National Association for Self-Esteem, I am keenly aware of the value of helping people build positive relationships that satisfy mutual needs and foster self-worth. Mutual respect and trust are valuable **end products** from cultivating caring relationships. When we create positive climates with and for others, we benefit by increasing the likelihood of getting our own needs met.

Getting along is not about giving in or giving up. It's about claiming our personal power while we build positive connections with others.

Wherever we go in life there are situations that test our "get along" skills. Perhaps we find it challenging to get along comfortably in business or social settings. We might feel uncomfortable establishing limits and boundaries. We encounter people who irritate and annoy us. We must deal with others who don't listen or even try to understand our needs. We may suffer from put-downs. All these situations—and more—sap our energy and drain our power. **When we experience such things, we often forget to tap the truth of who we are and the unlimited possibilities that life has to offer.**

This book takes us to places where getting along is vital—at work, with co-workers and colleagues; with customers and clients; and with our families and friends— wherever we go. It's a book about choices for building valued, long-lasting relationships in every circle of influence.

In every situation, you make a choice about what you think and do, about the quality of connection you want, and the actions required to create them. Get Along provides guidance for making your choices work for you so you can create positive, powerful, productive connections.

While there are plenty of books about relationships, Get Along offers the tools for doing just that in an engaging, easy-to-read style. Sanow and Strauss offer insights and wisdom you can put to work instantly. They understand the "art" of getting along!

I encourage you to take these tools and apply them. Build quality relationships with them that empower others and, at the same time, get your needs met, so go out there and get along!

Sharon S. Fountain, President
National Association for Self-Esteem

Table of Contents

Introduction
Enduring Connections Count!

An Enduring Connection *is a valuable relationship,*
long-lasting in nature, created with intent to honor needs and
sustained by choices to respect them.

Wouldn't you agree that life is about quality connections? Our success, happiness, and well-being are largely the by-products of our ability to get along well with others and cultivate positive relationships. By revving up the connecting spirit, we attract cherished friendships, valuable relationships, memorable moments, and an abundance of opportunities throughout our circles of influence. At the same time, we reduce the numbers of misunderstandings and conflicts that cost us dearly whether in the form of frustration, confusion, stress, lost revenue, heartache, headaches, or other draining experiences.

Connections—each one is unique, intertwined into our lives for different reasons and reflecting the multiple roles we play. Here are just a few examples from our personal and professional slice-of-life connections, which illustrate the endless opportunities generated by the connecting spirit.

Sandy's list looks like this:

- Years ago, I consulted with an organization regarding their communications programs and developed a synergistic connection with their communications director. When Paige told me that she was leaving to start her own consulting business, I suggested the possibility of us continuing our creative collaboration. As a result of sustaining that connection, we've had the good fortune to develop programs for many clients and we've both benefited by expanding our mutual networks and businesses.

- I tracked down the illustrators of my first book published nearly two decades ago, to illustrate this one. Their "service is our art" style coupled with their wit, wisdom and engaging personalities made an enduring impression on me.

- The local chapter of the National Speakers Association requested that members share the names of their favorite vendors for a directory of professional services. I responded with the names of some of the people I've worked with over the years who I totally trust to deliver quality work, and who are exceptionally service-oriented—a perfect demonstration of how good people skills and a focus on customer service multiplies your networks!

- Recently in celebration of Mothers' Day, each of my two teenage daughters wrote a tribute reflecting on what our mother-daughter relationship has meant to them. They shared from their hearts memorable moments of love, laughter, and favorite family traditions, from handmade Valentines to our heart-to-heart talks. Some of these became what my girls now affectionately refer to as "Mommy lectures," when I talked my heart out with the intent of "getting through" to them about the importance of getting along with others. Luckily, that huge investment of time and energy paid off— I hit the "mother lode!" Now as young women, they did indeed "get it" as I now see them adeptly navigating their way with their friends, classmates, and co-workers, not to mention the continuing opportunities for pumping up "get along" power at home—the eternal source of learning lessons in enduring connections! The importance of building positive relationships and guidance in how to construct them, is now part of their legacy to pass along for creating enduring connections in their circles of influence.

- After years of envisioning a new church facility and endless fundraisers to make it possible, our congregation recently celebrated the opening of our spacious sanctuary. It took nearly two decades of relationship-building to make that building possible.

- Recently, one of my clients asked me to provide a reference as part of her interview process with a prospective new employer due to our excellent working relationship. She recently landed the job and sees many opportunities for us working together again in her new position. (You never know where your connections might lead, offering totally new sources of business or whatever you may desire!)

- One of my childhood friendships from elementary school in California blossomed into a working relationship decades later in Virginia. After high school graduation, Elaine and I attended different colleges and lost touch with each other. My career took me first to Iowa, then Atlanta, and finally to Washington, D.C. At the time of our 10-year high school reunion, Elaine was still living in California but preparing to move to Washington, and she learned from one of our former classmates that I had also relocated there. When she called, we were both surprised to discover that we were both involved in the same field of consumer education. We re-ignited our friendship, and celebrated the births of our children, shared holidays, and marked many other milestones together.

  A few years later, I told Elaine about an opening at the association I was working for at the time. She got the job and we worked together for several years. Eventually, we both left the association; she recently recommended me for a consulting job where she now works. Our connection endures. In fact, our two daughters now attend the same college and are even in a class together. What a full circle! We share a precious connection to experiences from another time and another place, and are touchstones to each other's past.

Here are some of Arnold's connections:

- When Sandy and I met at a place called the Success Center, we discovered our common background in marketing, communications, and as former corporate spokespersons. Over the years, we have shared advice, ideas, challenges, and lots of laughter. We trust, respect, and like each other, and both of our professional networks have widened as a result. Through our mutual interest in effective communications and building positive relationships, we developed *Charisma Cards* (a deck of cards listing 50 ways to radiate a powerful presence and develop compelling connections). We've had a number of opportunities to refer each other to different clients. Our connection has been enriching in a multitude of ways.

- Several years ago, at the annual meeting of the National Speakers Association (NSA), I met a fellow speaker named Ron Davis. We

started talking and I was fascinated by his background. Not only was he one of the founders of the NSA, he was also the president of Security Associates, a trade organization for security alarm dealers. After the meeting, Ron said he had enjoyed our conversation and wanted to know if I would be interested in being the keynote speaker at his association's conference in Las Vegas. He did not ask for any of the usual references requested of speakers; he had confidence in my abilities based on the rapport we had already established. After the conference in Las Vegas, Ron and I continued to keep in contact. I later returned the favor and promoted him for a speaking job. Because I helped him and continued to maintain our relationship, he again offered me the opportunity to be the keynote speaker at the conference, the following year. A perfect example of what goes around, comes around!

- Over the years, I have kept in touch with five friends from elementary school. We went to middle school and high school, and spent our undergraduate college years together as well. Through this circle of friends, I have met many acquaintances who have since become friends. I even introduced one of the original five to a woman I thought he'd like—who later became his wife! We continue to meet at each others' homes, have helped each other out of jams, and our kids have become friends, too. Every year, we spend a weekend together to reflect on that year and share our goals and dreams for the next one. These enduring connections have served as a lifelong support team, and this bond continues to grow, becoming stronger and even more valued every year.

- As a result of the mutual trust and respect I share with many of my fellow speakers, we've developed a valuable network of colleagues and advisors—and friends. Over the years, we've made it a point to share referrals, contacts, and other beneficial resources with each other. This *quid pro quo* arrangement has resulted not only in the expansion of our businesses, it has also helped cultivate a supportive and encouraging environment for our professional and personal growth.

- One day our nanny, Ginger, was cleaning my office and noticed my speaking materials. She mentioned to me that her son-in-law, George, was the vice president of finance at a local university. Three weeks later, he called and wanted to know if I could provide a training program in presentation skills for some of his office staff. As a result, I not only developed a number of training programs for the university, but my connection with George has generated other opportunities as well as a highly valued friendship.

- While attending a networking event at a conference, I struck up a conversation with a fellow participant. He shared some of his thoughts about the speaker we had just heard, and I told him I was also a speaker. We developed an instant rapport, shared a few laughs, and exchanged cards. Five years later, I received a phone call from him. He was now responsible for making arrangements for an upcoming meeting; he had remembered our conversation and booked me because of the impression I had made years earlier. Enduring impressions make enduring connections!

- When one of my friends was looking for work, I arranged for him to meet with someone I knew would be a perfect contact for him. I met with them both, made introductions, and even paid for the coffee— thereby cementing two connections. Now, whenever I need a favor, they're more than willing to help me.

- At a recent party, I told a woman that I was co-writing a book about getting along. She said she was having trouble with her staff and could really use some help in that area. We exchanged cards, and two days later I was hired to lead a retreat for her organization.

... and the wheels of connection go round and round! In the last twenty years, we've had the pleasure and privilege of sharing the people-connecting skills contained in this book with corporations, associations, government agencies, and nonprofit organizations, as well as with our families, friends, colleagues, and even complete strangers. We know they work. We have studied the attitudes and actions of those who radiate "get along" power, and have identified exactly how they're able to so positively influence and empower others.

If you would like to:

- Gain instant rapport with any individual

- Widen your influence

- Build a powerful, engaging presence

- Expand your network of personal and professional connections
- Project a confident image
- Maintain the interest, respect, and trust of others
- Construct healthy and meaningful relationships
- Strengthen existing relationships
- Reduce tension and stress from energy-draining dynamics
- Manage conflicts proficiently
- Handle prickly behaviors
- Repair and restore disconnections
- Enjoy enduring connections

... and so much more—you're in the right place, because that's exactly what we're going to discuss. We promise not to waste your time on abstract theories that have no relevance to the real world. We know you're busy, so we promise to share tangible information that you can use immediately to engage interest, enhance cooperation, and increase your circle of influence.

These techniques have the power to produce many valuable, long-term benefits. In fact, we've seen almost miraculous results when people commit to improving their "connect-ability." We know that you, too, can enjoy more meaningful relationships and a more fulfilling, satisfying life, if you apply the suggestions you find in this book.

We're glad that you've invested the time and energy to buy this book; it is our sincere hope that you find it interesting and useful in pumping up your Get Along power and creating quality connections. This book is designed so you can extract nuggets of value quickly and easily—so read it and reap!

To your success,
Arnold Sanow & Sandra Strauss

Why the Need to Get Along is So Strong

The Connected Environment

Humans are creatures of community and thrive best in nurturing environments that promote connection and cooperation. Throughout every stage of our lives, supportive relationships play a significant role in contributing to our well-being, self-esteem, health, and quality of life. Living and working in a connected environment, whether among individuals or within organizations, is essential for the "right stuff" to root—only then do people bloom into their best.

Getting along is energizing. We thrive in climates that cultivate the connecting spirit and the excellence it inspires. On the flip side, disharmony disrupts and destroys, creating chaos that crushes cooperation, creativity, and our spirits. When we live, work, or interact in a demoralized, unsupportive environment, our needs go unmet, and harmful things can happen to our health, vitality, and relationships.

Many studies conducted around the world during the last several decades have validated the healthful role played by the human "connection factor" of feeling supported, cared about, and appreciated. Functioning in a compassionate atmosphere significantly reduces our risk of getting sick, whether from colds or cancer (and not surprisingly, heart disease) as well as other life-threatening illnesses.

According to research reported by Dean Ornish, M.D., in his book Love and Survival, loneliness and isolation increase the likelihood of disease and premature death from all causes by 200 to 500 percent or more, regardless of diet, smoking, or other risk-related behaviors. A number of large-scale, community-based studies examining the relationship

between social isolation, death, and disease from all causes were conducted around the world over a 15-year period. The research revealed that those who were socially isolated had from two to five times the risk of premature death when compared to those who had a strong sense of connection. We are creatures of community and our need for connection is at the very core of our being.

People who lack supportive relationships often make destructive lifestyle choices, choices that jeopardize their physical, emotional, and mental health. In addition, when people are subjected to chronic energy-draining interactions with others, the corresponding stress wreaks havoc on their bodies, minds, and hearts. Not getting along extracts an exceptionally high price indeed.

Throughout our lifetime, relationships that nurture and support us are vital, and especially critical to the healthy development of children and teens. Creating an emotionally "safe haven" is fundamental to fostering their feelings of self-worth and well-being, and to cultivating caring relationships as they grow. Supportive relationships at home and school have proven to dramatically influence children's choices and attitudes. Research from the National Longitudinal Health Study of Adolescent Health reveals that parent-child connectedness is the number one factor in helping to reduce the risk of teens participating in harmful, addictive, or destructive behaviors; school connectedness runs a close second.

Genuine connectedness is built on caring, concern, and commitment to nurturing the universal need for love, acceptance, and a sense of belonging. Plus, when parents focus on building supportive connections, kids are more likely to listen and follow their guidance. Endearing connectedness forges the most treasured enduring connections.

The need for connectedness carries into the world of work. Feeling connected and valued within the workplace is vital for bringing out the best in the workforce, cultivating peak productivity and performance. According to Jerry Harvey, Ph.D., professor of management science in the School of Business and Public Management at George Washington University, without the benefit of supportive relationships, a melancholy manifests itself in the workplace. He compares this to a condition observed in children who are separated from their mothers with corresponding anxiety and sadness called anaclitic depression.

Dr. Harvey uses this same term in his book, *The Abilene Paradox,* to describe the anxiety employees feel when separated from those they lean on for support. In these environments, communication is ineffective and employee needs go unmet. Feeling alienated and powerless from real decision-making can lead to a condition called *marasmus* or "wasting away," a deterioration of employee morale, motivation, creativity, and commitment—all of which are required for satisfactory performance and a rewarding work experience. Without supportive working relationships, this deadly form of organizational cancer is likely to have a metastastic impact on an organization's vitality. Working under these conditions becomes more like an act of survival and creates a wasteland of talent, potential, and productivity.

Getting along and enjoying caring relationships is indeed good medicine for our health, well-being, and success—at work, at home, and in all of our connections. After all, having supportive relationships is what doctors recommend, whether they're specialists in physical, social, or organizational systems. Research confirms that for us to thrive, connectedness is an essential requirement, and connectedness is about getting to the heart of our universal need to be nurtured, supported, and sustained. That most definitely is in harmony with the needs of every heart.

The Business of Bringing Out the Best

"In organizations, real power and energy is generated through relationships. The patterns of relationships and the capacities to form them are more important than tasks, functions, roles, and positions."

Margaret Wheatley

Building positive connections with both colleagues and customers is a boon to business. A cooperative spirit cultivates a culture that brings out the best in people and performance, keeping employees happy, energized, and productive. When we work well together, everything works better at work, and that carries into our contacts with clients and customers. That same spirit also pumps up profit potential. When smiling, satisfied customers say glowing things about a company's products or services, other consumers or clients are motivated to seek them out, increasing the company's market share.

Good interpersonal skills boost the bottom line in many ways—by helping to retain employees, improve morale, win new customers, seal deals, close sales, land clients, create a loyal following, secure repeat business, expand networks, increase job satisfaction, and more.

As customers, the feelings we experience in a business-customer connection are long-remembered. We recall how we were treated, how others made us feel, whether our needs were satisfied, what we thought about the people we interacted with, what the overall experience was like, and our general impressions. These satisfying customer experiences have such an enduring quality that we sometimes recollect this bundle of memories (and often recount them to others) years later.

In our role as consumers, with so many available choices, our satisfaction is largely determined by the perceived value we receive from the people who provide the goods and services we choose and whether they met our needs. If they do, they win our approval and probably our repeat business. If they don't, the business is bound to lose plenty—its customers, its reputation, and ultimately, its ability to sustain a profitable market share. The stakes are high when businesses are disconnected from what others seek. It pays to connect and collect all the benefits from doing so.

Our collective choices regarding how and where we spend our money and whom we choose as our merchants, vendors, contractors, agents, business partners, and others in the world of business all affect the bottom line. When those choices affect your bottom line, whether in the form of earnings, market share, a commission check, or a paycheck, building enduring connections becomes very personal indeed!

Keeping Connected in a Connection-Challenged World

"The more elaborate our means of communication,
the less we communicate."

Joseph Priestley

As we increasingly live in the fast lane, a few road signs might be useful to guide us along the way—words warning us when good connections are being overlooked, threatened, or endangered. Some possibilities might include: Yield to Connection, Stop to Connect, or Use Caution! Relationships at Work. Following these signs could make the paths we travel more satisfying, as well as directing us to some fascinating and fulfilling destinations we might have otherwise missed. These are signs for our times to keep us focused on the proper care required to cultivate good connections.

Our personal "connect-ability" is at risk of erosion more than ever from a culture being transformed by technology and increasing anonymity. The more plugged in we've become for the sake of speed and convenience, the more our once-traditional connecting points for personal relationships are disappearing. Our high-tech culture has ushered in bittersweet experiences; it has made connection faster and more fleeting, yet we're reaping more frequent episodes of disconnected humanity, a danger whose consequences may be more far-reaching than we suspect.

Phone calls and meetings are increasingly replaced by e-mails, which may leave us confused and trying to read between the lines. Complex automatic voice messaging systems wind us through a maze of computer-generated prompts, frustrating us when we just want to talk to a living, breathing person who can address our concerns. Cell phones interrupt personal conversations, disrupt meetings, and block us from conversing with the everyday people passing through our lives. We gas up our cars, pay by credit card, and drive off without a "thank you." Familiar faces that were once touchstones in our everyday lives—from the banker depositing our paychecks to the travel agent planning our vacations—are increasingly being replaced by automated systems or the Internet.

We now frequently walk, drive, and even fly without noticing or acknowledging the people who are sharing that slice of time and space with us, because we're too busy conversing with people halfway around the globe. For example, if you were seated or standing next to someone right now, that person could be starved for attention, for any human contact on any level—but how would you know? When we do reach out, we can never guess what effect our connection at that point in time will have on others. Even the briefest encounter can bring someone a moment of much-needed comfort or delight. For many of us, even an instant interaction can make a world of difference in whether we feel connected, visible, and cared about. That's why it's even more important to connect with intention and "show up" to extend our best.

Increasingly, we're losing the valuable connections of greeting and interacting with the fellow travelers we encounter along life's complex, multiple networks. Employees whose sole job is to serve customers may barely acknowledge their presence during a transaction. People walk along city streets, shopping malls, supermarket aisles, and office hallways, plugged into wireless networks rather than being wired to the moment and connecting with each other.

As we whirl past one other in dizzying style, frazzled from our fast-paced lifestyles, connectedness can indeed unravel, unless we're careful to keep weaving connecting threads back to one another. With technology changing the landscape of living, coupled with corresponding changes in today's cultural fabric, we risk losing something precious—the wondrous slice-of-time adventures with other human beings, the people who show up in our lives and make a difference. These are the most delicious fruits of life's connections, the unexpected pleasures that flow from people who make us smile, laugh with us, help us out, offer directions, take time to share, save the day, and more.

Personal "connect-ability" is indeed vital, as is our ability to be "high-touch" in the face of frequently more faceless connections. In our increasingly anonymous culture, when someone takes the time to notice, tune in, care about, or fuss over us, that benevolence ripples out in

wonderful ways. We're constantly creating currents of energy that envelope the people with whom we live, work, and share time and space—bathing them in the rich warmth of our kindness, understanding, and appreciation. It's all part of the interconnected nature of life. But the connections you make can create waves of positive, negative, or neutral energy. You must decide what message you want to send out to the universe and to all the people in it.

By awakening to the abundant pleasures and joy of joining, you connect at the core of what's meaningful and makes a difference to others and to your life experience. People connecting to people bring ordinary moments to life through extraordinary acts of valuable, high-touch humanity. When we create that "Wow, you noticed!" experience, a magical bond forms that leaves an enduring impression.

Connect-ability matters, because of the countless ways our connections count. We can nurture or neglect them, relish or reject them, cherish or chuck them. However we handle them, they all add up.

We may rather quickly forget neutral experiences that don't leave an impression on us one way or the other. The bad taste left from negative experiences we likely wish we could forget. But it is the compelling nature of our positive interactions that forge enduring connections—compelling vibrations of dynamic power and vibrancy, created in a place we call "The Connection Zone."

Creating
"The Connection Zone"

The Connection Zone is a dynamic balance of energy in which people honor each other's needs and enjoy the benefits that flow as a result.

Creating the Connection Zone experience is invaluable for short-term interactions to make enduring impressions (as in customer service), as well as for long-term personal and professional relationships, for sustaining their highly valued, enduring quality.

Whether it's for the short or long term, the Connection Zone experience is achieved through good communication. You enter "the Zone" by constantly monitoring people's universal human need to be:

> **H**eard and honored
> **E**ncouraged and empowered
> **A**ppreciated and accepted
> **R**espected and recognized
> **T**rusted and treasured

Every person you interact with has many needs that are represented in the HEART acronym. Of course, what we want or need from each other depend on the exact nature of the relationship. For instance, what we desire from our relationships at work, with our friends and families, within our community, and in our business transactions have many similarities. Yet, there are differences as to how we want or expect them to be fulfilled.

The following list describes in more detail some of what we want, need, or expect in various types of relationships.

In our personal relationships, we want:

- To know that when we speak, we are heard and understood
- To have effective, open channels of communication for expressing our concerns
- To have our feelings, ideas, and opinions honored
- To be encouraged to express our authentic selves and supported in our growth   and development
- To be accepted unconditionally
- To be acknowledged for the time, energy, effort, and other personal treasures we share and to be appreciated for them
- To be treated fairly and with respect
- To trust that promises and commitments will be fulfilled
- To be treasured and valued for who we are

In our working relationships, we want:

- To have effective, open channels of communication for expressing our concerns about work-related matters
- To have established procedures through which to settle differences and seek resolution
- To have our ideas and opinions heard and honored
- To feel empowered and supported in our work environment
- To be appreciated for our contributions of creativity, effort, service, and competence on behalf of the organization's mission and purpose
- To be treated fairly and with respect
- To be recognized as a competent and valued member of the organization
- To trust that promises and commitments will be fulfilled

In our business transactions we want:

- To be able to express our needs and have them honored
- To be sufficiently informed that we can make the best choices
- To be appreciated and valued for our business
- To be treated fairly and with respect
- To have confidence that products and services will be delivered in accordance with agreements, meet our expectations, and perform reliably
- To trust that promises and commitments will be fulfilled
- To air any grievances or concerns and have them heard, understood, and addressed

Paying attention to these important needs gets you to the heart of what people universally want from their connections, especially from their most significant ones. Good connections are predicated on meeting the needs and expectations of that specific relationship; fulfilling these needs puts you in the Connection Zone.

In the Zone, you explore common interests and needs, express your ideas, and talk about your concerns. Problems are quickly addressed and solutions sought and implemented. Especially for sustaining long-term connections, being in the Zone means that differences are honored and respected in a caring atmosphere of trust and support. Free of the stagnation caused by dysfunctional dynamics, the climate is right for bringing out the best in people and fostering the full expression of their gifts and talents. Everyone in the Zone benefits by feeling good about their relationships and supported in their needs.

When you focus on the HEART of what people want, need, and value, you enter the Zone and attract, sustain, and multiply dynamic relationships. It is pure joy to be in this energized space!

Enduring Connections Begin
with a Positive Intention

"You can outdo you—if you really want to."

Paul Harvey

How do you plug into the Connection Zone, and how do you translate the HEART of what people need into real life? By making a commitment to honor their needs in your interactions, appropriate for the type of relationship, and to regularly monitor whether their needs are being met. When you bring this positive intention into each interaction, it becomes your filter for everything you say and do. In order to create and sustain the best possible connections, you're aware that they can be very fragile, and if a person's needs are not being honored or their expectations have not been fulfilled, a connection is endangered. Your actions and attitudes must reflect good intentions or you're at risk of disconnecting from the Connection Zone. People will pull the plug right out of your connection and you may get zapped or burned in the process!

Keeping connected means sending out currents of positive energy that demonstrate your interest and support and sustained by understanding or seeking to understand, what others need, expect, or desire. Enduring connections are constructed with positive intent to create sound relationships coupled with the best you've got to give—bringing out your best (and your best behavior!). It's a simple equation (albeit a sometimes complicated one because of the unlimited nature and complexities of human thoughts, feelings, and interactions!), one that we call the Enduring Connection formula:

Personal Best + Positive Intention = Enduring Connection

Enduring Connection: A valuable relationship, long-lasting in nature, created with intent to honor needs and sustained by choices to respect them. By honoring needs and consistently choosing the attitudes and actions that respect them, you build quality connections of enduring value.

Personal Best: When you give your personal best to a relationship, it means you do your best to fulfill the needs and expectations of others while honoring your own. Your personal best is the expression of exerting the highest level of effort to provide the greatest value. It's demonstrating your commitment to meet or exceed the needs of people, which enhances and strengthens your connection.

We identify this expression of our personal best, the attitudes and actions of excellence, as the eX factor. Putting your eX factor to work creates extraordinary experiences for others, with corresponding value returning back to you. For a more detailed discussion of putting your eX factor into action, see Key #3: Energize the Winning Spirit.

Your personal best can take on another meaning when involved in difficult interactions or relationships. In such circumstances, it can be interpreted to mean managing the situation to the best of your ability and to "show up" with integrity and positive intent. Your intention may not involve creating a long-lasting connection, but at least one that is respectful and honors your needs, too. In these situations, your personal best is choosing to respond in a dignified manner, to bring your best to an interaction in order to make the best of it.

Positive Intention: Positive intention means bringing your commitment to honor the needs of others as well as your own into your interactions. Enduring connections are fashioned from the positive intention to create caring, quality relationships. This involves regularly monitoring whether the needs of everyone are being fulfilled.

During each interaction, the words you speak, the gestures you make, and the way you treat a person all make an impression and reveal your character. Often we're presented with split-second choices as to how to respond to someone. With a commitment of entering your interactions with positive intention, you respond to others in constructive ways, especially when at a crossroads of choosing your responses.

People who enter each interaction with positive intent are Conscious Connectors, a term we've coined for those who carefully choose how they relate to people with every interaction. They communicate their interest to others and show them respect via their words, actions, and attitudes.

To generate and sustain harmonious relationships, Conscious Connectors rely on the Enduring Connections formula. To become a Conscious Connector and create your own enduring connections, you must keep a positive intention in your heart and focus your energy (your personal best) on the people in your sphere of influence. To learn more about using this formula, read the following sections, which discuss each part of the formula in more detail.

Conscious Connectors
Make Enduring Impressions

In every connection, Conscious Connectors look for golden opportunities: to engage others, be attentive, relate to and serve their needs, support them, lift them out of ordinary experiences in unexpected ways, bring them joy, make them feel valued, and more. Enduring impressions are created by their personal commitment to bring their best to every situation; doing so often brings out the best in others as well.

Whether spontaneous in nature or carefully constructed, conscious connectors enrich the experiences of others; the impressions created by them endure. They fully recognize that without a firm commitment to personal excellence and positive intent, their connections would become susceptible to the ravages of indifference. They know those consequences would be deadly to their own vitality as well as the vibrancy of their interactions. Lethargy and indifference are fatal to relationships.

Conscious Connectors are the movers and shakers, the diplomats and the determined—the ones who make relationships extraordinary in whatever role they play. They see the possible in the improbable, and the best in the worst, and above all, they are committed to building quality connections and getting along. They're masters at maneuvering their way through the Connection Zone.

People love to be around Conscious Connectors because wherever they go they lift spirits, improve morale, increase support, generate cooperation, and command respect. Those who effectively tap their connecting power, whether for personal or professional purposes, are often celebrated for their abilities to:

- Lead and inspire others
- Put their passion into action
- Encourage a higher level of performance
- Communicate their ideas effectively
- Have their ideas accepted more easily

- Create an atmosphere of safety for discussing concerns
- Reach agreements faster and more satisfactorily
- Work in greater harmony
- Serve as agents of change
- Motivate others to work toward established goals
- Gain the respect, admiration, support, trust, and loyalty of others

They are skilled at harnessing these abilities to their connecting power. In their careers, their excellent interpersonal skills often mean they:

- Move ahead more rapidly
- Command excellent compensation and receive bonuses
- Acquire professional recognition and visibility
- Network with and gain access to influential people

When you're passionate about making your connections click, you don't sit on the sidelines waiting for others to take the initiative—you get busy clicking and get busy connecting! You move into action building a network of engaging encounters, often leaving a wake of surprised and delighted people as you pass through life. Whether with friends, family, or business associates, you're constantly cooking up ways to surprise, delight, encourage, support, and appreciate. It works wonders everywhere!

Make Positive Intention a Daily Habit

"When you look for the good in others,
you discover the best in yourself."

Martin Walsh

Whenever you interact with someone, asking "What can I do to make this person be glad we talked?" puts you in touch with the purpose and value of reaching out to connect:

- Solve a problem
- Relieve their stress
- Extend empathy
- Listen attentively
- Lift spirits
- Save them time or money
- Help them make money
- Nurture their potential
- Provide support
- Acknowledge their work
- Appreciate their contributions
- Give genuine compliments
- Surprise and delight them
- Enhance their self-image or feelings of self-worth

Interacting with purposeful intent not only benefits others; it also paves the way for attracting more of what you want. This people-connecting energy is empowering. It increases your confidence, wins support, lands positions of increasing power and influence, cements satisfaction in your relationships, and accelerates your success.

Watch how differently people respond and how moments are transformed when you put your positive intentions into practice! With intent to cultivate good connections, you always leave a long-lasting, positive impression behind.

By choosing to cultivate enduring connections, every moment becomes an opportunity to make others feel valued and to build or strengthen your relationships with them. Your actions will reflect this intention and command people's respect, admiration, trust, and confidence. An enduring connection is the treasure that's yielded from the investment of your personal best to create something valued by another; in turn, you gain invaluable gifts from it, too. It's pure gold and priceless!

Take your commitment to create positive connections with you everywhere—at home, to work, to school, to meetings, on the road, or anywhere you go! Use it with customers, co-workers, clients, kids, friends, partners, and particularly with any Prickly People (those thorny rascals who test your patience and your connecting power) to empower you in all your interactions.

With your intent to interact with others in positive ways, you enter each moment focused on delivering something of great value to share with them: the best of yourself. When this becomes your mantra, you make memorable moments of connecting magic!

WITH A NEED TO KNOW

Years ago, as vice-president of marketing for a trade association, I was asked to work on a business plan with several colleagues. Because of my experience designing business plans, I was given the lead on the project. At our first meeting, I realized that the pride of one of the team's members (who I'll refer to as Jack) had taken a hit because he hadn't been named chairman. Jack complained that he had also worked on business plans, that he was the best qualified, and that he should lead the group.

I could see that the project would stall unless we addressed his concerns, so the group spent an hour discussing them. Later, after a private chat with a few team members, we decided to offer Jack the co-chair. When Jack learned the news he immediately perked up, as did his attitude and collaborative spirit.

Being appointed co-chair was exactly what Jack needed to validate his expertise and address his need for recognition. It also made a difference in our relationship from that point forward: our communications improved dramatically, he spoke positively about me to our boss and other colleagues, and he even requested to work with me on other projects. When I took the time to understand his needs and try to meet them, our working relationship became one that neither one of us had to endure. —A.S.

RANDOM ACTS OF CONNECTION...

SENSATIONAL ACTS OF GOODWILL

My husband, Rick, enjoys schmoozing his way through life for the pure joy of it. He does it with intent, not to get anything out of it except the good feelings it naturally generates. However, he has certainly acquired quite a collection of goodies since his endearing manner invites unexpected delights.

For instance, he recently checked into a Doubletree Inn, commenting how much he valued the courtesy extended by the front desk clerk and how others probably took his service for granted. Rick didn't take that desk clerk's engaging manner for granted, because earlier that morning he had checked out of another hotel just half a mile away, disgruntled over its dreadfully poor service.

The next morning, Rick found himself honored as Doubletree's "Guest of the Day," and was showered with coupons, a free meal, a bottle of wine, and more. It wasn't about the stuff he got, but rather the connection he had nurtured that made a difference.

Another trip. Another connection, somewhere over the Atlantic. The flight attendant was making her rounds in the coach cabin taking the customary beverage requests. When she got to our row, Rick wryly replied, "Make mine a Frappaccino." He and I laughed, knowing the beverage cart was only stocked with the usual. To our surprise she returned with a Frappaccino! Then, he jokingly said, "What, no whipped cream?" Minutes later, she reappeared and apologized, "Sir, I'm so sorry. First class normally stocks whipping cream. Unfortunately, it's not on board today." She was serious. We were impressed.

Throughout the flight, we bantered back and forth, making this flight a most extraordinary one, much more than just warm bodies taking up space in seats 16 A and B. Then, she surprised us again. This time with a bottle of champagne saying, "It's been a pleasure serving you today. I hope you've enjoyed your flight." Extra WOW! Several years have passed and I have shared the special treatment she showered on us on that flight with my network of friends, audiences, and now you, the reader. Good feelings create good connections, goodwill, and enduring impressions. —S.S.

ARE YOUR CONNECTIONS ENDURING OR INDIFFERENT?

What we say can lead one way or the other. Conscious Connectors choose how they communicate in all ways, with everyone, everywhere. What they say and do make enduring impressions:

Enduring	**Indifferent**
How might I be of service to you?	I'm too busy right now to help.
Here's what we can do for you.	It's not our policy.
It's good to see you!	Yeah? Whadaya want?
Tell me more about your situation.	Ya gotta problem?
I would be happy to do that for you.	No way! I can't do that.
What can I do for you?	Sorry, no can do.

Make Every Moment Count

*"We do not remember days,
we remember moments."*

Cesare Pavese

A moment is fleeting. It comes and goes in an instant, sometimes passing by without our notice. But when we pay attention to what we do with millions of those moments—how we use them, invest them, and (daresay) waste them—it tells a story about our connecting spirit.

A mindful moment is one in which we focus on what's happening in that instant, and take a step to make it count toward the infinite desires of our heart. Mindful moments enrich our lives by highlighting our deeper awareness of our interconnected relationships—we make conscious choices to stay connected to life at its core.

Mindful moments become memorable when you take the time to involve yourself in the precious nanoseconds that construct your life—to notice, to care, to listen, to love, to nurture—being tuned in and attentive to everyone and everything. By doing so, you breathe life into your experiences, transforming the mundane and ordinary into the magnificent and extraordinary. When we appreciate the simple things, our focus becomes one of awe rather than *"Arrgghh! Now what?"*

Moments that make up life's connections are contained in everyday encounters, whether that means bantering with the receptionist, striking up a conversation in the check-out line, engaging a flustered ticket agent, or extending kindness to telemarketers. They want the same things we want, including being treated with respect and valued for who they are and what they do.

Every moment counts toward determining the quality and depth of your life; your legacy is built on how you decide to spend those moments. What you do with each slice of time influences your happiness. Stay mindful of your moments and make them memorable by attracting, creating, and keeping an abundance of rewarding connections.

Plugging into Your Connecting Power

"Life is not measured by the number of breaths we take,
but by the moments that take our breath away."

Source unknown

You can make magic happen anywhere. Wherever you go, think of the magic you can create to light up a face, lift spirits, lend support, or open a heart. Go out of your way to make someone's day. Be alert as to how you might help. Break out of routines. Stir up excitement. Put your passion into action. Go for the glow.

By committing yourself to forming enduring connections and expressing the attitudes and actions to keep them, you'll reap infinite rewards from the Connection Zone. Because building enduring relationships is so vital, the rest of this book highlights eight keys for unlocking and unleashing the magic of making and keeping compelling connections. These are designed to enhance your relationships, whether at work, with friends, within your family, and with other people in your life, as you strive to create valuable connections that enrich and endure.

The connecting spirit is all about building bridges to the HEART of needs—to hear and honor; encourage and empower; appreciate and accept; respect and recognize; trust and treasure. We absolutely thrive when our relationships support these needs. A wise soul once said, *"We're either pulling together, or we're pulling apart. There's really no in-between."* The power of the Connection Zone is all about deciding which direction you want your life to take, and harnessing your connection power to get there!

Cultivate Confidence:
The Cornerstone of Connection

Make the "Connection Zone"
Your "Comfort Zone"

Building confidence in yourself helps you develop the right mindset to master life's challenges, opening the floodgates for an outpouring of opportunities to make enduring connections.

If the thought of interacting with others sometimes takes you out of your Comfort Zone, you're not alone. Most people are susceptible to moments of self-doubt. Nothing is more excruciating than being ready to seize the moment and ending up losing out on an opportunity because your confidence falters under pressure.

If you find making comfortable connections with others is a breeze, you might want to skip ahead. However, even to the supremely confident, certain situations might inspire cold feet, a knot in your stomach, or at the very least, a bead or two of perspiration: entering a room full of strangers, dining with a prominent dignitary, delivering a presentation to a roomful of potential clients, or protecting your personal boundaries when others overstep them.

Even after a connection has been established, those pesky "maintenance issues" can arise, requiring a shield of confidence for masterful handling. A shadow of doubt crossing your mind can erode your confidence. Flooded with emotions ranging from slight apprehension to a full-fledged anxiety attack, you begin to doubt your social or professional prowess, which can significantly diminish your effectiveness.

Unfortunately, even momentary bouts of timidity have an impact. Negative thoughts can take control of your behavior and steer you in directions you don't want to go. Consequences ripple down the years, causing exponential damage to your future. Fearful of meeting new people or tackling new adventures or taking the lead on a project because you might make a mistake, you hold back, limiting your prospects for achieving the life of your dreams.

Building confidence is an essential building block to a dynamic destiny. Shaky self-esteem is a roadblock that can steer a promising future and promising relationships off course. If you find yourself stuck at a roadblock on the path to success, courage is the driving force to move beyond it. Courage is the energy that fuels your "connect-ability" and propels you upward and forward, determining the trajectory of your life.

Fortunately, courage also has a multiplying effect. When we meet life courageously, we learn to appreciate our skills and what we can offer others. We begin to relish the prospect of meeting new people, broadening our social and professional horizons, eagerly seeking new challenges on which to exercise our talent. We feel better about ourselves, more pleased with our increasingly confident self-image. Every success brings out a new luster in us, and reminds us of our glowing possibilities.

Yet without some strategies to shore us up when our confidence does take a beating, self-doubt can take root. When you're feeling insecure, it's difficult to think about connecting with new people, let alone connecting meaningfully. Because anxiety also has a multiplying effect, each time you pull back, unable to extend yourself toward the unexplored horizon, you jettison another opportunity. Since each opportunity is potentially rich with other possibilities, withdrawing means you might be limiting a whole chain of opportunities.

Shyness is a learned response, made up of a combination of attitudinal, emotional, behavioral, and physical responses that work together to protect you from the unknown. You learned many of these behaviors when you were young, or in a distant past that has long since faded from view. Your life has changed dramatically since then, as have your strengths, skills, abilities, and your unique worldview. If you underestimate your rich storehouse of gifts, talents, and capabilities – in effect, if you withhold your treasures – you lose out and so do those around you.

With some practice, a focus on courage, and a firm commitment to increasing your "connect-ability" skills, you can replace undesirable behaviors with a new code of conduct. With a little determination and careful application of the steps and strategies in this book, you can turn your own personal Comfort Zone into an authentic and thriving Connection Zone. This chapter will help you gain the self-confidence that can propel you into the Connection Zone and help you continuously reinforce your new assertiveness.

We know that by bolstering your confidence, you'll be better positioned to share your unique gifts and special qualities with the world. We want to make sure that you especially connect with those people who can make a difference in your life. Equally important, we want you to remember and embrace the enormous value you can bring to the lives of others, simply by reaching out and being present in their lives.

Woody Allen said that "eighty percent of success is showing up." Though simple, this is a formula you can apply for the whole of your life. Our prescription is that you "show up" with the intention of reaching out, interacting, and connecting with the people in your circle of influence. The greatest contribution you can give the world is the gift of your wisdom, radiance, and personal presence.

We work with many people who are uncertain as to how all this "relation-ship-building" stuff works. Our methodology begins with a simple truth that may help clarify the matter: everyone wants to shine, and sometimes all any of us needs is a little more polish to radiate absolute brilliance.

Connecting Counts: Do it Often ... with Confidence

"Every good thought you think is contributing its share to the ultimate result of your life."

Grenville Kleiser

We have tremendous power to affect the lives of others, to transform their experiences in a multitude of subtle, yet significant ways. Offering a friendly greeting, encouraging word, or compliment, or remembering someone's name, are simple, yet meaningful acts of connection. Often, we don't think about the impact a simple action can have on others: we might break the monotony of a routine day, brighten a face with our smile, or even lighten a heavy heart – gestures that make people feel valued and validated.

Gaining greater confidence and making all the connections you desire is within your control. You already have all the relationship-building skills you need, buried inside of you; they are just waiting to be called into action. When they're nurtured to their fullest, you thrive and flourish!

Careful tending of what you think and do hastens the growth of abundant possibilities. Your thoughts are like seeds, planting the possibilities of experiences, bearing either succulence or sorrow. By enriching the soil of your mental garden with positive thoughts about yourself and your capabilities, and by pulling out weeds of negativity or feelings of inadequacy, you cultivate the best environment for connect-ability.

Combat Shyness: Guerrilla Techniques to Attack Social Situations

*"Our duty is to proceed as if limits to
our ability do not exist."*

Teilhard de Chardin

More than likely, at some point we'll find ourselves in situations feeling socially challenged. Findings from different studies reveal that a majority of people surveyed, between 70 to 90 percent, admit to having had feelings of shyness. Whether it's walking into a room full of strangers, becoming the instant center of attention, or standing up to introduce yourself at a business meeting – even a sliver of gut-wrenching, heart-pounding anxiety can render you feeling inept. Being fortified with strategies to confidently handle this unease helps you over the hurdles.

Shyness is social anxiety, a learned response – a habit that doesn't have to be permanent. It's a combination of attitudinal, emotional, behavioral, and physical responses, working together and working against your greatest good. Social anxiety affects the quality of your life if you:

- Become nervous when initiating a conversation or meeting new people

- Spend more time alone than you would like

- Lack confidence in talking with people

- Pass up opportunities to meet new people

Anxiety often strikes when people underrate their abilities. If you have perfectionist expectations regarding your social aptitude, you're likely to condemn your behavior when it falls short of your exceptionally high standards.

If shyness is holding you back, explore what's keeping you from reaching out or speaking up. Since shyness is a learned behavior, use some of these strategies to help conquer it:

1. Pinpoint the fear: What is the nature of the fear? Where and when does shyness cast its shadow? Is it an occasional bout, or more persistent and pervasive? For example, if you're uneasy in large groups or when you're the focus of attention, you've identified specific areas to tackle.

2. Develop a plan to combat the fear: Think of the actions you can take to strengthen your performance. Set specific goals such as, "I will ask open-ended questions to keep conversations flowing."

3. Consider what you're missing: When you're tempted to stay stuck in familiar patterns, ask yourself, "What's my goal? What do I need to do now to move closer to that goal?"

4. Affirm your likeability: Never put yourself down or label yourself with negative names. Repeat positive affirmations throughout the day: "I am an interesting, well-liked, and valuable person." Refer to your mental notes when you slip into self-condemnation and need a boost. See Maximize Your Magnificence with Positive Self-Talk on page 47 for more information about affirmations.

5. Visualize yourself interacting positively. See yourself exactly as you'd like to behave in various social situations: greeting people confidently, being a lively conversationalist, skillfully mastering the social graces. Instead of seeing yourself being anxious, imagine yourself being totally relaxed and focused on having good interactions with others.

6. If an anticipated event is causing you heart palpitations, mentally rehearse the situation in minute detail—whether making a presentation, being introduced to important dignitaries, or meeting your fiancé's parents. Envision what's likely to happen and how you'll respond. Visualize yourself as the picture of composure, confidence, and competence; then step right into that picture when the long-awaited event finally arrives.

7. Learn relaxation techniques to manage stress and reduce anxiety. By controlling your responses to stress, you're better

able to control anxiety. See Stamp Out Stress! on page 56 for stress management techniques that help control anxiety.

8. Surround yourself with people who share mutual interests. It's much easier to start a conversation and maintain its momentum when your interests are similar. Join clubs and professional groups. Better yet, don't just join, get involved: serve on a committee or offer to help. Explore your community for a wide range of interesting civic, professional, or volunteer organizations.

9. Make others comfortable by reaching out first. Don't wait for others to reach out – remember, many people are fighting their own case of the butterflies. Don't be afraid to spread your wings and help others out of their cocoons.

10. Model the confidence you admire in others. Think of the confident people you respect, and observe what they do, how they move, the gestures they make, how they glide effortlessly through a room, and other qualities that create an air of self-assurance. Model similar behavior. For instance, how do your "confidence models" position their bodies when interacting? What facial expressions do they project? How fast do they speak?

How you position your body, set your facial expression, and modulate your voice can trigger certain emotions; just as your mood can affect your body language, your body language can affect your mood. If you hold your head up with your shoulders back and flash a wide smile, you project an image of confidence; similar feelings are likely to follow suit.

Call on your "confidence models" whenever you enter situations that might cause discomfort. "Strike the pose," take a deep breath, and tell yourself, "I breathe out fear. I breathe in confidence." Affirm "I am relaxed and at ease," or make other positive statements that can fortify you with feelings of greater control. Now you can move through the scene buoyed with an air of confidence. This may feel awkward at first, but by modeling the look of confidence, you begin to step into a different reality by creating a new image for yourself (and you might become the confidence model for others!).

11. Practice what you're going to say. Prepare for meetings, negotiations, presentations, and other occasions by anticipating the questions, issues, and other matters that might arise; determine ahead of time how you'll handle these situations. Spend time visualizing the scenarios, as well as rehearsing them in actual practice. For social events, refer to the list of handy conversation starters in Key #2, Rev Up Rapport.

12. Just talk! Strike up conversations wherever you go. It's more important to make any remark, even if it's about the weather or some other "small talk" topic, than none at all. The sheer act of talking demonstrates your friendly intentions.

13. Consider consulting a counselor or therapist if you find it difficult to overcome your anxiety in social situations. Professional therapists can offer tremendous support in working through your specific areas of anxiety, and provide an individualized plan for conquering the beast.

Being proactive can help you combat anxious feelings, boost your confidence in social situations, and enjoy connecting with people with greater ease.

Who Do You Think You Are?

"We can do only what we think we can do.
We can be only what we think we can be.
We can have only what we think we can have.
What we do, what we are, what we have,
all depend upon what we think"

Robert Collier

Your ability to connect with others and build dynamic relationships is greatly influenced by your self-image. Of all of the judgments you make, the ones you form about yourself are the most important because they serve as your life's guiding force. They will either support or sabotage your best intentions.

A positive self-image equips you with the confidence, determination, and resiliency to tackle life's trials and tribulations. When the waters get rough connecting with and getting along with people, you need to be able to rely on your internal resources and resilient spirit to create and maintain good connections,

If you see yourself in negative terms, diminishing your self-worth and reflecting a "less than" mentality, it will constantly play out affecting the quality and quantity of your relationships. A poor self-image churns out feelings of inadequacy that can destroy your goals and your ability to create and maintain positive and productive connections. Negative messages are destructive to your confidence and can erode your relationships in subtle, yet significant ways.

A negative self-image sabotages your best interests, brings you down, and wears you out. Poor self-esteem is demoralizing. As a way to make you feel more powerful, you might subconsciously activate defense mechanisms (such as unleashing insults, sarcasm, and other verbal abuse) that run counter to constructive connections. These obviously work against you and will keep you from creating the quality relationships you deserve. These and other destructive behaviors are discussed in more depth in Key #8, Handle Prickly People with Care.

BEYOND THE SHADOWS OF DOUBT

As a shy child, nobody would have guessed that Shy Boy Sanow would ever outgrow his inhibited nature and become a professional speaker – especially me! I resisted the limelight – now, I thrive when I am on the platform and teach others presentation skills. In fact, my journey from debilitating shyness to my success as a speaker has helped me to understand firsthand the power and influence wielded by confidence-building qualities.

For years, I was afraid to speak up at business meetings and other gatherings, afraid of sounding foolish. I sat quietly, too anxious to voice my opinions. When I was asked to speak before a group, I found an excuse to refuse. It became obvious that fear was hindering my professional growth, even preventing me from pursing my lifelong goal: to teach people how to use their own power to motivate and influence others. Determined not to let my shyness get in my way, I finally took a step that felt impossible: I joined Toastmasters International.

Toastmasters International is a professional association that teaches its members to speak publicly. Its meetings often focus on the skill of extemporaneous speaking, which gives everyone practice in responding to questions. At one of my first meetings, I was asked about the Arab-Israeli situation and given one minute to respond. I slowly stood up, my heart thundering. A minute seemed like an eternity. Maybe time stood still, but I sure didn't. I shook nervously and my chair shook along with me. All eyes were on me. I remained silent for the entire sixty seconds. Then it was over. Although I hadn't uttered one word, everyone clapped. Their applause was a gesture of encouragement that has supported me ever since.

I was determined not to let shyness get in the way of my lifelong dream of teaching people how to use their own power to motivate and influence others. As a professional speaker, I have since delivered more than 2,500 paid speeches. By devoting myself to overcoming my roadblock to success, I learned what I would eventually teach to hundreds of thousands: how to shine wherever they wanted their dreams to take them. —A.S.

What you believe to be true about yourself and what you choose to act on (as well as not act on) flow from your feelings of capability. We play a non-stop mental game of "red light/green light" in every aspect of our lives, choosing either to move forward or to put on the brakes. Often, the decision to take action or not is based on our analysis of the possibility for success or probability of failure.

If you think something is possible (you can make the sale, get the interview, land the dream job, access the right people), you give yourself the green light to move forward to make that your reality. Likewise, when you think something is impossible or not likely to happen (you will lose the sale, won't be invited, will be rejected, can't negotiate what you want), a mental stoplight brings your movements to a screeching halt. After all, red is a sign of danger and "impossible" may result in failure, so you might stop yourself from moving forward to avoid that risk. However, taking risks is usually all part of the process required to achieve your goals.

If you can't imagine yourself navigating social or professional events with some level of poise or panache, you'll be stuck right where you don't want to be. You'll stop yourself cold with criticism: "That's impossible. It's so not me." "I don't 'do' panache." Then, there you'll be . . . showing up with the same old behaviors that aren't getting you what you want!

Positive feelings about your people-connecting abilities build successful relationships. Learn to focus on new possibilities for expressing yourself positively and creating the connections you desire.

Call on Your Courage: See Yourself as Brave

"You have brains in your head, and feet in your shoes. You can steer yourself any direction you choose."

Dr. Seuss

Deciding to change requires an act of bravery. Start your transformation now by tapping into your reserves of courage and carefully tending your thoughts; what you say and do will follow. Your thoughts control your mental images, your feelings, your behavior, and your destiny. Focus on the images you want to manifest and take action in the direction of your dreams. The more frequently you exercise your courage, putting it to work for your best interests, the stronger and more resilient it becomes. When your confidence is secure, you can more easily bring others into your Connection Zone and watch your connections multiply.

Visualization accelerates skill acquisition and builds confidence. The science of visualization, also called mental imagery or mind simulation, is used by athletes, astronauts, pilots, high achievers, and others to successfully master their desired goals. Athletes use mental imagery to picture themselves winning and getting in the right mindset to win, whether that means scoring touchdowns, shooting baskets, breaking records, or whatever means victory. People in all walks of life, from students to business executives, use visualization to ensure masterful performances.

During the Vietnam War, U.S. prisoners of war used this technique to keep themselves mentally fit. Some mentally practiced playing the guitar or piano or typing on a keyboard. Colonel George Hall let his love of golf go right to his head: while confined, he mentally practiced every hole, visualized every stroke, and imagined himself playing the best games of his life. After his release, when he finally was able to get back on the links (seven years after his last real game), his golf game had actually improved! Through his investment of mental practice, he had collected a storehouse of positive images that actually netted him greater success on the green.

You can build and strengthen a confident self-image in the same way through regular mental work-outs. See yourself succeeding in every situation and make the images crystal clear: What are you doing? How are you acting? How are people acting around you? Concentrate often on this wise, courageous, and fully competent image: your true self. When your internal sensibilities begin incorporating these ideals, your sense of power will expand, as will your ability to influence those around you.

Mentally rehearsing ahead of time will help you feel comfortable when you put your new behaviors into action. This means leaving your Comfort Zone in the real world, but now you're pushing yourself in the direction of your goals. Now you can behave the way you've rehearsed – using your courage to push yourself ahead; to employ your untapped potential; and to empower your neglected skills, talent, gifts, power, and charm. You have within you all of the competencies you need for success; it's time you began harnessing them.

Keep confident images always in the forefront of your mind. Act in a manner that reveals the real truth of who you are—fully competent and confident.

Scan for Negative Viruses: Install Positive Updates

The endless assortment of messages, feelings, and attitudes we bring from our past into our present influences how we see ourselves. It also directly impacts our ability to relate to others. While growing up, we learned to judge ourselves and our capabilities based on how others saw us. Whether their judgments were complimentary or condemning (or accurate or inaccurate), we soaked up all that feedback, stuffed it inside our heads, and are still likely to be carrying it around. If the messages were disempowering, it's a heavy load and can weigh us down, as well as take us down. These messages form a kind of "database" of information, around which we form our sense of reality and our relationship to the world.

Your self-image serves as a sieve, filtering every experience and interaction and creates a running inner dialogue. You talk to yourself constantly about all of your experiences – what you think about yourself, the way you see others, how they react to you, and how you relate to them – it never stops. This ongoing, internal dialogue is your "self-talk," and it goes with you everywhere. When these private conversations are positive, they support you and work in your best interest. When they're negative, they're destructive and demoralizing.

Think of negative self-talk as outdated, erroneous computer data that was likely programmed by well-meaning but (sometimes) misguided souls. Negative inner dialogue is like a computer virus that infects the operating system, damaging or destroying it. On a human level, it's the equivalent of distorting the truth of your personal worth and value.

Negative self-talk belittles your potential, makes you feel undeserving and unworthy, and inhibits the achievement of your dreams, including enjoying fabulous relationships. It chatters on and on, often spinning out of control, feeding your brain messages that you blindly accept as your truth.

To override the destructive messages that formerly ran your personal operating system (you!), delete the misinformation by installing a new

DISCARD DESTRUCTIVE DATA

Your ability to connect with others is greatly influenced by your self-image. If you internalize negative messages, they're destructive to your confidence and can erode your relationships in subtle, yet significant ways. They're trash, so discard them now!

Negative Message	How it Could be Internalized
Don't mind her. just shy.	*People never pay attention She's to me. I'll just watch from the sidelines.*
You're a spoiled, rotten kid!	*I can get from people whatever I want.*
You're a brat!!	*People don't like brats. They must hate me.*
You're such a loser.	*Losers can't do anything right.*
If you have nothing , good to say don't say anything at all.	*I will avoid conflicts and not speak my mind.*
Be a perfect little girl (or boy).	*I know I'm not perfect, so why try?*

program – positive self-talk. This instructs your mind to carry out messages related to successful performance.

This time you're the programmer (and a most determined one!); this time you'll install the right software in the form of accurate, updated, verified data. To complete the installation correctly requires continual monitoring (a human form of virus scanning) for any toxic thoughts or infected data

that may creep into your brain, spreading error messages. Just as your computer is protected by regular updates, you must activate your personalized virus scanner every day, purging harmful and erroneous data. This prompts you to operate only with accurate data that produces desired results.

PLUG IN THE POSITIVE!

Always tell yourself good things about your capabilities and what you want to experience. Avoid any negative self-talk that reinforces what you don't want to happen. If you catch yourself slipping back into old, destructive patterns, counter the attack by rephrasing your thoughts in the positive.

Negative Self-Talk	Positive Self-Talk
I always seem to say the wrong things!	I know the right things to say!
I have a hard time making friends.	I'm good at making friends.
I'll never get it right.	I keep working toward what I really want, no matter what!
I don't know anyone here and I'm terrible at meeting new people.	There are many interesting people to meet here. Let's see what I can discover about them.
I know he won't want to talk with me.	He looks friendly. I think I'll ask him what he thinks about the conference.

Maximize Your Magnificence with Positive Self-Talk

"Peace of mind means the ability to be organized inwardly;
it means inner tranquility in the midst of confusion,
difficulty, conflict, or opposition."

Norman Vincent Peale

Positive self-talk expands your power; negative self-talk restricts it. Your personal power dramatically shapes your professional, personal, and social destinies, all with multiplying impact. Take the situation of entering a large ballroom full of unfamiliar faces. Immediately, if fearful thoughts take hold, you can talk yourself right out of a positive experience and the potential it holds:

Yikes, looks like I don't know a soul here. I'm so uncomfortable right now. I knew I shouldn't have come. I hate these types of events. I feel soooo awkward. Everyone else seems to be involved in conversations and I don't know where to go or who to talk to. I must look like an idiot standing here alone. Oh, there's Megan and Justin, but they probably don't want me to cut in on their conversation. I can't stand it anymore...Maybe I should just leave. Actually, that sounds like a great idea. I'll give it one more minute, then I'm outta here!

Positive self-talk awakens the courage that lies within. It boosts your self-image and sense of personal mastery. It directs your thoughts to expect positive outcomes.

This will be a good experience for me! It's up to me. I have to take the initiative, so just relax. I'll be fine. Hmmm? Let's see...there's a woman standing alone over there. I bet she'd appreciate a little company, so I'll go introduce myself. She looks friendly. That turquoise necklace she's wearing is really striking. I'll start by asking her about it. I'd like to also hear her thoughts about the new plans outlined during the morning session...

When you instruct your mind to carry out messages related to successful performance, it works to override previously stored information. It does work, but so must you, sometimes very hard, to re-program entrenched thought patterns, some of which can be extremely well-worn and deeply ingrained.

It's not unusual to sometimes fall back into old patterns. It would be wonderful if deciding to change a behavior (accompanied with a huge dose of determination) would immediately produce the new behavior. Poof! Old behavior gone! Hello, happiness! Dream on! Personal growth is rarely so neat, tidy, or instantaneous. It can be a very rugged journey indeed, but it is well worth the trek into the wilderness. You may even find yourself traveling longer than you would like, wondering if you'll ever "get it," maybe kicking yourself when you don't.

Pay close attention to your inner conversations. If you hear condemning, disapproving, confidence-crushing messages, they're not serving your best interests. Whenever you find yourself off-track, gently guide yourself back on course. Dump any destructive, negative messages that may still linger and want to take up residence in your brain. Ward them off by replacing them with positive messages to move yourself forward, one thought, one step, one action at a time. By switching to a positive sound track, you're changing your perception, reducing stress, averting potentially negative results, and laying the groundwork for promising possibilities.

Build Confidence and Extraordinary Connections, One Affirmation at a Time

"If you are distressed by anything external, the pain is not due to the thing itself, but to your estimate of it; and this you have the power to revoke at any moment."

Marcus Aurelius

An affirmation is a positive thought that, with repetition, helps change your belief by reinforcing an alternative image. It's a power-packed transformation agent that boosts your belief in your capabilities and enhances confident, quality connections. Affirmations are conceived in the mind, where they are born as powerful points of thought. As you change your thoughts, you change your reality. Thinking can reprogram your subconscious mind with new belief systems, new ways of being, and new behaviors, which results in a new personal truth when you experience a new reality.

Repeating statements that don't yet feel like the truth may feel phony at first, especially if they oppose your present situation or belief system. You might resist saying them, because they seem so foreign and out of touch with your current reality. You might even hear a resounding, "Yeah, right!" as you speak them, doubting their truth. Keep affirming what you want to experience, because your brain absorbs whatever "food" it's being fed – healthy thoughts that heal or those that gobble up our chances for achieving the success we desire.

It takes a lot of repetition to overcome previously programmed negative beliefs. If you keep at it, those old, erroneous beliefs will be replaced and you'll notice a new reality taking shape, connecting you to what you desire. When you develop new affirmations, use the "Four P" formula:

The Four P's

To charge up your affirmations, use the "Four-P" formula and make them Positive, Personal, Present Tense, and Powerful!

1. **Positive:** State your desire positively by focusing your words and thoughts on what you want, not on what you don't want. For instance, to secure more harmonious relationships, affirm "I am a patient, peaceful conflict negotiator," rather than "I will not argue and fight over trivial things." Your brain connects to the specific picture that is evoked by your words: in the first affirmation, the image is one of patience and peaceful resolution; in the second, arguing and fighting come to mind.

2. **Personal:** Make your affirmations personal using "I" or "I am" statements such as "I am confident in new situations." By making them personal, you're claiming the experience as your reality. Watch out for those nagging doubts that can surface after you make a claim that seems to counter your current reality (at least according to the negative self-talk).

3. **Present Tense:** Use the present tense as if it's already a fact. It may seem impossible now, but claiming something as fact can help create a new reality: "I have excellent communication skills." If you feel resistance to the claim, modify your affirmations to reflect the strength of your dedication to move you in that direction: "I am building excellent communication skills and I learn more with each encounter."

4. **Powerful:** Make your self-talk powerful by attaching it to positive emotions. We often have to feel something first to believe it. For example, imagine how you'll feel as a totally confident person or the power you'll feel delivering a successful presentation. Feel the power cursing through your body. Let that feeling resonate, deep down into your confident bones, and recall it often:

   I am attracting an abundance of interesting people.
   I am a powerful speaker.
   I speak with confidence.
   I am an excellent negotiator.
   I am confident.

Remember, you are a rich resource of talent and possess a tremendous personal treasure, and your gift is to share it.

THE SELF-ESTEEM TEAM

Building confidence is a process of developing the right mindset to master life's challenges. One of the most important roles parents play in their children's development is that of a cheerleader, providing encouragement and support to guide them through life's ups and downs and helping to create and fortify a positive self-image.

My husband, Rick, and I took this role very seriously from the start, speaking daily affirmations to our two girls. Even before they were born (it's never too early for some well-intentioned parent prodding!) we continuously praised their gifts and talents, and talked about how they would put them to good use in life.

Rick and I enthusiastically accepted the leadership of Stephanie and Stacy's "Self-Esteem Team." Throughout their growing up years, we read a library of character-building books, decorated colorful "I am lovable and capable!" signs to hang from their bulletin boards, made up silly songs (using their names) about being courageous and strong, and talked (sometimes lectured) about handling the challenges they faced with friendships, disappointments, and heartaches. They learned to associate the word "adventure" with another Comfort-Zone-stretching opportunity. They knew that one word alone meant they were in store for another life lesson and that their job was to boldly meet it.

Our girls also became the recipients of a steady stream of confidence-building notes – stuffed into lunch boxes and backpacks, posted on mirrors, crammed into overnight bags, and tucked into camp trunks, or whatever might serve as a touchstone when an extra dose of courage was needed. We only hoped the charms would work their magic and their messages would permanently "stick."

(Continued on next page)

(Continued from last page)

Recently, my oldest daughter called from college and asked me to locate a needed document. As I rummaged through her drawers of memorabilia and other treasures, I came upon a large box. Stuffed inside were notes of every color, shape, and size written over the years. I was surprised she had saved so many of them. It made me realize just how important those notes had been to her, serving as steppingstones for building confidence along the way.

This confidence-building habit evidently has rubbed off on her (I love it when a huge investment of parental energy has a "mother lode" payoff), because before she left for college I found attached to her bedroom mirror affirmations she'd written to prepare herself for life's adventures ahead.

We never truly outgrow the need to approach every event armed with affirmations that express our personal gifts, talents, and greatness. Take them into every arena to empower yourself, to build good connections, and to energize the excellence within. —S.S

Don't Beat Yourself Up: Build Yourself Up!

"A person seldom makes the same mistake twice.
Generally it's three times or more."

Marilyn Grey

It's a far wiser investment of energy to look for the humor in our imperfections rather than beating ourselves up over them. When you think you haven't performed up to your self-imposed ideals, let yourself off the hook a little, or you'll really get hung-up.

Stop the stinging self-talk – the "should's," "never's," and "can'ts." ("I should have known better!" "I never get it right!" "I can't get the hang of it!") Watch out for self-inflicted condemnation when you don't meet your own lofty demands. The constant comparison of how you (or your life) should conform to your expectations in an imperfect world can act as a wedge, severing your connections to happiness.

Instead, wrap yourself up with some comforting compassion, and build yourself up. Whipping yourself with words of woe will only take you down, and down is not the direction of your dreams. Just because you know the choices you want to make, doesn't mean it's possible to choose them every time.

Instead of condemning yourself for not acting fast enough or with enough consistency, acknowledge instead the progress you've made. Simply being aware of your desire to improve your people-connecting skills is a fundamental step in creating real change. When you pay attention to your choices for bringing more moments of connection into your life, you're already on your way, and you'll have many more opportunities to make successful choices.

Every time you take even the tiniest step toward what you want, congratulate yourself. Acknowledge each movement toward your goal, whether it's courageously stepping outside your Comfort Zone, speaking your truth, introducing yourself to a stranger, or giving a speech. In every

instant, when you switch a thought, a pattern, or a behavior to create positive change, that's progress!

Beating yourself up only takes you down. Build yourself up by acknowledging every effort that takes you closer to the connections you want to make.

SPEAK WITH CONFIDENCE

We project confidence through our words, tone of voice, and delivery. Adding filler words or sounds ("you know," "uhmm," "er," and "uh") or tentative language ("sort of," "I guess," "kind of," "well," "er," and the like) do not project a poised or polished image. People are not as likely to trust or have confidence in those with such dubious delivery.

Avoid giving voice to negative self-talk. A good way to make people question your abilities, for example, is to make this type of remark: "Sometimes I wonder where I put my brain!"

Avoid bringing attention to nervous behavior, as in the all-too familiar remark from the platform, "Excuse me, I'm a little nervous." Statements such as these undermine the aura of self-assurance you want to project.

If your intention is to influence or persuade others, avoid prefacing your remarks with statements that diminish your strength and power. For example, "I'm sure you won't agree with me, but ..." gives others permission to dispute your ideas.

Don't beat around the bush. Get to the point quickly without injecting self-defeating statements along the way.

Cancel Comparisons

"There is tranquility to be found in knowing that you are doing your best to make the most of yourself."

David Baird

from A Thousand Paths to Tranquility

"Look at that Melanie. She always seems so confident, so vivacious. What's wrong with me?" There will always be people who turn us green with envy. They're so refined, so savvy, and they seem to have it all. Logically, we know that nobody's perfect or gets it right 100 percent of the time, not even the Melanie's of the world. But chances are, it's the failure to measure up to our own self-imposed standards that renders us feeling "not good enough."

Most of us can be fairly hard on ourselves, maybe even brutal. While we may accept the flaws and shortcomings of others, we hold ourselves to a stricter standard. When you focus only on your flaws, you're probably discounting or overlooking your strengths and virtues. Work to counter that negative bias. Assess your strengths. Gain a more accurate, balanced image of yourself as a whole being, equipped with your own set of unique gifts, talents, and skills. You might not be the social butterfly you admire across the room, but your own set of "wings" will lift you up to where you shine, just in different ways. Learn to calculate all of your assets.

While we know that nobody's perfect, accepting our own flaws, faults, and faux pas is hard to do. We may judge ourselves unmercifully, tallying up what we perceive to be our social imperfections. Excellence has its rewards, but perfection is humanly impossible. Forget about having perfect conversational skills, interacting with others perfectly, meeting expectations perfectly, or whatever you believe is imperative to do perfectly in the interpersonal scheme of things.

Stop any self-condemnations with these perfect truths: "I am an extraordinary person. I am good enough right now!" Power up with these affirmations and use them as your mantra whenever you notice any self-talk becoming unfairly judgmental.

Stamp Out Stress!

"An ounce of renewal is worth a pound of repair."

Maggie Bedrosian

from Life is More Than Your To-Do List

With the many roles we play and tasks we perform, it's easy to have our attention scattered among multiple places and projects. Achieving a centered state occurs when your mind, body, and spirit are balanced and in alignment – infusing you with calming energy that helps clarify choices, discover solutions, and boost confidence.

Breathe! Deep breathing breathes life into you. With a faster tempo and intensified stress, we're just one breath away from an instantaneous relaxation tool. Proper breathing helps us to gain control, deal with situations in a more focused manner, speak more calmly, and approach situations with greater confidence.

Relaxation breathing is simple, and you can do it anywhere, anytime. Use your abdominal muscles to breathe more naturally (breathing through your chest promotes shallow breathing):

- Inhale through your mouth for two seconds, then hold your breath for three.
- Exhale through your mouth slowly for five seconds.

Take a few breaths of relaxation throughout the day to relieve stress and increase a feeling of well-being. Breathing this way sends waves of wonderful relaxation through your body:

- Inhale deeply while you focus on a calming idea, such as "I breathe in relaxation."
- Exhale, focusing on the thought, "I let go of stress."
- Repeat this several times to release and relieve stress.

DE-STRESSERCIZE!

Lift the weight off your shoulders with this stress-reducing technique: drop your head to your chest, then slowly roll it toward your right shoulder, your back, your left shoulder, and your chest. Repeat twice to the right, then three times to the left. Next, raise your shoulders as if to touch your ears. Do this several times daily; its effect is instantaneous and magical.

Doing this daily works wonders in reducing stress levels. Relaxation breathing quiets both mind and body, offers immediate relief, and can be practiced anywhere.

Learn to relax your muscles, where stress is stored and felt. Combine relaxation breathing with muscle relaxation. Progressive muscle relaxation (see box on next page) is an excellent way to release the tension you hold in your body. This simple technique involves tensing muscle groups to a count of four, then releasing them for five counts. This creates a wave of relaxation throughout your body and is especially beneficial if practiced at least once a day.

To progressively relax your muscles, follow these steps:

- **Arms and Hands**
  Clench your left fist and tighten your left arm
  Hold for a count of five, then relax
  Repeat the same procedure for your right arm

- **Head, Neck, and Shoulders**
  Tighten your forehead; relax
  Close your eyes and tighten; relax
  Clench you jaw; relax
  Tighten your forehead, eyes, and jaw together; relax
  Rotate your head several times; relax
  Shrug your shoulders up while pressing your head down; relax

- **Feet and Legs**
  Tighten your calves and thighs; relax
  Curl your toes downward; relax
  Force your toes upward; relax

- **Abdomen, Chest, and Back**
  Take a deep breath and hold it; then exhale
  Breathe deeply and slowly for 1 minute
  Tense your abdomen; relax
  Tighten your back; relax

Take Chances:
The Awesome Adventure of Risk-Taking

"He who is not courageous enough to take risks
will accomplish nothing in life."

Muhammad Ali

There's always risk associated with any activity holding potential for one of our greatest fears – rejection. The "R" word might send shivers down your spine, as you recall dreaded memories of feeling snubbed, spurned, ignored, ridiculed, or rejected. Activities such as striking up a conversation with a stranger, breaking into the middle of a huddled circle, or making cold sales calls might bring on the jitters as anything can when outcomes are unknown.

Any time you venture outside your Comfort Zone and into the world of the unknown, the possibility of rejection exists. However, if you aren't willing to take risks, you might get stuck in places of frustration and self-imposed limitation. You'll end up missing out, and that can cost you dearly – lost opportunities for creating endearing friendships, lucrative business relationships, and countless encounters for a richer, more meaningful life.

You might resist situations where rejection exists because the mere thought prompts a litany of negative self-talk: "They probably don't want to talk with me." "I'd only be interrupting them." "What if she says no?" Your imagination can throw a monkey wrench into your wildest dreams.

Remember, it's the meaning you attach to an event that determines your feelings about it. If you internalize the responses of others as personal rejection, you're reinforcing negative self-talk. If you withdraw, you're reinforcing behavior that sets you up for a lifetime of limitation. If people turn you down or don't show interest, avoid writing them off or making assumptions.

When others are preoccupied in a conversation, they may be addressing a critical issue requiring their immediate attention, which has nothing to

A DATE WITH DESTINY

*"Take into account that
great love and great achievements
involve great risk."*

The Dalai Lama

I was invited to a party hosted by professional single women – a great place to be as a single guy, except I felt intimidated for a number of reasons. When I arrived, I could see I wasn't dressed appropriately for the event, plus the women seemed somewhat aloof, or at least absorbed in their networking. I sought some comfort at the refreshment table.

A striking woman, fashionably dressed, caught my attention, but she was engrossed in another conversation. I wanted to meet her but that would take an act of courage on my part. As I stood there, munching on about two dozen carrots, I asked myself, "What's the worst that could happen?" Rejection, of course! But it would only last a fleeting moment, so I decided not to let it stop me. Anyway, it would save me from overdosing on carrots!

I gathered up my courage, joined the group she was in, and introduced myself. Nancy and I immediately hit it off. I asked her for a date and she said yes. I asked her for another, and another, and seven months later, I asked her to marry me. My entire future changed based on one decision to break out of my Comfort Zone and into a Connection Zone.

Had I stayed frozen at the refreshment table that night, my life would be totally different. I might still be hanging around snack bars munching on carrots. Fortunately, Nancy is now my "24-carrot" gold mate and we enjoy sharing lessons with our son, Stephen, about the importance of confidence and the value of courage. —A.S.

do with you. It may be purely a matter of timing. If someone doesn't accept an invitation, the real issue might be lack of interest in the topic or event, not you. If your call is ignored or you're cut short, it may mean they have other pressing priorities.

Don't let turn-downs or turn-offs stop you from starting up future conversations, extending invitations, making or returning calls, and all the other opportunities gained by reaching out to others. Congratulate yourself each time you do. Every connection contains fertile opportunities. Don't miss out on the abundant harvest!

See risk-taking for what it is – a necessary means to achieve positive, enriching, and rewarding connections. Be adventurous! When you take risks and engage others, you open up new opportunities for building your dreams, forming outrageously wonderful relationships, or furthering your financial future.

IT'S IN THE CARDS!

Follow your heart to achieve your dreams
Go ahead! Let your diamond traits shine!
But watch for clubs that beat you down
and squash those dreams to smithereens!

Remember the spade for digging out
From all of life's tight places
'Cause when you do you'll surely find
Your life is filled with aces! — S.S.

View the four suits in a card deck as symbolizing life's journey. Following your heart and radiating your diamond qualities serve as powerful allies when the clubs whack away at both your dreams and self-esteem. Remember, like the spade, there's always some type of tool, new choice, or option for handling every challenge. Deal 'em out!

Move in the Direction of Your Desires

"Throw your heart over the bars and your body will follow."

Trapeze performer

Movement – even the smallest action – exerted in the direction of your desires gains momentum and moves you closer to your dreams. The tiniest steps you take to enhance your connect-ability, consistently taken, will yield precious gifts of increased confidence, interpersonal skills, and personal power.

Change is possible when you select actions that catapult your heart in the direction of what you truly want. So move forward, and grow. Continue exploring ways to express the best within yourself, expand your social and professional networks, create and maintain fabulously fulfilling relationships, reach out beyond your Comfort Zone, expertly manage challenging situations, and connect with people for the sheer joy of a splendidly shared moment of humanity.

Moving in the direction of your desires pulls you along the path to expanding your confidence and gives you the power to:

- Choose thoughts, attitudes, and feelings that produce positive connections

- Create desirable outcomes in your interactions by making new choices

- Direct your personal and professional destinies through enhanced connections

- Choose empowering responses when involved in challenging interactions

- Cultivate positive, productive, and meaningful relationships

- Celebrate the success that accompanies rich, rewarding, and outra- geously wonderful connections

Baby steps, little strides, giant leaps – eventually, they'll all take you to the destination you desire. With increased confidence and personal power, you can create a lifetime of enduring impressions!

Key #2:

Rev Up Rapport!

You're Never a Bore with Rapport!

"He liked to like people, therefore people liked him."

Mark Twain

Rapport can be defined as "bringing agreement, harmony, and accord to a relationship." Isn't that what we want in our connections—to discover points of mutual interest or common ground, reach agreements, live and work together in harmony, and enjoy our interactions along the way—with more ease? Rapport is the magic ingredient for getting along with our customers, coworkers, colleagues, committee members, families, friends, neighbors, and everyone else we encounter in any role, anywhere, anytime. Getting along means smoother sailing, fewer hassles, and more fun!

The key to revving up rapport lies in expressing the same qualities that people find attractive. It's the Pleasure/Pain Principle in action. We move toward the people we like—those who are easy to get along with, who make us feel comfortable, who bring out our best qualities (including our smiles, laughter, and good feelings).

In the reverse, we move away from those who bring us discomfort—those with whom we find nothing in common, or who grate on our nerves, make us see red, hold up our plans, don't meet our expectations, give us headaches, or provoke other negative responses.

The relationships that bring us pleasure and good experiences are likely to endear as well as endure, generating fond memories, long-lasting

NO-FAIL RECIPE FOR REVVING UP RAPPORT

To cook up good connections, bring these ingredients "to the table" in every interaction:
- A positive, upbeat attitude
- Listening ears
- Buckets of encouragement and support
- Plenty of positive words
- Genuine interest

Combine your finest ingredients. Season with tasteful humor and enthusiasm. Savor the sweet life, making good impressions and long-lasting relationships!

Delicious connections boil down to three basic elements:
- What you project
- How you present yourself
- How you make people feel

impressions, and joyful feelings. In contrast, the relationships that bring us discomfort and cause negative experiences are likely to test our endurance; although their accompanying impressions, feelings, and memories may also last, we probably wish they wouldn't.

The ability to rev up your rapport is critical to creating enduring connections. Without it, you're more likely to suffer the pain and stress of troubled relationships and disappointing connections. You may also miss out on wonderful opportunities and their power to transform. All are typical fallout from choosing a life of disconnection.

"Get Along" Qualities that Create Enduring Connections

Make a positive impression and strengthen your people-connecting power by regularly projecting the following qualities:

- Authenticity
- Appreciation
- Compassion
- Confidence
- Engaging style
- Enthusiasm
- Friendliness

- Good communication skills
- Humor
- Neat appearance
- Positive attitude
- Social skills
- Respect
- Sincerity

Qualities that Crush Connections

If you slip into any of the negative behaviors listed below, remember that these traits typically turn people off or turn them away:

- Abrasiveness
- Apathy
- Coldness
- Insensitivity
- Insincerity
- Lack of appreciation
- Lack of confidence

- Lack of humor
- Negative attitude
- Poor body language
- Poor communication skills
- Poor social skills
- Profanity
- Rudeness

Not only does rapport enhance your personal and professional relationships, it can also boost a company's bottom line. Communicating with insight, perception, and empathy strengthens your efforts to keep customers happy, gain and maintain their trust, regain favor with disgruntled clients and customers, and increase the likelihood of getting their repeat business and their referrals. Likewise, building good rapport with colleagues increases the quality of your working relationships, with corresponding impact on productivity, creativity, cooperation, morale, and overall job satisfaction. Either rev it up, or risk losing vital connections that are costly if not created or maintained. There's always a payoff to having good rapport. It acts like a magnet for good things to flow.

*"Getting people to like you is merely
the other side of liking them."*

Norman Vincent Peale

THE CHARISMA CONNECTION

*"I treat people the way I want to be treated, and
respect the way they want to be treated."*

From Charisma Cards—50 Irresistible Ways to Energize
Your Personal Magnetism

Arnold Sanow and Sandra Strauss

Charisma enhances your ability to create and keep
enduring connections. It's a people-connector because the
energy that's emitted is magnetic in nature. While some come
by it naturally, charisma can also be cultivated through
conscious choices to connect with others in compelling ways.
We think of it this way:

Connecting
Habits
Attracting
Really
Important/**I**ntriguing
Shared
Moments of
Attention/**A**ppreciation/**A**cknowledgment/**A**musement—
we need them all!

MAGNETIC BY NATURE

Growing up, I watched my dad connect with people evvv-erywhere we went. He was a master at transforming the briefest encounter into something extraordinary. He'd strike up a conversation while gassing up the car and drive away with a new story to tell. Dad could put a radiant smile on the most disgruntled face and light up rooms with his jovial spirit.

My brother, sister, and I knew that going anywhere with him meant evvv-erything took longer—we were forever delayed by Dad stopping to give someone a compliment or a hug, or share a story or a joke. Sometimes it annoyed us when we were in a hurry to be someplace, but mostly we wondered how he seemed to always cause such a commotion. One day I asked him why he did what he did. He said, "Because it makes a difference how I experience that moment. Whether it's only a smile or a kind word, it makes a difference to me. Hopefully, it makes a difference to others, too."

This endearing quality served him well in his business as the owner of a variety store. His rapport-building expertise attracted customers because he talked the language of connection. My dad's companionable nature was like honey to the small town folk that swarmed to his store like bees.

With other dreams to fulfill, my dad cashed in his good fortune early, selling the lucrative business to a man who was "rapport challenged." Where customers once had been greeted with a beaming smile and genuine concern, Mr. "No Charisma" stayed off the sales floor. Customer traffic dwindled. Without that magic honey that was once the store's hallmark, customer traffic dwindled and within a few years, its doors closed. The business died from neglect and showed me firsthand the absolute power of rapport and the magic of making magnetic connections. —S.S.

Build Rapport with the "Meet and Greet 4"

"If someone is too tired to give you a smile, just give him one of yours."

Source unknown

Research has shown that we have about 90 seconds to make a favorable first impression. That's not much time to decide whether a relationship will blossom and grow or wither and die. With so much at stake, you need to grab the moment and rev up the rapport, because here's another fact: first impressions rarely change. So remember, as you're evaluating other people, they're doing the same to you, judging your character, personality, likeability, attitude, credibility, suitability as a friend or associate, and more. So meet, greet, and be merry!

A good first impression is a powerful tool for carving out future relationships with others, winning their trust, respect, and confidence. We like and trust those who are most like us, so finding points of common interest helps cultivate the confidence we want others to have in us. How and what we communicate, both verbally and nonverbally, are potent factors in enriching the soil for building good connections.

The foundation for building rapport is based on the exchange of a few basic communication signals. We call the four most fundamental signs the "Meet and Greet 4." Although they are simple, these signals are crucial in maneuvering through social and business occasions. Disregarding gestures as basic as smiling and shaking hands can leave others wondering or distrustful.

1. SMILE

"A smile is the light in the window of your face that
tells people your heart is at home."

Judith Byrne

Its language is universal. A smile is the connecting point of a relationship, whether personal or professional. It signals interest and conveys care and concern. It lights up faces and brightens the atmosphere. A smile takes you up; a frown takes you down. A smile can make or break a connection; its absence can leave others worried or wondering what you're hiding behind that frown. At work, a smile is a service essential. It speaks volumes and sends a powerful message that affirms the sender's focus on the needs of others. A friendly face promises immediate comfort, like an S.O.S.—a beacon of help and support. It demonstrates a willingness to communicate and sends a signal that prompts others to reach out in return. Even an "unseen smile" can travel through fiber optic cable, sending out goodwill and making a powerful connection. A smile costs nothing, but pays off in big dividends.

NO SMILE, NO JOB

An article in The Washington Post reported that an Amtrak ticket agent lost his job because "he didn't smile enough." The agent admitted that he couldn't pretend to be happy when he wasn't, so he chose not to smile. Losing his job probably didn't improve his ability to smile, made even more difficult after being fired and unemployed!

Tight-lipped, wimpy, half-smiles signal discomfort or insincerity. So, go ahead and radiate a great big, genuine grin!

THE GIFT OF A SMILE

Hope Price, a long-time member of our congregation, was famous for the radiant smiles she beamed to everyone. She always made people feel good with her kind words. Everybody loved her and she loved them back. But it wasn't until her memorial service that her daughter shared with us more about the smile that had become her mother's signature.

As a young woman, Hope believed everyone else had special talents. Frustrated that she couldn't identify any special skill of her own, she asked a dear friend what she thought Hope could do well.

Why, Hope, you have a wonderful smile! Your smile is a gift to so many.

A gift?

Yes! What does a smile do?

It makes you feel good!

Exactly! That's what your smile does for others. It makes them feel welcome.

Never before had she considered smiling to be a gift, but greeting people with a big grin and kind words came easily and naturally for her. From that day forward, she was fully aware of her simple but valuable gift, radiating genuine smiles every-where. She never put on a "put-on" smile. They were always authentic, connecting, and caring. Wherever she went, she lit up the world around her.

What do smiles do? They connect us. Hope connected positively to others everywhere she went. Her smile opened doors, ushered in new opportunities, and created friendships and goodwill. Hope's gift was literally right in her face and it was priceless! —S.S.

2. SHAKE IT UP!

In American culture, a handshake is a customary first physical point of connection; how you shake hands says a lot about you. A sensational handshake conveys warmth, friendliness, and confidence; a bone-crushing handshake is often perceived as a power play.

Be the first to extend your hand. As you extend your right hand, make eye contact and smile, while offering an introductory remark or an energized "Hello!" Give about three firm shakes, then release your grip. The good vibes a handshake generates are part of the engaging bond you're forming by showing others that you're interested.

Point of caution: avoid shaking hands if you can't offer a clean, dry hand, such as if you've been noshing away on barbequed buffalo wings or hitting the chocolate fondue pot and it's all so finger-lickin' good. Simply offer an apology for obvious reasons; they'll likely appreciate not having to "grip and grin" right then!

3. THE NAME GAME

Ahhh!—the sweet sound of your own name! People love to hear others address them by name, even if they know it was just gleaned off a credit card or name tag. In our increasingly anonymous world, it's refreshing to hear your name in conversation. It's flattering and makes us feel important. When leaving voice-mail messages, be sure to include the person's name as an effective part of your relationship-building efforts.

Remember Names (You Really Can!)

Many people say they can't remember names. Of course, if we believe that we can't, we probably won't. Often, we forget names because our attention is focused elsewhere during introductions, possibly buried amidst a flurry of mental observations: "She looks like my college roommate." "Who does this guy remind me of?" "What a beautiful necklace!" "It's my lucky day! Miguel is with the XYZ Company! Wonder if he can connect me with the CEO?"

There are many different strategies you can use to help you remember names. The easiest and most effective is to fully concentrate on a person's name during the introduction, and repeat it immediately to cement it into the cerebrum: "Ramon, it's great to meet you!" "Crystal, how wonderful to meet an associate of Jason's!"

Memory-Making Ideas

Follow the steps listed below to enhance your ability to retain new names:

- Focus on remembering names during introductions and mentally repeat each one several times.

- Look for a personal connection. For instance, does one of your relatives share the same name? "Vernon—That's my favorite uncle's name!"

- If it's an unfamiliar name, inquire about its origin: "'Houston'? Does your name perhaps reflect any Texan roots?"

- Sometimes asking about the correct spelling or pronunciation of a name is useful, especially if it's unfamiliar. With our changing global landscape, even some common names are spelled or pronounced differently, such as Michael and Michel.

- Use the name frequently in conversation.

- If you forget a name, simply ask the person again: "I'm sorry. I was a little distracted the last time we met (or 5 minutes ago). Please refresh my memory. Your name is…?" They may need a refresher, too.

- If you really should know someone's name, but can't recall it during introductions, let others introduce themselves with a quick save, "Have you two met?" This usually works wonders and saves everybody embarrassment.

- If you don't remember someone's name from a previous event, reintroduce yourself to them. When you offer your name, others usually reciprocate (gratefully, since they might have forgotten your name, too).

- Ask for a business card (if it includes a photo, that's especially helpful for future ID reference).

4. WHAT'S YOUR M.O. (Marketing Opportunity)?

We're always selling our capabilities, gifts, talents, and ideas to those we meet. What we say in just a few seconds can attract the immediate interest of others. By creating a "personal commercial"—a concise, crystal clear statement of what you want others to know—you have a personalized marketing tool always ready on the tip of your tongue. Having a personalized M.O. is valuable for many reasons:

- It answers the inevitable questions, "What do you do?" or "What's your area of interest?" in both professional and social circles.

- It helps people focus on potential topics of conversation.

- It can lead to new business connections for you (you wouldn't want to lose an opportunity for some free advertising!)

THE SNOWBALL EFFECT

As a speaker and marketing strategist, I try to "walk my talk" and practice what I teach, including the need for a personal commercial. I consider it a business essential and have mine ready to deliver in an instant. Yet, I'm surprised at the number of people who haven't crafted theirs and miss opportunities as a result. My personal "sound bite" has nurtured valuable connections at networking and social events, meetings, and even casual encounters, because people learn immediately what I do and how my expertise might be useful for them or someone they know.

For example, with my passion for skiing, I occasionally serve as a member of the ski patrol in Pennsylvania. I once rescued a skier, and later as he was recovering, he asked me what I did. On top of that mountain, we were far away from our business environments, but my M.O. "rolled out" quite naturally, starting a conversation that snowballed into other connections. Two weeks later, he called and invited me to speak at his company. Jackpot—an avalanche of opportunity! We never know from where good things flow. Just be prepared so they don't run off. —A.S.

When networking in professional circles, your statement should define what you do for a living, for whom, and the results your work provides.

- I present programs to help businesses increase profitability by exceeding their customers' expectations.

- I develop communication strategies to help small businesses effectively market their services and grow their operations.

- I help teens explore career paths that utilize their gifts and talents.

- I help people gain confidence in creating successful connections in both their personal and professional lives.

- I produce marketing materials to help businesses strategically position their products and services to consumers.

If you're not employed or simply not interested at the moment in promoting your professional interests, consider a positioning statement that reflects what you'd like people to know about you, such as the following:

- I volunteer as a mentor to help children improve their reading skills.

- I am a student majoring in Environmental Sciences at GW University and interested in protecting our earth's natural resources.

- I am actively involved in planning and implementing fundraising events for our community food bank.

"Mixing and Mingling 101": Connection Courtesies

"Courtesy is the politic witchery of great personages."

Baltasar Gracián, The Art of Worldly Wisdom, 1647

Customs may change, but common courtesy never goes out of style. There are many unwritten rules about basic courtesies that can help in the mixing and mingling of life. Since people judge our behavior on the basis of their own expectations, by extending courtesy and respect at all times, you can enhance the possibilities of meeting their approval and avoiding accidental missteps. Following is a list of common courtesies:

- **Acknowledge the presence of others.** This lets them know they're not invisible. At the very least, say "hello." Give your attention to everyone in the group. If you're having a conversation and someone is standing nearby, alone, invite him or her to join you (if it's not a private conversation).

- **Break into conversations.** Move to within 4 to 5 feet of a group you want to join. Establish eye contact and smile, indicating your interest. When you see or hear a natural place to jump into the discussion, ask a question or offer a suitable quip. Then, introduce

YOU DON'T HAVE TO SAY A WORD!

Excellent eye contact, positive facial expressions, open gestures, nodding, good posture and body positioning, and supportive verbal encouragers (such as mmhhmm, aah, and the like) are nonverbal cues that boost your connections with people. For more information about the power of body language, see Key #4: Boost Your Communication IQ.

yourself and restart the conversation by asking a question or referring to an earlier comment.

- **Take turns.** Although communication traffic does not have road signs, there are definite rules of courtesy. Since you have no blinkers to indicate you want to turn, you must signal your intentions: to pass the conversation to another person, use eye contact, or direct a question or comment to him or her. Word of warning: if you're caught with a non-stop talker, avoid giving cues that say "keep on talking," such as nodding, smiling, or uttering "mmhhmm's". Wait for a pause and then change the subject or gracefully exit.

- **In search of.** When you're ready to change partners, a good segue is to ask for help:

  - "I'm looking for the meeting planner for the association. Do you know who she is and where I might find her?"

  - "Do you know anyone here that I might talk to about fundraising?"

- **Explain your plans.** When you're ready to change partners or you have another agenda, let people know the reason for your departure by telling them what you want or need to do:

  - *I promised to meet my colleague here this evening. I need to see if he's arrived.*

  - *Please excuse me, I was intrigued by what Osmond said during his presentation and I'd like to talk with him.*

  - *Would you excuse me? I want to say 'hello' to an old friend I just spotted.*

  - *I need to talk with Marisa, our client's project manager. We have to catch up on a few details.*

- **Give reasons for actions that might appear rude.** For instance, if you interrupt a conversation to ask an urgent question, apologize and explain why it's important. When people learn why you're making a "rude" action or comment, they usually understand. This also reduces the reactions often precipitated by gestures of rudeness (such as "Who does s/he think s/he is!").

- **Speak in a respectful tone of voice.** An engaging voice resonating with respect is an inviting connector.

- **Monitor others' interest.** Listen to the topic of discussion and be mindful as to whether everyone in the group can participate. Avoid "talking shop" or carrying on about any one topic when it's not pertinent to the interests of others, such as a diatribe on youth sports when others present don't have children in sports.

- **Double your pleasure.** If you want to move on, but don't want to leave a conversation partner alone, extend an invitation:

  - *How about if we check out those enticing appetizers over there?*

  - *I want to say 'hello' to the new chair of our outreach committee. Would you like to join me?*

  - *Would you like to see if we can locate the meeting rooms for the next session?*

- **Make a graceful exit.** When you sense it's time to move on during a networking function or meeting, end on a note that is professional and polite. Bring closure with a smile: "I've really enjoyed talking with you." "It's been fascinating learning about your adventures." "I'll definitely remember what you told me about ..." Exchange business cards or contact information, and initiate a follow-up step that indicates your level of interest:

  - *I look forward to continuing our conversation the next time we meet.*

  - *I'll call you next week to set up a time for us to get together.*

  - *I'll e-mail that information as soon as I get back to my office.*

  - *I'd be happy to share your name with my training staff.*

FINDING THE PEARLS IN THE OYSTER NETWORK

They say the world is your oyster. So, if you think of people as human oysters containing pearls of possibilities, don't clam up ... get cracking! Vast treasures are revealed by opening up and connecting. Seeds of rich opportunities are found within everyone, just awaiting your discovery. At the same time, it's essential to remain open and receptive so others can discover the precious gems in your personal cache, too.

We're all a part of the good 'ol Oyster Network; your power is multiplied by tapping into its connections. What do you want? What do you need? Your answers might be found within the person standing next to you in the check-out line, or cheering at your daughter's basketball game, perhaps vacationing on a tropical island, sitting next to you on the train, or living next door or down the street.

We've received many business leads from unexpected "oysters"—attending school plays, shopping in supermarkets, waiting in line at airports, through our kids' friends, volunteering, attending community meetings, and even landed a contract as the result of presenting a success workshop to inmates in a detention center! Life is one gigantic pearl-diving adventure! Always look for the treasures.

Don't Sweat the Small Talk!

*"Ultimately, the bond of all companionship,
whether in marriage or in friendship, is conversation."*

Oscar Wilde

Do you sometimes find it challenging to strike up and carry on a conversation? Do you experience anxiety from long, uncomfortable silences? Have you ever missed opportunities to meet someone intriguing or important because you didn't know what to say? Are you ever afraid of saying something that might make you sound "stupid"?

Fear is the enemy of connecting—fear of saying the wrong thing, making a stupid remark, or enduring painful, awkward moments of not knowing what to say. Feeling ill-at-ease in social interactions keeps people miserably stuck in uncomfortable places. They end up watching others meet the people they want to meet, have the fun they want to have, and enjoy life the way they wish they could.

For those who are "conversationally challenged," plenty of mental energy is exerted (often in anguish) while searching for something to say, anything, to connect with people. Others seem to never be at a loss for words, effortlessly engaging anyone and everyone in a seemingly endless discourse. But being a good conversationalist is not necessarily an innate talent. It is a skill that can be acquired and enhanced, simply by having the right tools to start up a conversation and keep it flowing.

If you sometimes feel conversationally challenged, we offer a few basic rules to ensure more success and less stress in your personal and professional endeavors. One basic principle of communication is that people enjoy talking about their personal interests, so focusing on them and their pursuits can take away the pressure. Another is (as the saying goes): "Feel the fear and do it anyway!"

The few "starters" listed below offer a stream of topics to help the conversation flow:

- Say something flattering. Start a conversation with a compliment. Perhaps it's something you notice about the person—an attractive jacket, a fashionable hat, a colorful tie, or a unique piece of jewelry he or she is wearing. Is someone sporting a tan in the dead of winter? That's likely to lead to a lively discussion about some intriguing travel destination they recently visited.

  People love being acknowledged, so comment on something positive you've heard or observed about their work, their involvement in the community, or maybe about a family member who is making headlines, such as a daughter who made the winning shot in a recent game or a relative who was awarded some special recognition. Perhaps you were at a meeting together and she made an interesting comment. A good starter might be, "I really enjoyed what you had to say about... " Just remember, compliments should always be genuine.

- Relate to the present moment or experience. Explore ideas relating to the current time, place, and situation, or what's going on around you. Reflect on the occasion. For instance, if you're attending a meeting, conference, or networking function, here are some suggestions for starting up conversations.

  - *Are you a member (of the sponsoring group)?*

  - *How long have you been a member?*

  - *What value have you gained from your membership?*

  - *How often do you attend?*

  - *Tell me about some of the interesting sessions you've attended at the conference.*

  - *What are some of the most valuable ideas you've gained at this meeting? How have they been useful?*

  - *How do you think the recommendations of the speaker would make a difference if implemented?*

  - *Is this your first time attending?*

  - *Do you live in the area?*

- **Observe your surroundings.** Natural conversation starters flow naturally from your environment. When visiting someone's office or home, look around for potential topics. Notice how the room is furnished; scan the walls, desktop, or décor for clues. Do they have pictures of family members? Celebrities or dignitaries? Special collections, trophies, or awards? People enjoy talking about what's important and meaningful to them, so ask questions about what you see.

- **Go fish!** Probe for areas of common interest by fishing for some tasty morsels of mutual interest. When you find one, milk it for the sweet juice it offers in building a connection. Springboard a conversation by exploring a variety of topics using ideas from this list. The art of conversation is like a game of leapfrog, hopping from topic to topic, until landing on one that sticks. Exploring common interests is also like digging for gold; it may take some time to discover those nuggets, but when you do, they offer rich treasures to mine for more. Eureka!

CONNECT WITH COMMON INTERESTS

I was on the list of speakers being considered to present a keynote address at a national conference. When I went to meet the person responsible for selecting the speaker, I noticed a National Ski Patrol certificate on his office wall. That kicked off our hour-long conversation about skiing, which landed not only the opportunity to speak, but an invitation to join him and other patrollers out in Aspen, Colorado. It reinforced to me the value of focusing on common interests. —A.S.

- **Hobbies and special interests.** Do they like to golf? Ski? Climb mountains? Volunteer? Are they history buffs? If there's a match, you're in luck because the conversation can easily delve into what you know and enjoy.

- **Reading interests.** "What do you like to read?" This is another topic that pinpoints their interests and can target a whole world of possibilities, from best sellers to investment strategies, parenting, boating, collecting antiques, spiritual exploration, historical fiction—literally a bookstore and library of ideas.

- **Weekend activities.** Weekends are often packed with adventures and demonstrate special interests or commitments—whether it's running in a 10K charity event, mountain biking, camping with the Scouts, or hot air ballooning. Inquire about their upcoming weekend plans, or ask how they enjoyed the last weekend.

- **Goals and dreams.** Most people hold dreams in their hearts, so nudge your way into them. Ask what goals they may be working toward and what inspired them to pursue them.

- **Travel.** Travel opens up a world of discussion. Our global network now has people scrambling all over the planet. The question, "Do you have an opportunity to travel often?" usually gets people talking about some rather intriguing experiences. If they are globe-trotters, probe for further topics:

  - *What are some of the biggest travel challenges you've encountered?*

  - *Tell me about some of your favorite places you've visited.*

  - *What other places would you like to visit?*

  - *What are your travel plans for this year?*

- **Personal opinions.** Many people can't wait to speak their minds. Asking them, "What's your opinion regarding ...?" can provide you with additional ways of opening doors to other areas of conversation. For instance, if you're attending a meeting about making money on the Internet, ask the obvious question: "What's been your experience with Internet marketing?

- **Current events.** Suggest a topic from the news or something you may have seen on TV, heard on the radio, or read about in a magazine or newspaper, or on the Internet. Choose from world, national, local, or lifestyle concerns, or draw on some of the wackier news features, inquiring, "Did you see ...?" Did you hear about ...?"

- **Challenges.** Ask people about the challenges they're currently encountering. People often enjoy the chance to have others listen and serve as sounding boards. To address work-related challenges, you might lead with, "What do you like about your job?" followed by "What are some of the challenges you face in it?" Challenges are found everywhere, so the topics are truly unlimited, whether they're parenting, balancing career and family, taking care of an elderly loved one, or volunteering.

- **Advice.** Ask people for advice on matters related to their expertise. People enjoy being acknowledged for their wisdom, experience, or perspective. Asking questions such as, "What is your opinion about ...?" or "What would you suggest?" opens the door for their opinions to flow.

- **Origins.** Inquiring about how something started can launch a tidal wave of conversations:

  - *When did you get interested in catering (financial planning, collecting butterflies, graphic design)? Where has that interest led you?*

  - *How did you meet the host (the CEO, your partner, the featured speaker)?*

  - *When did you realize you wanted to become a cruise director?*

  - *How did you get the idea for your book?*

  - *What was it like to grow up on a farm (in another country, in a small town, in New York)?*

"No Sweat" Small Talk Tips

"In conversation, keep in mind that you're more interested in what you have to say than anyone else is."

Andrew A. Rooney, Pieces of My Mind

The following steps can help you get the conversational ball rolling:

- **Be ready with an opening line.** There is no one comment that works everywhere because life simply isn't that tidy. Effective openers can springboard off a statement made during your introduction or from your shared current experience, such as:

  - A query about their unique name

  - An observation about the city you're in

  - A question about their interest in the meeting you're both attending

  - A remark about a piece of jewelry or vibrant color they're wearing

  - An observation about the dramatic story delivered by the speaker

  - A comment about the ambience of the event

  - A remark about the large number of people attending

  The purpose of the opening line is to make a connection and start the process of exploring common ground. Generally, the more you reveal about yourself, the more others reveal about themselves. During introductions, tossing out a snippet and providing more than just your name gives the other person permission to do the same. At a networking event, start by introducing yourself, including your professional affiliation; at a party, you might talk about how you know the host and ask them about their connection as well.

- **Build conversational bridges that take you to new topics to explore.** To move a conversation in a different direction, use statements that create a new flow for discussion: "That reminds me of ..." (Take it away!) "Your comment about ... reminded me of ... "

ENDURING A DOSE OF DISCOMFORT

The motto posted on my computer reads, "If you don't ask, you don't get." It's a daily reminder that opportunities come to those who reach beyond their Comfort Zones. That motto could be adapted to "If you don't connect, you don't get."

I can honestly say that I now enjoy getting out of my Comfort Zone, but it wasn't always that way. When I first started attending networking events, community mixers, and association meetings, I waited for people to introduce themselves to me; I was more comfortable waiting rather than reaching out. I noticed that I wasn't alone. Many others seemed to be waiting as well, reaching out to the food or beverage table instead of connecting with each other.

Fortunately, someone offered me a bit of advice in developing rapport and the connections it could yield: (1) pretend you're the host, and (2) realize that most people standing alone are desperate for someone to talk to. Taking the advice to heart, I began assuming the role of host, introducing myself to everyone. I learned that by offering to make others comfortable, I could offer both comfort and conversation. When I felt any discomfort about my new "role," I asked myself, "What's the worst that can happen?" The worst that ever happened was that someone didn't feel like talking.

In the many years that I have followed this sage advice, I have met many interesting people, formed valuable relationships, and gained experiences that have enhanced my life in countless ways. Think of the people in your own life you wouldn't have met, the relationships that might never have developed, or the opportunities you might have lost, had you decided not to reach out and connect. Enduring connections might be hard to endure at first, but their value is long-lasting. —A.S.

- **Play the host.** Even if it's not your official duty, taking on a host-like demeanor can help you more easily meet and greet your way around the room: "Hi, I'm Hector. Glad you could join us this evening!" Consider volunteering for the greeting committee or to host a meeting, giving you a built-in opportunity to start conversations with everyone who attends.

- **Abolish the fear of rejection.** While this may be easier said than done, focus on your goal, whether it's to have more friends, more opportunities, or more confidence. Do you want to expand your network? Have more fun? Meet interesting people? Secure more business? Take steps to move in the direction of your goal. Remember, many people are uncomfortable approaching others and will welcome your friendly gesture (rather than finding solace dipping nervously into the guacamole!) Be sure to review Key #1: Cultivate Confidence.

- **Talk to the person standing alone.** It's downright awkward to be in a group setting and not be interacting with others. Reach out to people on the sidelines or to those not talking with anyone. They will undoubtedly appreciate your gesture for sparing them any more moments of anguish.

- **Make yourself approachable.** A friendly smile is the beginning of many intriguing connections. Maintain good eye contact and be open with your body language. Don't wait for others to make the first move or to speak first. Take the initiative and listen to the sound of free-flowing conversation; it's music to your ears, and others might enjoy being a part of the symphony, too!

- **Join Toastmasters International.** Build confidence whether speaking to one person or 100 by participating in a supportive learning environment. With chapters around the world, it's a convenient way to improve your speaking and listening skills. Contact them at 1-800-WeSpeak or www.Toastmasters.org.

DON'T GO THERE!

Here are some things to avoid in conversations:

- Gossiping

- Talking too long about yourself

- Talking about an illness or operation in detail

- Dominating the conversation

- Bragging (this is different from promoting your achievements)

- Being critical of others who have different opinions

- One-upsmanship

- Interrupting

- Using unfamiliar terminology

- Displaying insensitivity regarding race, religion, gender, age, or sexual preferences

- Asking personal questions

Learn What Makes Each Person Tick

"All persons are puzzles until at last we find in some word or act the key to the man, to the woman; straightway all their past words and actions lie in light before us."

Ralph Waldo Emerson

Establishing a sense of congruence or similarity with other people is an important element of building rapport. When you understand other people, and are attuned to their needs and desires, they are more likely to feel as though you're on the same wavelength.

Learning what makes people tick facilitates understanding and connecting with them. This is especially useful in negotiations or when you're involved in sales or customer service or other situations in which sorting out all the options is critical. Here are some guidelines that will help you hone in on their needs:

- What do they value?
- What's important to them?
- How do they like to spend their time?
- What are their goals?
- What motivates them?
- What makes them happy?
- What do they get excited about?
- What are their current concerns?
- What's their current lifestyle?
- How might a product or service fit their current lifestyle?
- Who are the important people in their lives, personally and professionally?

NAILING A NEED

When shopping recently for a new car for our daughters, we each had our own priorities. While safety and economy topped the list for my husband and me, Stacy, my youngest daughter, was tracking how "cool" the car had to look and how she would look in it. After a few test drives, the choice was narrowed to an economical, sporty model with an excellent safety record in either a blue or silver exterior. My oldest daughter, Stephanie liked either one, so it was Stacy's choice from here; she liked them both and couldn't decide.

The sales rep asked her what she needed to make a decision. Stacy said she couldn't decide between the two colors, so color was now the key to the sale. She sat in the silver one, then in the blue one, and still was torn between the two. The salesman knew his sale was just a color choice away. Perhaps because Stacy was wearing a blue outfit, he commented on how the blue car matched both her outfit and her eyes. That's just what she needed to hear to close the deal and make her "baby blues" really sparkle! —S.S.

Get in Sync: Reflect a Familiar Image

Being synchronized, or "in sync," is the ability to tune in to others, to create a rhythm of similar movements and behavioral cues that orchestrate a wonderful harmony. Being in sync means having rapport; it means playing up your similarities to establish a stronger connection, to create that "You, too!" experience. It means reducing the distance or differences between us.

Often subconsciously, we synchronize ourselves to those around us, picking up subtle signals and modulating our behavior in response. When we're in sync, an invisible energy serves as a connecting current between us. Connection is easier, almost effortless, as we sense that others understand us and our needs. That's because when people reflect our own behaviors, they're mirroring a very familiar image back to us.

People like people who reflect their own image. When we're with people who mirror our own (or similar) qualities, we're smack in the middle of our Comfort Zone and it feels divine, nothing scratchy or irritating rubbing us the wrong way, frustrating us, or getting under our skin. It seems as though we can more easily understand and relate to each other's needs.

Being out of sync means being out of step, out of tune, and not on the same wavelength. We're out of our Comfort Zone; making connections is challenging as we struggle to find common ground. Our familiar ways simply don't work the same. We're not as prone to like or trust those with whom we have difficulty establishing rapport, which can mean lost opportunities on both sides of the chasm.

One key to revving up rapport and increasing our harmony with others is learning to reflect their behavior back to them. This means using simple and effective connecting devices that plug us in to the same wavelength and speed up our "connect-ability." The result can definitely create electric connections that offer high-voltage opportunities!

The technique of reflecting a person's body language is called matching and *mirroring*. It is done by selectively mirroring body movements,

posture, tone of voice, and rate of speech. The object is not to parrot someone's behavior, but to convey congruence by subtly giving them a glimpse of their own behavior. When you match their behavior naturally and respectfully, you're telling them (on a subconscious level) that you're "with them."

To reflect someone's body language, synchronize your movements at a comfortable tempo without being obvious. Focus on their facial expressions and reflect them back. If they smile, you beam back; if they look worried, indicate your concern. Match their stance, use similar gestures, tilt and nod your head, breathe at the same rate, and adjust the tone, tempo, and volume of your voice to match theirs. Body movements can be easily synchronized without others being conscious of your mirroring them by design. Remember, the keyword for effective use of this technique is "subtle."

Make Sense Out of Sensory Preferences

Neuro-linguistic programming (NLP) studies the structure of how humans think and experience the world, including how we process information through our senses. Each of us has a dominant mode by which we interpret our experiences, primarily either sight, sound, or touch. You can usually identify someone's sensory preference through visual cues and by listening closely to the words they use. Our vocabulary is peppered with clues and reflects our sensory preference, using words that relate to sight, sound, or touch: "I see what you mean." "I hear what you're saying." "It feels like the right choice." Taste and smell play a relatively minor role in processing information, although these also appear in our vocabulary: "Such a sweet deal!" "I smell a dirty rat!" "It stinks!"

Our sensory preference even affects how we learn:

- Visual Processors understand and remember better when information is presented visually
- Auditory Processors do better when they hear information
- Kinesthetic Processors "get it" when they can apply the information through touch and a "hands-on" approach

When we are able to track someone's sensory preference and relate to it, we're tuning in to their sensory channel and speaking their language, the language they process through sight, sound, or touch. Typically, people can shift from one sensory mode to another. But when stress escalates, as in times of negotiation or confrontation, people often become frozen in their preferred sensory mode. They have more difficulty expressing themselves and find it harder to understand other sensory modes. Therefore, it's especially important to get in sync with a person's preferred sensory style. Otherwise, you may be locked out of a vital connection at a time when understanding is needed the most.

Getting in sync with a person's preferred sensory mode puts you on their wavelength. By matching their mode, you're tuned in to their sensory channel, which is beneficial for gaining their trust, especially when trust is fundamental to the communication or negotiation at hand.

Sensory Modes of Communication

Visual Processors think in pictures, gesture with their hands, talk fast, dress impeccably, and have an astute eye for matching colors from memory. They're well-groomed and concerned about their personal appearance, and they enjoy stylish surroundings. They "see down the road" and like to be in control so they can capture the vision and create it.

When speaking, they may look up to the left and right as if to catch the vision from the corners of their eyes. Visual Processors use words related to sight.

Visual statements include phrases such as:

- *I see.*
- *Look at it this way.*
- *The way I see it …*
- *It appears …*
- *I can see how that might work.*
- *Let me make this clear.*
- *I get the picture.*

Auditory Processors respond to the quality of sound and are sensitive about noise levels and tonality. They tend to gesture from side to side, but their gestures are more subdued than those of Visual Processors. Auditory Processors enjoy words and conversation, and are frequently employed as broadcasters, lawyers, counselors, teachers, professional speakers, and writers.

When speaking, their eyes move from side to side, rather than making a lot of direct eye contact; too much eye contact tends to distract them. Although our society encourages direct eye contact to reflect confidence and strengthen connections, Auditory Processors have difficulty with this. Their vocabulary is peppered with words related to hearing and sound.

Auditory statements include phrases such as:

- *I hear you saying ...*

- *What you're telling me ...*

- *It sounds like ...*

- *I hear you loud and clear!*

- *Sounds good to me!*

- *Let me tell you.*

Kinesthetic Processors process information through touch, movement, and feelings. Comfort is king to them; how something feels is their top priority. They often speak very slowly, quite possibly because it takes longer to put feelings into words than it does to translate mental images or sounds. Kinesthetics often choose on-the-go careers—athletes, emergency response and medical personnel, and sales professionals, as well as people who like working with their hands such as chefs, carpenters, electricians, and plumbers. Because of their kinesthetic nature, they use words related to touch and feeling.

Kinesthetic statements include phrases such as:

- *I sense ...*
- *I have a good sense where we're headed.*
- *It feels right to me.*
- *I'm not following you.*
- *It's hard to figure ...*
- *Wish I could put my finger on it.*
- *You have everything you need at your fingertips.*
- *Walk me through it one more time.*

Project a Pleasing Presence

"Nothing succeeds like the appearance of success."

Christopher Lasch

Each of us is an individual marketing package that communicates our social, professional, and personal identities to the world. Where do you want your personal "package" to take you? Successful people recognize that an impeccable personal appearance can transport them straight into their desired circles of influence. Like it or not, those who are tastefully dressed and neatly groomed are generally given more respect and granted more privileges. By "packaging" yourself for success with the style that suits both you and those you want to reach, you project a powerful presence and create a winning edge.

An attractive appearance makes an immediate impression; it can make or break a connection. In addition to enhancing our own self-confidence, paying attention to our appearance increases our connect-ability with others. If we don't make a good impression, we may not get a second chance to develop a relationship that otherwise could introduce our products or services, make a sale, start a friendship or romance, expand our networks, or take us where we want to go. Being "turned off" is often terminal!

Many people who are in positions of authority have more freedom for personal expression in their fashion statements, whether it be quirky, outlandish, or outrageous. However, their personal appearance still affects those they want to influence. For the rest of us, we can't go wrong by showing up well-groomed and tastefully dressed.

While some of the conventional standards of wardrobe and fashion are more relaxed nowadays, guidelines still exist and are considered appropriate to maximize impressions made in the workplace. In social settings, dressing correctly for the occasion never goes out of style. Since we're judged by our appearance, follow conventional wisdom to make a desirable impression for projecting your best.

Here's a checklist for producing a pleasing, polished, and professional image:

- Project an overall appearance that is clean, fresh, healthy, and fit, and reflects a sense of well-being

- Always wear clothes that are free of wrinkles and stains; make sure your apparel fits correctly, is suitable for your age and style, doesn't clash, and is appropriate for the occasion

- In professional settings, make sure your shoes are polished

- Wear subtle, natural-looking makeup

- Keep your nails well manicured, whether they are polished or not

- Make sure you have attractive, well-maintained teeth and fresh breath

- Wear tasteful jewelry that is not excessive or noisy (no jingling bracelets or dangling earrings)

- Keep your hair clean; wear styles and colors that are both traditional and flattering (kept away from the face); hairpieces should look natural and fit right

- Use perfumes sparingly; some people are chemically sensitive or may find a particular fragrance objectionable

Appearance counts and speaks volumes. Your appearance gets you noticed, opens doors, ushers in new opportunities, and wins friends and business deals—you have an array of possibilities, all enhanced by your pleasing, powerful presence.

Go for Their Funny Bones

"A good sense of humor helps to overlook the unbecoming,
understand the unconventional, tolerate the unpleasant,
overcome the unexpected, and outlast the unbearable."

Unknown

It's almost impossible to smile or laugh and not relate positively to people around you. Laughter is contagious and has a magnetic appeal. The energy surrounding humor is naturally uplifting. It magically raises spirits; it's kinetic, connecting energy in motion.

Humor is a tonic for togetherness—sharing laughter and smiles brings people closer. Imagine how we could transform the atmosphere every-where, if only we could bottle it and ship a case or two to those in need of a gigantic dose! People like to be around those who amuse them because of the good feelings stirred up by laughter.

If you're caught in a snag or snarl, search for any tidbit that might offer a shred of humor. Having a sense of humor cushions against life's inevitable blows, busts, and boondoggles, and keeps up the spirit we need to endure them. Besides, taking life too seriously takes its toll, both on us and our relationships. Whenever we're being too serious, too stressed, or spending too much time sweating the small stuff, it's time to tickle a few funny bones, starting with our own. By looking through the lens of laughter and lightening up on both ourselves and others, the energy around us lifts, as well. When connections are beginning to fall apart from too much tension, they often get bonded back together with a little "glueshtick"—a little humor to patch things up.

When we poke fun at ourselves, about the silly things we do or the wacky things that happen to us, and laugh about our imperfections and our predicaments, others usually join in. It makes us more real and more approachable, as well as more memorable, because people tend to remember the moments of divine comedy—when we reveal our imperfect selves and our silly sides. The funniest people we know expose their foibles, flaws, and fumblings without attempting to disguise them. They bring out the wisecracks, let them shine, and transform them into comical authenticity!

Creating joy is charismatic; laughter signals the presence of a joyous spirit. Humor comes in many forms—from the subtle to the sublime, from a clever quip to rolling-on-the-floor outrageous. It all has a positive effect and people delight in it.

Real humor abounds everywhere; we just have to be ready to scoop it up and have some fun with it. Laughter is the glue that joins humans together and produces memorable snapshots of long duration—enduring connections are bound to develop.

THE GIFT OF WIT

Humorist Michael Aronin learned to laugh at himself early in life. Born with cerebral palsy, his life has had its share of challenges, but humor helped softened the blows. As Michael tells it, at the age of four, when he was just learning how to walk, he fell down on a shopping trip with his mom and was unable to lift himself. As his mother and a passer-by helped him up, he quipped to the woman: "You know, I really should-n't drink this much so early in the morning." Oh, Michael!

"Laughter's always helped me survive, even during the toughest times. Humor is my way of putting people at ease about my disability. Everywhere I go, I use humor as an intro-duction. It transforms every interaction. We're only here for a while and what better legacy to leave behind than a legacy of laughter." What an attitude!

We can attest to Michael's ability to "leave 'em laughing." He serves as a frequent emcee during our local National Speakers Association chapter meetings, has appeared in comedy clubs across the country, and is a frequent guest on radio and TV. His quick wit is enviable and his timing impec-cable. Whenever Michael is on the platform, the entire room lights up with laughter.

What's So Funny??!!

"Humor is a set of attitudes and skills that we can use to move from 'grin and bear it' to 'grin and share it'."

Joel Goodman

You don't have to be a professional comedian to be funny. You just have to have a willingness to look at the lighter side of life. Here are some ideas for adding a little humor to your rapport:

- **Use humor that's appropriate, timely, and tasteful.** Being the target of someone else's bad taste or poor judgment is never funny. Avoid telling stories or jokes that focus on race, ethnicity, gender, disabilities, sex, sexual orientation, or other subjects that may be disrespectful, critical, or condemning to others.

- **Scan your material for irony or double meanings.** Humor is often based on them. One of our speaking colleagues, Ron Culberson, a humorist, suggests putting together two unrelated points with an unexpected spin to capture the laughter you're after. The following story is a good example of this.

- **Use self-effacing humor.** Make a joke about yourself, never about anyone else. Some possible areas to focus on include your height, weight, disability, career, looks, hair (or lack of it), or a personal situation.

- **Glean funny or strange stories from the media.** Humorous or bizarre events appear right along with the headlines every day— bungling crook capers, parodies on politicians, and other humorous everyday events add welcome comic relief to a stressed-out and all-too-serious world.

- **Collect funny jokes, stories, and anecdotes.** Gather stories with humorous twists. For endless resources, check out search engines on the Internet with the keywords "jokes" or "humor," or drill down even more specifically: "business humor" or "parent humor." File them away in your collection for adding a light-hearted accent. If telling jokes or stories doesn't come naturally, be sure to invest some time to polish them up with a little practice. Always remember the punch line and work on your timing for flawless delivery.

- **Keep a list of humorous quotations.** Check out the library, bookstore, or Internet. Do an Internet search using "humorous quotations" as the keywords for peppering your conversations or presentations with humor.

- **Watch comedians in action.** Observe how they weave together stories along with their impeccable timing, delivery, and gestures.

HUMOR SOMETIMES COMES IN SPURTS

In honor of my parents 50th Golden Wedding anniversary, my brother, sister, and I captured some of our family's treasured times in a poem, "50 Cherished Golden Moments." We shared it with friends and family during the festive celebration.

Later that evening, when our family had gathered together for dinner, my brother was helping dad squeeze mustard onto his hot dog. My father had Parkinson's Disease which made some of the simplest movements difficult. The clogged mustard bottle suddenly erupted, accidentally squirting Dad in yellow goo.

Dad had always been quite the quipster whose fitting remarks knew how to capture a humorous event. Even though the disease had slowed and slurred his speech, it never robbed him of his humor. A grin lit up Dad's face as he slowly drawled, "Another Gulden moment!" The man had quite literally become mellow yellow! Even though the disease had taken away so much of his agility, his humor remained forever intact. —S.S.

- **Increase your humor IQ.** Repeat often the affirmations, "I am very humorous. I see life in a humorous way." Keep looking for humor everywhere and you'll likely see funny things popping up all around you.

- **Inject an element of surprise.** Liven up your life with unexpected surprises that generate laughter. Think creatively about how you might spark up the routine by adding more fun and your personality to the mix. Add humor to your emails or presentations, when appropriate. Might a particular presentation gain some laughs with a shower of confetti that "explodes" from a fake microphone? How about a funny photo or cartoon? Think out of the box—more laughter is usually found there.

- **Put a message on your voicemail that gets people grinning.** With so many message prompts sometimes required for getting to the right department (and the corresponding frustration that results), adding humor can be a wise investment! With the element of surprise, we're whisked out of the realm of the routine to enjoy the lighter side of life.

Stay on the humor quest. Don't give up, even if your humor doesn't appear to be working. Just keep looking through the lens of laughter and remind yourself that life's imperfections are a rich treasure chest of humorous material.

In addition to its high connect-ability quotient, laughter also has other beneficial attributes. It makes you feel better, both emotionally and physically. When you laugh, a stress-relieving chain reaction takes place, flooding your body with natural "feel good" compounds called beta-endorphins. The result—you feel better and so does everyone else who shares the laugh.

Just one light-hearted comment can open the door to connecting smiles and connected humanity. Think of life as a situation comedy. If you go through life looking for more humorous material for your "act," you'll see the world as an opportunity for gathering funny stories and harvesting humor.

FOCUS ON THE FUNNY

Mine the gold from the treasure box of your own life experiences for humorous material—moments of sheer embarrassment (looking back, they probably were hysterical) or other events that touched hearts and funny bones with levity and laughter:

- Family gatherings

- A blind date

- Moments when you wanted to "curl up and die" from embarrassment

- Kid antics

- Pet tricks

- Holiday happenings

- Times you blew it and knew it

- Fashion emergencies (weird things that happen with the clothes we wear)

- Language disconnects

- Travel calamities

- Mixed up luggage or gifts

- A funny thing that happened at a serious or somber event

- A workout fiasco

- Funny failures of miscommunication

- Fixing things

- Humorous anywhere happenings

Humor is a matter of focus. So, take a FUNdamental approach to living. Look for the *fun* before *da mental*. That way you'll focus and find what's funny first, before analyzing all the reasons why life should be taken seriously. Honing in on the humorous nourishes the soul, lightens up your surroundings, and connects you to others.

LIGHTEN UP!

We found this circulating on the Internet, demonstrating how flight attendants and pilots have given passengers a few giggles in the air by glibly modifying routine messages:

There may be 50 ways to leave your lover, but there are only 4 ways out of this airplane.

Folks, we have reached our cruising altitude now, so I am going to switch off the seat belt sign. Feel free to move about as you wish, but please stay inside the plane 'till we land. It's a bit cold outside, and if you walk on the wings it affects the flight pattern.

Your seat cushions can be used for flotation. In the event of an emergency water landing, please take them with our compliments.

As you exit the plane, please make sure to gather all of your belongings. Anything left behind will be distributed evenly among the flight attendants. Please do not leave children or spouses.

Last one off the plane must clean it!

Energize the Winning Spirit

The Winning Spirit is the expression of the actions and attitudes of excellence. Putting the winning spirit to work is connecting energy in motion, bringing out the best in people and their experiences. Its potential exists within everyone, and can be nurtured by recognizing and appreciating their special gifts, talents, and contributions. Encouraging the winning spirit is vital for sustaining the actions and attitudes that create enduring connections and the spirit of cooperation.

Putting Excellence into Action

"All things come to those who go after them."

EJ Marshall

Do you find that you experience something most extraordinary when interacting with people who have a clear intention of making people their passion? When people "show up" to express their best, they simply shine—they are jewels of priceless, high-performance energy! Their "diamond power" makes an extraordinary difference when all those jewels within them, their collection of gifts and talents, really get "glowing" and radiate out to all the people in their circle of influence. It's the eX factor that makes all the difference:

eX factor = the attitudes and actions of eXcellence that create eXtraordinary eXperiences

Whenever you plug in the eX factor, excellence is definitely in the air! In customer service, it's a refreshing breeze that simply blows the competition away... the dazzling attitude, the friendly smile, the engaging manner, the focus on needs, and the expert knowledge of how to make every interaction most extraordinary. In the workplace, the eX factor cultivates the right atmosphere and a climate of cooperation for nurturing creativity, productivity, and dynamic connections. In our personal connections, it means the commitment to fully express our potential and support others in that same goal. It's the winning spirit within us, our eX factor, that fires up our passion for expressing our best in countless ways.

Make a Choice and "Glow with It"

It's up to us to put our eX factor to work. Consistent choices become our habits. We can choose habits that create enduring impressions if we think of them as the right CHOICE:

> Choosing
> Habits
> Of
> Increasing
> Continuous
> Excellence

What would life be like in our worksites, our schools, our homes, and our communities if we all chose habits of increasing continuous excellence, all the time? We would simply astound ourselves and one another!

When you focus on your eX factor, in addition to being of service to others, you're also serving your own best interests. That's because when you truly share your gifts, talents, and expertise, you discover greater purpose, meaning, and significance in the process. Expressing your best reinforces wonderful feelings of positive self-regard with direct benefits to your health, well-being, and relationships. By recognizing that how you "show up" really does make a difference, the eX factor is indeed most eXtraordinary!

The Distinctive Difference of a Dazzling vs. a Deadly Attitude

"We either make ourselves miserable, or we make ourselves strong. The amount of work is the same."

Carlos Castaneda

Your attitude reflects your thoughts and feelings and is revealed in your voice, your words, and your facial expressions. Your attitude has a direct impact on the quality of your relationships and helps determine whether you engage people or turn them off. Your attitudes direct your destiny in both subtle and significant ways.

Positive attitudes (we call them Dazzling Attitudes) are like powerful magnets. A person with a positive attitude looks on the bright side and tries to see the best in everyone and everything. They attract the interest of others with their optimism, enthusiasm, and love of life. Positive attitudes also seem to magically bring out the best in others, too.

What's it like being with those on the flip side, the people who complain, blame, and see the worst in others? Uncomfortable? Miserable to spend even a few moments in their presence? Do you find yourself concocting excuses to keep interactions with them brief or avoid them altogether? Negative attitudes (we call them Deadly Attitudes) are naturally repelling. The only thing these attitudes attract is a chain of avoidance strategies by people who don't want to catch them!

Dazzling Attitude Traits	**Deadly Attitude Traits**
Optimistic	Pessimistic
Courageous	Fearful
Patient	Impatient
Thoughtful	Rude
Cheerful	Complaining
Caring	Uncaring
Interested	Bored
Helpful	Grumpy
Confident	Conceited
Warm	Cold
Enthusiastic	Apathetic
Supportive	Critical
Friendly	Aloof
Motivated	Lazy
Authentic	Fake
Forgiving	Vengeful

Attitudes are contagious. Dazzling Attitudes are worth catching; Deadly Attitudes are like a plague, contaminating connections and breeding bad feelings.

Attitudes are contagious. Is yours worth catching?

What You Get From an Attitude

Attitudes are choices. You have the power to choose how you look at, think about, and respond to every person, event, or situation in your life. You are in control of your attitude, every moment, with every interaction.

The attitudes you choose will determine the quality of your interactions and, ultimately, the quality of your life experience. What do you want in abundance? Happiness? Harmony? An exciting, fulfilling life that is rich in meaning and purpose? Unlimited possibilities? Awesome connections?

Different attitudes create different experiences or outcomes, all part of the natural law of cause and effect or reaping what you sow.

The outcomes associated with a Dazzling Attitude often lead to:

Success	Friendship
Achievement	Happiness
Respect	Patience
Love	Multitude of positive opportunities
Motivation	Well-being
Support	Positive self-image

The outcomes associated with a Deadly Attitude often lead to:

Stress	Money problems
Frustration	Loneliness
Worry	Depression
Envy	Boredom
Dissatisfaction	Health problems
Employment problems	Negative self-image

By adopting the attitudes and actions that help to create the experiences you want, you direct your destiny. At any time, you can decide to speak, think, or respond differently. This means changing habits or patterns that aren't producing the results you want. By knowing what you want in both your personal and professional relationships, you can choose the right attitudes to create the outcomes you most desire.

Dazzling Attitudes propel people toward positive experiences. Successful people typically operate with positive thought patterns—a major reason for their success. Positive personalities shine their optimism on difficult or challenging situations and extract any kernel of good they can find. They accept what can't be changed and make the best of it. They see the possible in the impossible, the good in the bad, and the glimmer of hope in seemingly hopeless situations.

Train your brain to project an optimistic attitude. It will serve you well in expressing the winning spirit.

"There is real magic in enthusiasm. It spells the difference between mediocrity and accomplishment."

Norman Vincent Peale

BOTTOM LINE
ASSETS OF AN ATTITUDE

Consumer surveys repeatedly confirm the value of a good attitude. When customers are asked why they don't return to a business, their overwhelming response: "An attitude of indifference by the owner, manager, or employee." Consumers don't like doing business with people who have rotten or indifferent attitudes.

Enthusiastic employees with optimistic attitudes are valued for their high performance and the positive results they generate. They're excellent assets in their ability to connect with customers and clients as well as coworkers. Companies often bank, quite literally, on the value of positive employee attitudes, which typically translate into greater profitability, better employee relations, and an enhanced work atmosphere. People with winning attitudes are well-recognized for their ability to create a culture of cooperation and teamwork. They're usually quite skilled in getting along well with their colleagues, establishing camaraderie, and making people feel good. Skills can be taught, but attitude is an inside job.

The bottom line: a good attitude is not only an asset but a requirement in many companies—those without the right attitude may not be hired (or might get fired) if a good attitude is missing in action.

Believe it or Not!

"The greatest revolution of our generation is the discovery that human beings by changing the inner attitudes of their minds, can change the outer aspects of their lives."

William James

Your belief system paints a picture of your world, how you relate to it, and what you attract into your life as a result. What you believe to be true, whether it's a belief about a person, situation, or event, is your personal reality. It doesn't have to be supported by fact; in your mind it is your truth. Your choices regarding how you act or respond to people or events are based on your beliefs.

Do you actually believe it's possible to enjoy outrageously wonderful relationships? If you don't, you've just formed a negative belief (that it's not possible to have outrageously wonderful relationships). What you believe to be true becomes your reality! If you don't believe something is possible, it won't be. Your mind responds by falling in line to support your beliefs. If you believe something is impossible, your mind focuses on all the ways to support that impossibility—which then becomes your new reality.

If, on the other hand, you do truly believe that somehow, some way, those quality connections are possible, your mind works overtime to unearth the ways to make those experiences real. With positive mental conditioning, your thoughts are able to hone in on the strongest course of action. By feeding your mind messages that something is possible, your mind goes to work cultivating all the possibilities for making them your reality.

Your beliefs, as formless and intangible as they may seem, will eventually manifest themselves in tangible ways. Therefore, if you want an abundance of friends, harmonious working relationships, and endless

opportunities for enjoying an extraordinary life, you must believe in their possibility, and that you are attracting them to you. Claim whatever you desire as your reality and imagine how you will feel receiving it. Beliefs coupled with feeling are powerful elements of manifestation. Visualize yourself receiving everything you want; picture these images often, along with the feelings of getting your heart's desire. Visualize with vigilance, and don't let appearances, setbacks, or obstacles get in your way. Picture what you desire with passion and never, ever, give up on your dreams! For more information about the power of visualization, refer to Call on Your Courage: See Yourself as Brave, on page 42 in Key #1: Cultivate Confidence: The Cornerstone of Connection.

IT'S A BEAUTIFUL DAY!

A beloved friend in all of his networks of connections, Spencer Bartley exuded enthusiasm everywhere. He was a networking dynamo, perpetually focused on helping others and connecting people to one another for their mutual benefit. He constantly looked for the good in others and in every situation.

His signature phone greeting, "It's a beautiful day!" reflected his winning attitude and exuberance for life, whether it was pouring rain, sleeting, or blizzard-like conditions. But then, his attitude was never really about the weather; it's how Spencer approached every day—seeing the possibilities, not the problems. You'd never really know if Spencer was having a bad day because he simply radiated optimism.

(Continued on next page)

When I learned that he was in the hospital undergoing chemotherapy and radiation treatments for cancer, I called to give him my get well greetings. He answered the phone in the very same way, with the same gusto: "It's a beautiful day!" It actually stunned me to hear the upbeat tone of his voice.

Spencer told me that his hospital experience was a good thing because by being in the hospital he had gained insights into the needs of medical professionals and patient-centered care, perspectives he wouldn't have gotten otherwise. Already he was envisioning ways to turn this health challenge into a positive experience, and as always, Spencer wanted to be a force for good. In spite of his declining health, not to mention the dreariest, soggiest Washington spring on record, Spencer continued to greet nurses, doctors, friends, and family with his signature saying.

On June 21, 2003, on the first beautiful day of summer, the man with the unstoppable attitude died. During his memorial service later that week, many gathered to celebrate his joyous and generous spirit. When I saw the casket lining embroidered with, "It's a beautiful day!" I smiled in spite of great sadness in the passing of this most remarkable man. It was a perfect reflection of how Spencer lived life, a tribute to how he greeted every day as beautiful, no matter what. Those few words became his legacy, a reminder of the power of an attitude and the difference it makes in the minds and hearts of others. —S.S.

Attitude Adjusters to See the Light

"Happiness is a function of accepting what is."

Werner Erhard

Even extremely positive people have moments when they grumble, groan, and glimpse the worst instead of the best in life's ever-changing events. The difference is that they don't dwell on them, and they work feverishly to find the good in a bad or undesirable situation. Keeping an optimistic attitude in the face of negative events is a challenge to even the most optimistic of souls.

It often takes some tools to shift perspectives during difficult, discouraging, and trying times. Optimists live for the light and look hard to see rays of hope filtering through the darkness. To put an optimistic spin on negativity, and break away from gloomy, dismal, or depressing thoughts, use these attitude adjusters to light your way:

Flip Side Exercise

"Nothing worries the pessimist like the optimist who says there's nothing to worry about."

Source unknown

This mind-bending game is based on the principle that a kernel of good is usually planted inside every situation no matter how dismal it may appear. Holding to this belief can miraculously twist your perspective when the unexpected happens. For example:

- If you hate your job, at least you have one.

- If you don't have a job, new opportunities await you.

- If you're involved in a fender bender, thank your lucky stars that you weren't injured.

- If your computer crashes, while it is definitely tear-your-hair-out frustrating, it can be repaired or replaced (hopefully, your files were all backed up to make it less of a technological tragedy!).

Trying to find the flip side of your negative attitude may be laborious, especially when life's complications multiply stress. At these times, you have to dig down deep and put your frustrations in perspective to remember what's really important. It takes some doing to focus on what's good, rather than bad, since our minds usually start cranking "full speed ahead" when it comes to the inconveniences, the impossibilities, and the difficulties that are stirred up by life's many surprises.

C.O.D. (CRUSHED ON DELIVERY)

My niece, Arlene, really didn't want anything after my mother-in-law died except Nana's heirloom china. It reminded her of fond family gatherings and most of all, wonderful memories of her dear grandmother. When the shipment of 12 place settings arrived nearly all broken, Arlene called me to vent. She was crushed (along with the china) and shared her disappointment in having to discard the whole set. As we talked about it, an idea struck from a Girl Scout project my daughter and I had worked on years before, using broken pottery to decorate planters for the patio in colorful mosaics. As I described the process, Arlene's anguish began changing with this new aware-ness—she could still display Nana's china, but in a different way than expected. In fact, she thought she might even decorate an entire table!

The next day I received a shipment of my mother-in-law's gold china, circa 1920, and wondered about their condition as I opened the box. Before even unwrapping the plates, cups, and saucers, I could feel the telltale broken pieces within. Although there were still some settings left to enjoy, the pattern had long since been discontinued. So I shipped off those broken pieces to Arlene to put them to good use as golden accent pieces for her new table. We had made lemonade out of "Humpty Dumpty" lemons. With some attitudinal gymnastics, we were able to shift our angst into acceptance of what was, seeking solutions out of the box, to see new possibilities. —S.S.

To focus on the flip side, try this: carry a pocket-size notebook with you everywhere. When something goes wrong (which is simply life in process, just not according to your plan), write down what happened. Then, look at the flip side (remember, you may have to dig deep to see what might be good about it). Another option is to record these events at the end of the day, with the goal of discovering that kernel of good. Viewing your challenges and frustrations from a "What's good about this?" perspective can change your attitude:

- Lost your job? While the timing or financial situation may not be perfect, you're now free to put your talents to work in a new place with the potential for greater opportunities.

- Broke your leg and wearing a cast? Your cast will capture signatures of friends, plus you'll get extra attention, special privileges, and some TLC, too. Your bones will eventually heal and you'll cast out that cast.

- Didn't get into your first pick of colleges? Your other choices will also offer new places to dream, learn, explore, and make friends.

By seeing a glimmer of good in every situation, your attitude will at least be headed in an optimistic direction, and that is the start of something good!

> *"A pessimist can hardly wait for the future*
> *so he can look back with regret."*
>
> Source unknown

Ground Yourself in Gratitude

Too often, life's challenges can infect our attitude, sapping our energy and rendering us unhappy and less productive. We resent the very presence of uncomfortable and undesirable experiences, cursing them as the scourge of our happiness. We may question, "Why this? Why now?" Happiness is always a choice, although not always the easiest option to select.

To combat the negative forces that suck our energy and enthusiasm, take a gratitude check. Take a moment to reflect on and appreciate the multitude of gifts so often taken for granted—family, friends, the beauty of nature, and life's simple pleasures and treasures. When you feel depressed, lonely, angry, jealous, or impoverished, it may seem nearly impossible to embrace any feelings of being grateful. However, this is exactly the time to count your blessings. When your heart is aching, your career is in question, or a relationship in doubt, take stock. Look hard, and don't overlook the obvious. From your perspective, you may not have the whole pie, but some of the slices are delicious and yours to enjoy right now. Concentrating on what you have, rather than what you don't have, grounds you in gratitude.

> *"You can never get to peace and inner security without first acknowledging all of the good things in your life. If you're forever wanting and longing for more without first appreciating things the way they are, you'll stay in discord."*
>
> Doc Childre and Howard Martin, The HeartMath Solution

Simplify Your Life and Watch Your Attitude Improve

> *"Everyone is trying to accomplish something big, not realizing that life is made up of little things."*
>
> Frank A. Clard

The stress and strain of life in the fast lane can take their toll. Examine what might be at the root of your stress, and explore ways to reduce it. Monitor the causes of your stressors and the impact they have on your life. Determine what you might be able to change to help elevate your attitude. Then commit to taking action. To learn more about relaxation techniques to help you counter stress, see Stamp Out Stress on page 56 in Key #1: Cultivate Confidence: The Cornerstone of Connection.

A DAILY DOSE OF HUMOR

Filling a room with laughter is the personal signature of John Jay Daly, veteran speaker, who's well-known throughout Washington for his hilarious ad libs and quips. John's career in marketing, public relations, and professional speaking has been punctuated not only with his wit, but with his innovative approach to increasing public awareness and communicating the needs of the many associations he has served. The combination of his light-hearted perspective, commitment to excellence, and media savvy has earned him numerous awards, including one for the National Speakers Association-DC, which was named in his honor.

His award-winning talent in the communications field and positive approach to life took on a new focus when his wife, Lu, was diagnosed with Alzheimer's Disease. One of John's major roles today is serious business—meeting the demanding challenges as caregiver to his wife. John has also put his talents to work helping people better understand the disease and its impact on caregivers, as well as to gain more Congressional support for long-term research to find a cure.

He has also found ways to put his gift of humor and positive attitude to work to help him cope with the challenging effects of the disease, which can be so heartbreaking. "Developing a sense of humor is the elixir for a happy life," John noted. "Moaning and groaning are counterproductive. Besides, who wants to be around someone who is constantly complaining? I've resolved never to be one of those. By remaining optimistic, despite the obvious difficulties of this disease, I help my family cope. My 20-plus years as a commanding officer with the Navy Reserve taught me the importance of being in charge of morale."

Dealing with the deteriorating health of a loved one is one of life's most challenging tasks. Yet John maintains an optimistic attitude and an extraordinary sense of humor in spite of the difficulties. He's putting his talents to work in the service of others and counts his blessings daily—all reflections of his success champion spirit.

From Success Champions℠—the electronic newsletter by Sandra Strauss about the attitudes and actions that energize excellence

www.SuccessChampions.com

Champion the Winning Spirit

"Encouragement is oxygen to the soul."

George M. Adams

Encouragement: the act of giving courage, hope, or confidence. By encouraging the human spirit, you create an environment that nurtures the expression of excellence in others and often enhances your relationships with them, too. Giving encouragement demonstrates to others that you believe in their ability to succeed and that you support them. Encouragement inspires others to work with you and for you, instead of against you.

Encouragement is powerful motivation that inspires us to tap our diamond potential and strive toward our deepest aspirations and the expression of our best. It provides a support system that keeps us drilling deeper to discover even more dazzling gems buried within. It empowers us to take risks, explore possibilities, and "take it to the next level," which pumps up our courage and performance. By encouraging and appreciating others, you build confidence, garner respect, and champion the winning spirit.

"The best minute you spend is the one you invest in people."

Ken Blanchard

Workplace Woes ... or Wows?

"When people go to work, they shouldn't have to
leave their hearts at home."

Betty Bender

In our 25 years of working with corporations, associations, government organizations, and nonprofits, one of the major complaints we hear repeatedly is that people don't feel appreciated. How much does appreciation matter? In a U.S. Department of Labor (DOL) survey, 46 percent of people who quit their jobs did so because they felt unappreciated. Nearly

A CHOICE MOVE

One of my former suburbanite friends, Jason, commuted from Virginia to Washington, D.C., five days a week, fighting snarled traffic and arriving every morning with a miserable attitude, then reversing the process and arriving home totally depleted. After increasingly time-consuming and stress-producing bumper-to-bumper episodes, he decided it was time to make some lifestyle choices. Although Jason enjoyed suburban living, he recognized that stress was taking its toll. He knew it was time to make a move, so bought a townhouse just 15 minutes from work.

Without the morning headaches and hassles, Jason's attitude improved dramatically; he now arrives at the office renewed instead of resentful. He had lived in agony until he realized he had to make a change; then, after analyzing his options, he finally moved (literally!) into action. Jason made adjustments that were within his control to improve the quality of his life and his attitude. —A.S.

half quit because they didn't believe their employers valued their contributions, so they left presumably in search of employers that would satisfy their need for appreciation. Appreciation really does matter!

In other research, senior managers were asked what they believed were the priority concerns of their employees. Did they want more money? Prestige? Advancement? Supervisors believed employees were motivated mostly by good wages, ranking appreciation near the bottom of the list. In contrast, first on the employees' list was receiving appreciation for their work—a finding confirmed in many other surveys conducted by human resources experts in recent decades. This doesn't discount the value of fair wages and other important motivating factors, but for long-term loyalty and happiness, employees are usually motivated more by receiving recognition for their contributions.

Unfortunately, without the knowledge of how much appreciation is valued by employees, managers aren't as likely to give their employees what they need.

Not showing appreciation comes with an extremely high price: reduced productivity, less creativity, poor morale, and a disgruntled staff.

We all need to feel appreciated. Even a small dose of appreciation can change attitudes, motivate behavior, influence opinion, increase cooperation, improve morale, gain respect, and enhance our working relationships.

In a world where recognition is so highly ranked in motivating others, it pays to validate people for their contributions. Showing appreciation and valuing what people do is a powerful motivating force! To encourage the winning spirit, make it a point to regularly acknowledge the time, energy, effort, creativity, and other personal treasures provided by people. No matter your role, look for ways to acknowledge their contributions and show your appreciation. Let them know how much you value them and that you care, not only for what they contribute, but also for who they are.

Fault Lines

"Our worst fault is our preoccupation with the faults of others.
If you want to get the best out of someone, you must look for
the best that is in them. People can only use their strengths
to excel, not their limitations."

Kahlil Gibran

Unfortunately, far too many of us don't recognize the power of appreciation. Instead, we focus on the faults and foibles of our partners, colleagues, and children, nitpicking, criticizing, and condemning them, admonishing rather than appreciating them. It would be so much more sensible (and realistic) to recognize that mistakes are a part of life, as distressing as they may be, as are the complications that result from them. Rather than focusing on faults, it's far more beneficial to take the time and effort to recognize others as the incredibly talented beings they are and to acknowledge their achievements.

MORSELS OF MAGIC
FOR THE UNAPPRECIATED SOUL

"The greatest humiliation in life is to work hard on something from which you expect great appreciation, and then fail to get it."

Edgar Watson Howe

During our communication workshops for leaders and managers, we ask participants to write ten positive things about one of their employees. Although some complete the assignment with ease, this often proves to be a challenge for many. Some of the reasons they mention:

- "I never get any appreciation, so why should I give any?"

- "I didn't receive much appreciation when I was growing up, so I'm uncomfortable giving it."

- "It embarrasses me to recognize or reward people for their good work."

- "I don't have time to show appreciation."

- "I pay them. That should be enough."

Do you have an excuse that keeps you from showing your appreciation? If so, let it go. Give appreciation abundantly and let it be heard! Do more than silently appreciate others; unspoken appreciation can't inspire or motivate. Speak up and let your words work their magic. Let people know how much you value them for who they are as well as for their contributions. Their performance will positively reflect your praise.

It doesn't matter who we are or what we do, dishing out daily doses of appreciation pumps up positive feelings and perform- ance—they are morsels of magic!

FROM THE GROUND UP

While Arnold and I were on our way to a seminar, the gorgeous landscaping of the conference grounds caught our attention. As we passed one of the groundskeepers, I remarked how beautiful it looked and inquired, "Did you do that?" He beamed back a sheepish smile, and exclaimed: "Lady, you just made my day. We don't usually hear from others about our work or even if it matters to them. You just gave me a reason to unload this mulch. Thanks for noticing!"

Just a few moments... a comment about a lovely view . . . a quick connection, forever remembered. I hope when he's tired of all the hauling and heavy work, he'll recall that some people do notice and appreciate his work. When people actually pay attention to what we do, don't we tend to give it more effort because it's valued? —S.S.

There's Hunger on the Home Front, Too

*"You know you're the 'rock' in the family
when everyone takes you for 'granite'."*

Source unknown

Are you guilty of taking at least one of your personal relationships for granted? Or are you actively nurturing the needs of those you love? Because our personal relationships are so entwined into our everyday experiences, we can easily forget to acknowledge how valuable and important they are to us. We might believe our loved ones will always be there for us, intricately woven into the multiple layers of our lives. But the fragile nature of life, just a heartbeat away from misfortune, shows how quickly those threads can unravel.

PLEASE FEED US!
WE'RE STARVING!

"There is more hunger for love and appreciation in this world than for bread."

Mother Teresa

"Hey, we're hungry! Our hunger pains have gone global. You can hear them everywhere, echoing across the land—from those seated behind desks, standing in classrooms, boarding trains and planes, driving buses and trucks, making marketing and sales calls, and doing our best job possible wherever we are.

"Our hunger pains are insatiable, but food won't stop the gnawing emptiness we feel. We want to be fed with sustenance for our spirit: appreciation. Appreciation is the only thing that eases our desire to be acknowledged and recognized for the countless things we do right. We are starving for recognition and exhausted from working so hard, devoting our lives to our jobs, and giving everything we've got. We're hungry to hear the words that can make it all worthwhile. When we know that what we do is appreciated, it motivates us immeasurably.

"So ladle it up and heap it on—praise for our successes. After all the effort we've put forth, the creativity we've cooked up, the solutions we've provided, the things we do for you and your bottom line—it's good to know you care, you notice, you appreciate it, and above all else, that what we do matters to you."

No matter our age or the multiple roles we play, we never outgrow our desire to be acknowledged or appreciated for who we are, what makes us special, and what we do. You can't see it, but we each wear a marquee that reads:

> **Show (or tell) me often
> that you value who I am
> and what I contribute!**

Show and Tell was always our favorite part of kindergarten (actually, it still is—that's why we're speakers!) and it's still part of our philosophy. Take the time to show your appreciation and tell your loved ones how much their energy and efforts mean—it makes magic, lights up eyes, creates smiles, and fills hearts.

While you may believe that your family and friends must surely know how much they're loved, valued, and appreciated, they may think otherwise—their opinions are based on their perceptions of what's said or actively shown. Merely thinking about how much you appreciate and value a person misses the mark (mainly, the heart). If the important people in your life have to wonder whether they're appreciated, they might seek approval elsewhere, weakening and unraveling that critical connection. Disconnection often disintegrates into discord and despair.

Even when you think your relationships are rock solid, don't ever take them for granted. With your generous investment of appreciation, you'll sustain precious connections and reap the rewards from a lifetime of caring.

*"The deepest principle of Human Nature is
the craving to be appreciated."*

William James

Words and Ways that Work Wonders

"Failure to provide recognition leads to psychological malnutrition. Approach people knowing they wear a sign on their forehead that reads: MMFI-AM: Make me feel important about me."

Robert Henry

How do you feel when someone notices something you've contributed in terms of your time, talent, creativity, or other resource, and gives you a compliment? It lifts you up and boosts your self-regard, right? Receiving a compliment is an instant boost to our self-esteem. It's the Pleasure Principle in action. It makes us feel good when others recognize us for our efforts. Likewise, what thoughts and feelings get stirred up when no appreciation is expressed? Maybe a mixture of aggravation and resentment:

• How ungrateful!

• I'll never do that again!

• Next time he'll have to find someone else to do his dirty work!

• I invested so much time in preparing that proposal and not a word of thanks!

It's human nature to desire acknowledgment and appreciation when we put our time, energy, or other resources into something. Not receiving them usually revs up resentment. Without recognition, whether at work, at home, or in a volunteer capacity, a wall of resistance often builds. These kinds of bitter feelings serve as a destructive negative force, promoting "withholding" behaviors and eroding good connections.

Too often, people hear from others about their wrongdoings, how they're doing something the "wrong" way or not meeting expectations. What a difference in both output and attitude when people notice and comment about their exemplary performance and everything they're doing right! We love to be caught "doing something right." It brings magical rewards of continued performance and expressions of excellence. It awakens the best within us and reinforces desirable behavior.

Wherever you go and whoever you encounter throughout your day, look for the good, the special, the appreciated, and the extraordinary—and tell them. Even if it's not your official responsibility to do so, your appreciation makes a difference; whether it's the concierge at a hotel who suggests an outstanding restaurant, the housekeeper who tackles the dirty mess, the cashier who rings up your purchase with a smile, the receptionist who answers the phone with an engaging tone, or your teen who cuts the grass without asking. Tell them what a difference their actions and attitudes make.

When you see desirable behavior, praise it. Be specific as to the difference it makes to you: "Your smile just changed my day." "What a joy to walk into the house and see it so well organized!" Genuine compliments can fuel hearts with hope and reinforce commitments to provide the exceptional service or behavior you want to see repeated.

Appreciation reflects the value placed on our investments of time, energy, and effort. Each act of appreciation is a steppingstone, paving the way for a future filled with greater willingness and cooperation.

> *"I can live two months on one good compliment."*
>
> Mark Twain

In Praise of Praise

> *"People do not live by bread alone.*
> *They need buttering up once in awhile."*
>
> Robert Henry

Praise people for their efforts! Praising people on just about anything works wonders and is a tremendous motivator; but all too often, whether at work, home, or school, it's an underutilized tool. Be sure to extend only genuine praise and sincere compliments; don't say anything you don't mean. Most people have fairly accurate "radar systems" that detect any smattering of insincerity.

Practice positive praise. Being noticed in a positive way is a very high compliment. You get better results when emphasizing what people do

right, rather than giving power to the not-so-good, the bad, or the "needs improvement." Praise the abundance of excellent grades on your daughter's report card, rather than scolding her for the wayward C or D. Praise your staff for pushing to break the sales record, rather than criticizing them for not meeting the division's goal. By praising the behavior you reinforce the value of the desirable behavior: "Your creative idea really wowed our client today!" "I really liked the way you handled that customer!" "You did an exceptional job on your presentation this morning!"

Avoid negating the positive effects of praise by adding a disclaimer: "Good job! Too bad you didn't do it like this for our earlier customers." This saps all the power out of your praise as the recipient internalizes the message, "Yeah, but not good enough!" Avoid attaching any negative remarks to praise.

Be on the lookout for signs of success. Focus on finding what has worked or is working well, rather than focusing on mistakes and failures. Congratulating people on the smallest of victories reinforces the winning spirit.

> *"Praise does wonders for our sense of hearing."*
>
> Arnold Glasow

Show Your Gratitude

> *"Become a talent scout among people and put your discoveries into words of appreciation. Remember, it's OK to send flowers, but they have a limited vocabulary."*
>
> Glenn Van Ekeren

Showing your appreciation comes in many forms—the more creative, the more it's likely to get their attention. A simple "Thank you!" is a dynamic people connector; anything beyond that is pure gravy for our hungry souls. Sending a handwritten note, personal letter, or gift as a gesture of appreciation nets big returns. While e-mails are fine for many routine acknowledgments, don't let cyberspace totally replace good old-fashioned, more personalized and meaningful displays of appreciation, especially for exceptional displays of service or effort. Saying "Thank you!" through your words or actions each time anyone does anything for you helps create magical connections.

Extending your appreciation in meaningful ways is also a good way to solidify and sustain connections. For instance, if a sales agent learns that her customer has a penchant for collecting gadgets, and sends a special gizmo to add to her collection, that scores points in the "Wow, you noticed!" department. It's not so much the gift, but the recognition that the agent was tracking her customer's interests. Being in alignment with a person's thinking is a natural draw.

When we appreciate people for their efforts, we energize their performance. Creating a supportive environment helps people feel safe to tackle their jobs, explore new ideas or ways of doing things, express creativity, and consider options to achieve "the impossible."

By developing an "attitude of gratitude," thanking people for their help, their time, their service, their thoughtfulness, their care, or their support, you're setting up a continuing series of happy returns that works wonders everywhere. In turn, it is usually rewarded by receiving more help, more concern, more caring, more support, more loyalty, and enhanced connections—more of all the good things you want.

GENEROUSLY DISTRIBUTE
DAILY DOSES OF APPRECIATION

To fire up the best in others, focus on these questions:

1. What will I do today to show my faith in others?

2. How will I encourage others to do their best?

3. What specific actions will I take to recognize people for who they are and what they can achieve?

Awesome Acts Appreciated Anywhere

"Too often we underestimate the power of a touch, a smile, a kind word, a listening ear, an honest compliment, or the smallest act of caring, all of which have the potential to turn a life around."

Leo Buscaglia

Extend appreciation everywhere—at home, at work, at school, and wherever you want to acknowledge those who make your life brighter. Here are a few ideas:

- Do the unexpected; it never fails to capture hearts
- Provide praise delivered with a smile
- Give recognition
- Write a letter of praise
- Affix a note of praise to a "can't miss" location—a mirror, computer, door, car, backpack, or suitcase
- Scribble a note on a white board or message center
- Send a greeting card with a message appropriate for the occasion
- Send an electronic thank-you card
- Post a public note of praise
- Catch people doing something you admire and lavish them abundantly with compliments
- Give credit where credit is due
- Drop a roll of Lifesavers with a note of thanks, acknowledging how they "saved the day"
- Send flowers, candy, bear grams, fruit baskets, or other treasures or treats at unexpected moments
- Purchase inspirational books and send them along with a note
- Select a gift related to their special interests

- Create a special award in recognition of their accomplishment or contributions

- Organize a "Just Because!" celebration: decorate with colorful balloons, crepe paper, and a banner extolling your appreciation, and load on the munchies. Whether at work or home, this acknowledges people you care about for the incredible value they bring—for who they are and what they do. The unexpected celebration creates delicious goodwill. Celebrations can also spotlight appreciation for achieving a goal, pushing out extra performance, exceeding expectations, and the like.

- File away (preferably in your contacts database) the names of the important people in your life and the things that matter to them: their birthdays, the names and ages of their children, their hobbies, and so on.

- Have an Appreciation box centrally located and ask others to regularly drop notes of appreciation into it. Read the messages at staff meetings or around the dinner table, or create a special ritual for a time for good feelings to flow.

Here are some ideas especially for the workplace:

- Celebrate "Employee Appreciation Day"

- Have fun with food: declare "donut day," host a "bagel breakfast," throw a spontaneous pizza party (it's amazing how much value you gain from a slice or two!), and toss an ice cream sundae soiree or a chocolate fantasy feast (chocolate in any form is a people pleaser!)

- Stuff an appreciation "goodies" box with "appreciation prizes" and have regular drawings

- Start a Wall of Fame, posting letters from customers or vendors praising any employee (or post them on the company bulletin board)

- Send an e-mail thanking the appropriate staff with copies to supervisors or other managers

- Make people feel like they're an important part of your business by involving them in decisions that directly affect them; people need to feel like they belong

- Give gift certificates to a favorite restaurant or store
- Take staff out for lunch or cater an event
- A free spa treatment would be a most appreciated and perfect way to unwind after an intense period of peak performance
- Send cards beyond the customary holiday season; remember birthdays or employment anniversaries
- Make up a poem or limerick that features an individual's appreciated performance
- Give people proper credit for their ideas

P.S.: We love to hear how people are being acknowledged and appreciated at work and would appreciate hearing from you! Please tell us what's working at your workplace, send us a note at:

info@getalongwithanyone.com

FROM STRESSED OUT TO ASTOUNDED

The night before giving a seminar, I was working at a frenzied pace and balancing several other projects as well. Before running out to gather needed materials, I scribbled a note for my 16-year-old daughter with instructions to grab whatever she wanted for dinner, since I would be late. This is not my typical style—I enjoy cooking and appreciate family meals as an important time for building those enduring connections. But this day was definitely made for simplicity. Since my husband was off on a business trip, Stacy was left to fend for herself.

When I arrived home that evening, I walked into a magic moment. Soothing music played in the background. The table was set for two with candles glowing. The Caesar salad was ready for last-minute tossing, and three red roses adorned the center of the table. Next to them was placed a handmade card that read:

Dear Mom:
I've been noticing how hard you have been working lately. I appreciate every single thing you have done for me and our family. I recognize the hard work you do and I'm shocked at how you are so good at balancing your priorities and still manage to sit down and spend time with me, even if you're up to your nose in work! Keep up the good work, Mom! You can do it! I believe in you with all my heart.

I love you, XOXO

Stacy

After reading the card, I looked up and into her face to see pure delight in catching me off guard and pulling off a moment of sheer joy. She made magic that evening, transforming chaos for me into a moment I will always cherish. Her card has since been tucked inside my "Treasures" box, my collection of priceless "keepers," each one a reminder of how all those moments of taking time to notice, care, and appreciate have added up to make a world of difference and create an enduring connection. —S.S.

MOOSE ON THE LOOSE!

There's an old saying, "Appreciate, to be appreciated." This really came to life for me quite vividly on a business trip to Anchorage, Alaska.

It was September and the tourist season had died down. After finishing up a speech at 6:00 p.m., I decided to stay overnight to take advantage of the beautiful scenery and great bike trails and catch a flight home the next day. Although it was raining and no one was biking, I live by a "Carpe Diem" philosophy and wanted to seize the day. I was told by the locals that the bicycle shops were closed, but I called Anchorage Cycles just to check. Luckily, the owner answered and said he'd open up for me.

At the bike shop, he greeted me with a smile. I looked at his assortment of 75 bikes, finally spying the most expensive one. He said, "I really appreciate your interest in bikes, especially on such a rainy day. Here, take my best bike." I then asked about the fee. "Normally we charge $25 a day. Why don't you just give me $10."

I was amazed that anyone would open their store for one customer and give him a special deal. Then, he noticed my city slicker shoes and said, "You can't ride in those shoes. What size are you?" Amazingly, we were both the same size, so he said, "Here, take my shoes." He went on to load me up with an energy food bar, map, water bottle, binoculars, and even "bear repellent spray," a good thing to carry in grizzly country. He told me about all the bike paths and where to find the best scenery. Then, he gave me his phone number, just in case. All for a $10 sale!

As I rode along the bike path, enjoying the scenery, I reflected on how his enormous generosity had made such a difference in my biking expedition, transforming a rainy day into a special occasion. Suddenly, up close and very personal, several mammoth specimens of Alaska's wildlife caught my attention. Straight ahead, on the bike path, were four moose! I had been warned about encountering bear, but wasn't sure at all about moose handling. No one was around to ask, so I called the bike shop owner's number and fortunately he answered. His sage advice: "Turn around."

I'm not sure if he saved my life that day, but the generous spirit of the bike shop owner sure made a big impression—and I lived to tell his tale! By sharing with him how much I appreciated his opening the store for me, he poured out his generosity in return. —A.S.

Give Abundantly

"We make a living by what we get,
but we make a life by what we give."

Henry Beecher

Giving abundantly is putting your winning spirit to work. The act of giving is the universal principle of energy in motion that nets happy returns for both the giver and the receiver. Investing your time, energy, and resources generates a payoff—sometimes immediately, sometimes in the future. Yet don't expect a return from where you have given, or flowing from some invisible re-payment plan. Your "rebate" may come in the form of referrals from unexpected sources, new doors opening with outpourings of opportunities, cherished connections, or an influx of unexpected surprises. Giving activates possibilities that simply wouldn't exist without your decision to give.

When you give more value or service to a client, you receive more value back—contracts are renewed (and often expanded), and others seek your services as well. When customers are given superior service, they tell others and become your goodwill agents; they give you more of their business, and you gain new customers. Giving your time, energy, and other personal resources create powerful bonds that reap an abundance of rewards and treasured connections in both your personal and professional relationships.

The gift of the winning spirit is very much alive in the hearts of volunteers. As a volunteer, you might not realize how much of a difference your time and service makes. It does. Even the smallest gestures of kindness and compassion have a gigantic impact. Stuffing envelopes for charities brings dollars to cure diseases, provide homes, protect our planet, and grant last wishes. What you give and the amount you give is never the issue; whatever is given serves a need. Your connection to giving always makes a difference.

Genuine giving is done freely, without expectations of getting anything back. Although there will be a payback in some form, somewhere down the road, you may not see the direct link. Of course, as long as you truly

BANKING ON CONTINUED INTEREST

Think of every relationship as an individual bank account. Just as you make deposits and withdrawals from your bank account, you can overdraw from your relationship accounts. To accrue interest on your account, you have to keep making deposits. Think of each of your personal and professional relationships. What can you do to enrich them? Be sure to maintain your relationships with a healthy balance of give and take.

don't expect anything in return, you'll never be disappointed, just surprised in the outcomes that result. However, if you harbor an expectation of equal exchange in the recesses of your mind, you'll likely suffer disappointment. Perfect parity doesn't exist. Life doesn't dole out precise equality—sometimes you give more, sometimes less; sometimes you receive barrels full, sometimes a smidgen. In the long haul, it usually balances out—not in a precise equation, but in direct proportion to your overall giving.

Givers are those who ask, "How can I make a difference right now? How can I make experiences for others more meaningful or memorable? How can I add more value—At work? In my family? In my community? How can I contribute to something of value beyond myself?"

Don't overlook or diminish any of your gifts. Every time you offer a smile, a helping hand, a willing heart; share an encouraging word; brighten a moment; or take the time to support, listen, or understand—you're giving a valuable part of yourself. Share your abundance and value yourself for your commitment to giving.

True giving is a joy because it connects you to the limitless potential within you. It opens the floodgates to receive an endless flow of abundance from the rich reservoir of possibilities.

"The best use of life is to spend it for something that will outlast it."

William James

IT ALL COMES BACK

My husband, Rick, is a vocational expert witness and consults on personal injury cases regarding wage-loss issues and how the injury affects the wage-earning capabilities of his clients. Several years ago, one of his clients who had suffered a severe back injury impressed Rick with her remarkable "nothing-can-stop-me" attitude.

When the case was settled, he felt compelled to return her payment for his services. I thought this was an extraordinary gesture on his part since he had invested so much of his time on her behalf. His caseload is a continuous stream of heart-wrenching stories, people suffering from so much loss. Yet her unstoppable, upbeat attitude had such a profound effect on him that he was moved in such a way to make that choice.

The following week while vacationing in Seattle, we took a boat out on a lovely lake so Rick could get in some waterskiing, a favorite sport from his younger years. However, while attempting a maneuver perfected long ago (and not practiced since), he wrenched his back and his waterskiing adventure came to an abrupt halt. He reeled in pain as we made an emergency trip to a local doctor, who made some adjustments in his back, prescribed some medication, and then said, "No charge."

We were stunned. (I know, you're thinking I must be making this up—a doctor who doesn't charge for his services?!) When we expressed our amazement, he simply said, "You're on vacation and you don't need a doctor's bill to spoil it!"

Needless to say, that doctor made quite a connection and an enduring impression on us. We were shocked at his amazing outpouring of generosity, and years later we're still talking (and now writing) about it.

No, I am NOT suggesting that you don't charge for your services. It just so happened that two people decided to do something most extraordinary. With the first experience still so fresh in our minds, we connected the two giving-and-receiving events together. It did, however, clearly serve as a demonstration to us of how it all does comes back in the universe of giving. —S.S.

Grow a Garden of Blossoming Connections

"People love us not for who we are, but for how we make them feel."

Ralph Waldo Emerson

Beautiful gardens don't just happen. To make them grow, blossom, and flourish into full vibrancy takes time and requires careful cultivation—preparing and nourishing the soil, providing the plants with an optimal environment, and tending to weeds and pests. Without nurturing conditions, they won't grow into their glorious grandeur.

Relationships are like gardens: cultivating winning attitudes and encouraging excellence yields the greatest harvest of respect and energized behavior. When we maintain a sunny outlook, give everyone opportunities to grow, and value their unique gifts, people flourish and bloom into their best. Once in bloom, keep feeding them words of appreciation; tell them how much they matter, and don't let them wither. Perennially vibrant relationships stem from carefully tended connections, season after season!

WORDS TO LIVE BY

"Keep your thoughts positive because your thoughts become words. Keep your words positive because your words become actions. Keep your actions positive because your actions become habits. Guard your habits and keep them positive because your habits become your values. Keep your values positive because your values become your destiny. Every day is a new beginning and we must always remember that the nurtured seed always produces the abundant harvest."

Mahatma Gandhi

Key #4:

Boost Your Communication IQ

Get on the Same Wavelength

"Whatever your grade or position, if you know how and when to speak,
and when to remain silent, your chances of real success
are proportionately increased."

Ralph C. Smedley

It's easier to get along with people who are on the same wavelength. Each of us is an individual broadcasting system transmitting signals everywhere we go. In every role we play in our personal and professional lives, the messages we send out affect the quality of our reception. High-quality communication is clear, engaging, and in tune with listeners' needs—people tune in and stay tuned. Just like radio frequencies, if people can't hear, understand, or relate to what's being transmitted, they'll hear garbled messages and get static—they'll tune out and find another station (or person, in this case) that suits them better.

We're always broadcasting messages that reveal a lot about us by what we say and how we say it; these messages play a significant role in the type of connections we make along the way and the way we relate to others. Each of us is responsible for the quality of our own communication. We can boost our communication IQ and improve the quality of our connections by improving how we deliver as well as receive all those messages and signals. Whether we're presidents or parents, managers or marketing representatives, students or supervisors, communicating clear messages and getting good reception from people is fundamental to our success.

How well you communicate determines how others perceive you and your message. Constantly monitor your transmissions; if something is weak, work to strengthen it so your communication is clear and you improve your chances for getting good reception.

With effective communication at work in your relationships, you get along better; its empowering nature brings out the best in your connections and receptivity. In turn, a healthy communication IQ is instrumental for tapping your potential, influencing others, achieving your goals, and constructing a network of supportive connections.

LOOKING FOR QUALITY COMMUNICATORS

"The art of communication is the language of leadership."

James Humes

Research confirms that good communication skills are the conduit for developing and preserving constructive, dynamic relationships. According to the American Management Association, the number one quality employers seek in job candidates is effective communication skills. Perhaps this reflects AMA's research that 90 percent of all problems in organizations are attributed to the direct results of poor communication. Nearly half of the executives from a Wirthlin Worldwide survey of Fortune 1,000 companies ranked good communication as the number one critical quality needed for leadership-driven CEOs.

Communicate to Connect

"Good communicators are open to my ideas. They respect me. They know who they are and what makes them 'tick' and they want to know the same about me. They foster my growth while attending to their own. They are proud of their accomplishments and of mine—for our mutual benefit."

A Get Along seminar participant

Isn't it a thrill to talk with people who are great listeners, who hear every word you speak, and who understand exactly what you say?

Have you ever received outstanding treatment by a customer representative who handled your situation with such amazing grace, who went so far beyond the call of duty to resolve your problem, that he or she far exceeded your expectations?

Have you experienced meeting someone who seemed to be so much on your wavelength and so responsive to what you wanted that they earned your trust almost immediately?

High-quality connections are truly magical! No question about it—the ability to be on someone's wavelength, to be in tune with each other's needs, and to clearly communicate ideas is the lifeblood of quality connections. To create them, you must take care to constantly monitor the quality of your communications.

Good communication is a balance of honoring your own needs as well as the needs of others. Building and maintaining positive connections means getting to the heart of what people want and need, as represented by the acronym HEART. This acronym was first introduced in Creating the Connection Zone and is highlighted again here because communication is so critical for having these needs fulfilled. These qualities help to

cultivate respect, and build positive and productive relationships by respecting our mutual needs to be:

- Heard and honored. We want to be heard and to have our ideas and feelings honored. When others are attentive and truly listen to our thoughts, opinions, and feelings, and seek to understand our perspectives, we feel validated. Being heard and honored provides a supportive, compassionate environment in which we feel safe to express our truth.

- Encouraged and empowered. We want to feel encouraged and empowered in our relationships, not discouraged and drained. Encouragement is fostered through an atmosphere of supportive connections and builds confidence in our capabilities, sustains us through challenges, and helps us to achieve our personal goals and desired outcomes. We're empowered within the flow of positive energy which enhances the expression of excellence in our attitudes and actions.

- Appreciated and accepted. We feel valued when we're acknowledged for our time, energy, creativity, talent, and other contributions; showing appreciation boosts positive feelings in others and helps create positive environments. We also want to be accepted as unique individuals, which includes being respected for our personal beliefs and values.

- Respected and recognized. Respect is an attitude communicated through verbal and nonverbal behaviors, which is extended and maintained through positive communication patterns. We also want to be recognized for our contributions of time, talent, energy, and other resources, which nurtures healthy self-esteem.

- Trusted and treasured. The ability to trust others is critical for establishing and sustaining relationships of integrity. We trust the individuals, businesses, and institutions that consistently uphold their commitments. We also want to feel treasured for who we are and what we bring to a relationship.

These qualities help to produce positive work and living environments, enhance credibility, inspire cooperation, encourage effort, and more—all vital for creating, solidifying, and maintaining enduring connections.

How's Your Communication IQ?

Take the following test yourself, then ask two people you know well to rate you on the same statements. Rate yourself on a scale of 1 to 5 on the statements below:

> 1-Never
> 2-Almost never
> 3-Sometimes
> 4-Almost always
> 5-Always

Do you ...

____ Give people your full attention when they speak?

____ Project genuine interest in conversations and negotiations with others?

____ Try to maintain a good balance between speaking and listening?

____ Avoid giving advice before you're asked?

____ Wait until someone finishes talking before speaking?

____ Maintain good eye and face contact?

____ Ask open-ended questions to encourage others to talk?

____ Respond to others by communicating in a positive way?

____ Ask about the meaning of any unfamiliar words, phrases, or jargon?

____ Restate instructions or expectations to be sure you understand them correctly?

____ Withhold all opinions about what's being said until you have all the information?

____ Listen for the meaning or feelings behind the speaker's words to confirm your understanding of them?

____ Note the speaker's expressions, gestures, and tone for the intended meaning?

____ Make mental notes to help you remember the main points?

____ Try to see a situation from the speaker's perspective when you disagree?

____ Focus on listening even when you disagree?

____ View conflicts as opportunities to understand the issues better?

____ Allow people to vent their feelings and concerns?

____ Provide supportive and constructive feedback when others speak?

____ Seek to negotiate mutually satisfying solutions when disputes arise?

GREAT COMMUNICATION
DOESN'T GRATE ON YOUR NERVES!

Good communication creates GREAT outcomes:

Gets problems solved faster

Reduces stress levels

Empowers and energizes; builds healthy and caring relationships

Achieves goals; allows for expression of concerns

Teamwork is fortified, ensuring trust, support, and cooperation

---

Scores:

90-100: You've got excellent communication IQ!

80-89: You're using some excellent communication skills. You're tuning in to the main ideas, but you may be missing important messages and distracted at times.

70-79: Listening is music to other peoples' ears! Explore more ways to connect to the interests of others.

69 and under: Tune in and listen up! You're likely to be frustrated by a disproportionate share of miscommunications. Recognize that listening is a skill and concentrate on developing it daily.

Stop, Drop, and Roll Out
Your Listening Ears

"We have been given two ears and but a single mouth, in order that we may listen more and talk less."

Unknown

Listening is the critical component for making your critical connections. We need this vital communication tool for gathering information, following instructions, making choices, extending compassion, launching new relationships, and spicing up our lives with the joy that flows from connecting. Listening requires our personal attention and active effort for us to create and keep constructive connections.

On the job, poor listening has been linked to the loss of billions of dollars as a result of mistakes, lost opportunities, and decreased productivity. Poor listening is costly on the home front, too; needs that go unmet cause discontent, disappointment, and disconnections. We want to be heard and understood everywhere and at all times!

Distractions, judgments, and other barriers thwart our best intentions for effective listening. Other obstacles that get in our way include personal agendas, negative self-talk, noise, physical appearance, past experience, prejudice, status, and self-absorption. Our brains go to work filtering and sorting data as we take in images, tones, and expressions, recall similarities, make comparisons, attach labels to appearances, or activate patterns of behavior that don't work well for us. Our minds also wander; we think about irrelevant matters or rehearse what we're going to say next, which pulls our attention away from the speaker. Working to minimize or eliminate all this interference significantly improves our ability to listen, process the intended meaning, and connect with the speaker.

IT DOES A BODY GOOD

Research from the University of Maryland's School of Medicine revealed that effective listening is a major component in personal stress management—it lowers blood pressure, slows pulse rate, and improves chemical regulation of body processes. It's therapeutic and good for your physical and emotional health, not to mention essential for quality connections!

"A good listener tries to understand thoroughly what the other person is saying. In the end he may disagree sharply, but before he disagrees, he wants to know exactly what it is he is disagreeing with."

Kenneth A. Wells

Stop ... Drop ... and Roll. To enhance listening, we've adapted the sage advice from fire safety professionals to stop, drop, and roll out your listening ears. This guidance helps prevent connection fires fueled by conflict, confusion, and misunderstandings:

- Stop to listen. Giving others your full attention is the greatest gift you can give. When you stop to listen, remember what you want—to create positive connections.

- Drop your reactions. Focus on what others need first. Push your reactions out of the way to give space for others to state their case, or tell you what's on their minds. Finding out about the concerns of others, what they value, and how you can satisfy those needs has a big payoff in creating quality connections.

- Roll out your listening ears. Pay attention. By listening, others know that you care, you're focused on their needs, and you're open to communication. You establish an environment that builds and supports positive communication. Your willingness to listen also increases the probability that you will be heard by others, since language is like a boomerang: what we put out usually comes back to us.

Activate Active Listening Techniques

"Courage is what it takes to stand up and speak; courage is also what it takes to sit down and listen."

Winston Churchill

From the sheer number of words and their interpretations, communication is plagued with problems and ripe for confusion and misunderstandings. Of the estimated 800,000 words in the English language, we regularly use only about 800. However, there are 14,000 different meanings for these most commonly used words, averaging about 17 meanings per word! We can significantly reduce this communication chaos by applying active listening techniques.

Active listening builds rapport with those with whom we want or need to share our thoughts and feelings, and enhances the receptivity of our messages. It makes others feel valued, because they know their thoughts and feelings have been heard. It's also an excellent tool for focusing the main points of communication, keeping it on track, understanding the speaker's intended meaning, and helping to correct any misunderstandings or assumptions.

Active listening has been compared to getting into another person's "movie" and understanding their concerns and the feelings that are going on in their real-life dramas. When you know more of the details and concerns surrounding a situation, you're more equipped to take on a supportive role.

One of the biggest challenges of being the listener is the need to remain attentive. When we step into the role of watching someone's personal "movie," we gain a privileged perspective into their character, the backdrop for the scene, and the supporting players involved. There's always something interesting playing on the big screen of life! We just need to focus our attention and be a supportive player, listen to their "dialogue," and focus on the big picture. From this wide-screen perspective, we're better able to gain greater insights, and be much less judgmental "movie" goers!

Roll out your listening ears with the active listening techniques listed below to increase your understanding and correct interpretation of what's being communicated.

> ## *WHAT DO YOU MEAN?*
>
> Some remarks can be easily misinterpreted. The question, "What do you mean?" is a useful tool that gets to the bottom of an issue. By posing this question, you get immediate clarity rather than reacting to a presumed attack, wondering what a person may have meant by it, and then stewing over it. This opens up conversation and gives your partner the opportunity to explain and reconnect: "It wasn't my intention to hurt you. This is what I meant by that statement ..."

1. Clarify

Clarifying serves two purposes: to make the message clear, and to confirm that your understanding is accurate so as to eliminate misinterpretations.

As the listener, check out what you hear and ask yourself questions to clarify:

- What has the person told me?
- Am I totally clear on agreements, expectations, or instructions?
- Am I confused about anything?

Ask for clarification. If something is confusing or unclear, follow up with questions or statements to reduce confusion:

- *Are you saying that ...?*
- *Would you say that again?*
- *What do you mean?*
- *I don't understand.*
- *Am I to conclude that ...?*
- *Is it true that ...?*

When making requests for people to handle tasks, projects, or other assignments, be sure to clarify your expectations by outlining the specific conditions you have in mind. Sometimes, we take for granted that others know exactly what we have in mind—that is, until we see a totally different result than expected! You may have a clear picture of what outcome you expect, while others may clearly have a different idea. It's always interesting to see what develops without defining expectations! So, be specific in defining exactly how you want something done. If there's latitude for creativity, then enjoy the creative outcomes. Otherwise, provide specific instructions to make sure everyone is on the same page.

CUT DOWN TO SIZE

I asked my husband, Rick, to trim the bushes as I was hurriedly dashing out the door early one Saturday morning. When I returned, I was shocked to see my "Heavenly Bamboo" looking like Hell! The graceful stalks had been whacked back to the ground! His interpretation of the word "trim" was obviously different than my own. If I had taken the time to clarify how much I wanted trimmed, it would have prevented a "clip-tomaniacal" disaster! —S.S.

If you're assigning the task, make sure that everyone is clear on expectations. Your instructions should answer questions the person receiving the assignment might have, such as:

- What am I supposed to do?

- How am I supposed to do it?

- When does it need to be completed?

- How well am I supposed to do it? What level of quality is required? What is considered acceptable regarding the effort to achieve satisfaction?

A PRESIDENTIAL DETAIL

The images inside our heads can be so different. We may think we've got the identical picture in focus, down to the last detail. However, different interpretations of even the same word can lead us in totally different directions, as I discovered one morning headed toward Washington D.C. for a very important meeting with the president of a trade association.

I arrived in a section of the highway dedicated exclusively to carpoolers just one minute before the restricted lanes become safe for motorists driving alone. So you can be in violation one minute, and perfectly safe to travel free of any ticketing worries the next. Since I'm not a regular commuter, I didn't realize the sanctity of that one minute.

The blue flashing light of the patrol car was colorful evidence that those sixty seconds do indeed matter. I rolled down my window and explained to the officer that I had entered the carpool lanes one minute earlier because I couldn't risk being late for an urgent meeting with the president. His expression changed instantly. I thought it was due to my obvious distress that the officer issued only a warning. It wasn't until I was heading down the road that it stuck me—the compassionate officer probably had assumed I was on my way to the White House to see the President. Fortunately, that assumption turned into a blessing and I arrived in time for my meeting with the "other" president. —S.S.

A CLEAN SWEEP

A child's bedroom is an inner sanctum of sorts, their personal space for stashing their cherished treasures. To teach personal responsibility, parents often require their children to periodically clean this "hallowed ground." It seems to be a natural part of the growing up process, a rite of passage that kids must survive in order to obtain the rights to do anything else!

You have an image of what a clean room looks like. So does your kid. When they match, bingo! You're lucky if he or she did what you requested and you got what you expected. It's when expectations differ that the nagging and arguing begin.

The success of that cleaning process is largely determined by how you define "clean room." The better your child understands what's expected, the greater the chance you'll obtain that result without the hassles and headaches. Be specific and make a checklist (or draw pictures if they don't read) of what you want and display it prominently.

A clean room means ...

- Trash emptied

- Toys picked up

- Clothes hung up

- Bed made

- All toys, books, clothing, and other things that don't belong on the floor put away

- You get the picture ...

The same clarification is required whether you're serving as supervisor, manager, volunteer coordinator, committee chair, CEO, or whatever your role. Define what you mean and always provide people with the specifics to ensure that your picture and theirs is a photo finish!

If you're the one being asked to handle the task, clarify using these same questions. When the task is in progress, or if you have any concerns about expectations, clarify by asking:

- *How am I doing?*
- *Is there something I should be doing differently?*
- *Is there anything else required?*

2. Empathize

Empathy is the capacity to understand, validate, and respond to the experiences of another person. By being empathetic, you encourage communication and build connection. This demonstrates support and that you've tuned in to his or her feelings. When our feelings are not validated or acknowledged, it denies our own sense of reality, and frustrates us that others either cannot share or refuse to share how we feel.

Well-meaning people sometimes try to cushion sensitive feelings but end up diminishing them instead. Denying, discounting, or trying to change someone's feelings won't make them go away or seem any less real; expressing empathy validates his or her truth.

It doesn't matter that we may not be able to offer solutions. Being a sounding board for someone else's troubles provides a valuable form of relief, giving them the opportunity to voice their concerns or talk a problem through, which might even guide them to a revelation or possible solution.

Empathetic listeners ...

- Listen for the feeling being expressed, such as frustration, disappointment, or embarrassment
- Observe nonverbal behavior, such as facial expressions, shaking the head, or frowning
- Reflect back the presumed feeling: "It sounds like you're feeling really angry." "I can see how you'd be upset after waiting so long for the appointment." "From what you've told me, I can understand your frustration."

WOULD YOU SAY THAT AGAIN??

A few announcements that appeared in church bulletins (which have since circulated through cyberspace) show a light side of the need for clarity. We're sure members of these congregations enjoyed the accidental humor:

- Bertha Belch, a missionary from Africa, will be speaking tonight at Calvary Memorial Church in Racine. Come tonight and hear Bertha Belch all the way from Africa.

- Low Self-Esteem Support Group will meet Thursday. Please use the back door.

- Announcement in the church bulletin for a National Prayer and Fasting Conference: "The cost for attending the Prayer and Fasting conference includes meals."

- Ladies, don't forget the rummage sale. It's a chance to get rid of those things not worth keeping around the house. Don't forget your husbands.

- The peacemaking meeting scheduled for today has been cancelled due to a conflict.

- Next Thursday there will be tryouts for the choir. They need all the help they can get.

- At the evening service tonight, the sermon topic will be "What is Hell?" Come early and listen to our choir practice.

- The church will host an evening of fine dining, superb entertainment, and gracious hostility.

- Potluck supper Sunday at 5:00 p.m. Prayer and medication to follow.

- The ladies of the Church have cast off clothing of every kind. They may be seen in the basement on Friday afternoon.

- Weight Watchers® will meet at 7:00 p.m. at the First Presbyterian Church. Please use large double door at the side entrance.

Source Unknown

Avoid asking, "Why do you feel that way?" They may not know. It's more helpful if you state what you observe: "I see something is upsetting you."

Avoid saying, "I understand how you feel." You really don't know exactly how a person feels. Instead, be specific:

- *Losing a sale after working so hard must be upsetting.*

- *Not having an item in stock must be disappointing, especially after you made a special trip to buy it.*

- *After spending so much time studying, not getting an 'A' on the test must be a huge disappointment.*

- *You must be furious that they wouldn't extend the deadline!*

- *Losing such a valuable client seems so unfair, after all the creativity you've invested in them.*

- *I know you've worked hard on that proposal—it must be devastating not to have landed the contract.*

3. Paraphrase/Summarize

To paraphrase or summarize means to repeat back what you've heard being said. It wraps up the content communicated to you and shows that you understand the situation. Paraphrasing does not mean parroting the words being spoken; rather, it's a natural summary of the comments. It focuses on the content expressed and is especially useful for clarifying instructions as well as confirming intent.

Effective summarizing statements include:

- *So, you think ...*

- *You mean ...*

- *What I hear you saying is ...*

- *In other words ...*

- *From your perspective ...*

- *From what you've said, I understand ...*

- *If I understand this correctly, what you're saying is ...*

- *Is it correct to say ...?*

To ensure that you correctly interpreted the speaker, repeat back what you believe was said. If you misinterpreted the message, it gives the speaker an opportunity to clarify, so you're both on the same page. However, be cautious if you ask others to repeat back what you say in order to confirm their understanding. While this is appropriate for younger folks, adults often view this as a childish gesture.

Avoid the summarizing questions, "Do you understand?" or "Does that make sense?" When people are asked these questions, they will often say they do (even if they don't) to avoid looking stupid.

Stick to What Clicks

"The most basic of all human needs is the need to understand and be understood. The best way to understand people is to listen to them."

Ralph Nichols

How often do you find yourself going in circles regarding your communication patterns? Do they produce the desired results? We might very well know that what we say or do isn't getting us what we want, yet we charge right ahead and do it anyway! What happens? No surprise—the same old thing! The trick for good communication is to stick to what clicks. Do what works well and drop what doesn't. Here are a few proven tricks that keep communication clicking:

- **Listen up!** Seek to understand others first—this wins their respect. Listen without interrupting, letting others fully express their concerns and feelings. Give your full attention. Don't let your mind wander off or use the time to prepare your comments. Show that you're all ears.

- **Be an animated listener.** Silence is often viewed as a sign of disinterest, so be a lively listener. Give others verbal and nonverbal cues to encourage communication. An animated listener looks at you, expresses empathy, provides feedback, uses responsive body language, nods, and offers nonjudgmental statements or verbal encouragers, such as the following:

  - *I see.*

  - *I hear you.*

  - *Oh?*

  - *Uh-ha!*

  - *Interesting.*

  - *Tell me more.*

  - *I'd like to hear.*

  - *No kidding?*

- *Wow!*

- *Let's discuss that.*

- **Connect through nonverbal clues.** Using engaging nonverbal cues, as described below, communicates a readiness and willingness to listen. Also, see Understanding BodySpeak: It Goes Without Saying on page 171 for more information on nonverbal communication.

  - Smile: A simple smile provides a sense of warmth and increases your likeability.

  - Eye contact: This is one of the most important ways to establish rapport because it shows interest and invites interaction.

  - Open posture: An open posture (not crossing arms or legs, not turning or focusing in other directions) sends the signal that you're more approachable and open-minded. An open posture is the sign of an open mind!

  - Leaning forward: A slightly forward posture shows interest and affirms that you're positioned to listen.

  - Nodding: Nodding (not nodding off!) demonstrates interest and attentiveness, and encourages others to speak. Research shows that listeners who nod at their conversation partners significantly encourage them to talk more; if a listener doesn't nod, it can bring a conversation to an abrupt close.

- **Think territory.** See Think Territory on page 177 for a discussion about monitoring personal distance.

- **Define needs.** Find out what others want. When people's needs are recognized, they're more likely to be happy campers/workers/clients/family members. Successful relationships are maintained when needs are kept in balance. When everyone shares their perspectives on what is desired, mutual understanding is enhanced and goals achieved. By having a better awareness of your needs, others are also more likely to respect them in the future.

- **Consider the timing.** Timing is an important issue in deciding the appropriate time to address concerns. Avoid encounters when there isn't sufficient time to discuss a matter thoroughly; when either of

you is exhausted, angry, or distracted; or when you don't want your conversation overheard. When we're angry, we're more rigid in our thinking and not as receptive to hearing others; likewise, we're not as likely to be heard. Finding solutions is also more difficult when we're blocked by angry emotions.

- **Talk in a setting that's conducive to listening.** To increase a good listening environment, eliminate distractions. Is it too noisy? Too hot or too cool? Is the phone ringing all the time? Are people interrupting their conversations by taking phone calls? Are there other people around? Eliminate any distractions to encourage quality communication.

- **Speak from your own perspective.** By sharing your viewpoint, others learn more about your reasons, which sheds new light on situations. Use "I" statements ("I feel ..." "I believe ..." "I think ..." "I notice when ...").

  Avoid using too many "I" statements consecutively, which can become a source of irritation. Other options include ("It seems to me ..." "My feeling is ..." "It's been my experience ...").

- **Avoid defensive statements.** Using "you" statements increases defensiveness and may ruffle a few feathers ("You're always dumping too many projects on me! You never tell me what's most important.").

  Instead, try something to smooth those feathers: ("I get confused when you don't keep me updated on priorities because I don't know what's most important to you."). Speaking from your own perspective of noticing, thinking, believing, or feeling reduces tension and keeps communication flowing.

- **Maintain respect and dignity.** Respect is an attitude communicated to others through your voice, choice of words, and body language, all of which reflect your character. It's important to respect and honor needs, differences, and dignity. When needs aren't honored, dignity is denied.

ARNOLD'S EMBARRASSING SHOPPING ADVENTURE

When I was the awkward age of 11, and getting more embarrassed about being seen with my parents, pre-teen "Hell" was going shopping with my mom. I had my own ideas about the clothes I wanted and how they should fit me. Nonetheless, I followed my mom around our local Sears store in search of new attire.

Suddenly, without warning, my mother yelled across the department to a salesperson, "Do you know where the HUSKIES are located?" That one word, "Huskies," released for all to hear, sent waves of humiliation through my whole body. I felt every eye was focused on me (and my "husky" physique). I wanted nothing more than to hide my beet-red face!

To this day, whenever I hear the word "Huskies," it reminds me of that most embarrassing moment, when threads of my dignity and respect were unraveled in a big way. Be sensitive in respecting the needs of others to avoid bigger than life problems. —A.S.

Give Feedback Tactfully and Receive it Willingly

"Don't mind criticism. If it is untrue, disregard it; if unfair, keep from irritation; if it is ignorant, smile; if it is justified it is not criticism, learn from it."

Source unknown

Criticism is a loaded word, with its ability to send shockwaves of self-esteem-crushing magnitude. As a result, the term "constructive" is sometimes used as an adjective to cushion anticipated blows and preserve the receiver's self-esteem. A more popular vernacular choice has evolved for communicating desirable behavior—"feedback." We prefer using the term feedback because even the adjective "constructive" often sets defense mechanisms in motion.

Whether seen as criticism or feedback, the fact is that our many roles in life require the need to both give and receive it. Whether as parent to child, teacher to student, supervisor to staff, colleague to colleague, customer to business representative, plus a myriad of other relationships in our relationship-rich world—we need to know how we're doing, and we need to let others know how they're doing. It's valuable information that can help us grow. It also serves as a teaching tool for gaining skills and knowledge.

Giving Feedback

When you give feedback, people learn how their behavior is affecting you and helps them to modify it. Feedback is valuable for improving both the performance and the relationship, which might otherwise splinter from the wear and tear of continuing undesirable behavior.

The goal of giving feedback is to create a change in future behavior. While you can request behavior changes, you cannot demand that others change their attitudes, feelings, values, or priorities. This can be frustrating, but it's not within your control. For instance, you can ask your staff to attend a weekend event, but you can't require them to have a good attitude about being there. You can ask your siblings to participate more in the care of an aging parent, but you can't change their sense of priorities or feelings about providing that additional support. People are naturally more inclined to modify a behavior when they understand that it's in their best interest to adopt it, such as if their performance review is riding on it, their job is on the line, a relationship is at stake, or a privilege may be withdrawn.

Telling others what you think, feel, or want helps them understand your perspective and the reasons for it. We're usually more willing to make adjustments when we know how our behavior affects others and why they are requesting a change.

When you give feedback, follow the guidelines listed below to create an atmosphere more conducive to maintaining integrity and respect:

- **Be strategic.** Before discussing the matter, identify the exact nature of the problem, what's causing it, and why it's a problem. Determine the best way to present your comments, and make a list of the changes you want to communicate.

- **Pick a good time and place.** Make your comments timely, either at the moment the behavior is occurring, or soon after—the receiver is more likely to understand what you're talking about. To respect privacy and preserve dignity, avoid locations where your comments could be overheard. Check the timing. Are both of you receptive? If not, the other person may be tuned out and your intent may be more easily misinterpreted and more likely to ignite defensive reactions.

- **Express empathy and acknowledge the challenges of the situation.** Receiving feedback is uncomfortable for everyone, even if they are handling it well. Show concern about what the other person may be thinking and feeling, and how you recognize the difficulty that's causing the undesirable behavior. This reinforces your support and makes your comments more palatable.

- **Include positive messages to preserve self-esteem.** If only a negative viewpoint is conveyed, without reinforcing what's right about a person's behavior, criticism can be very disheartening. Including positive statements as part of the feedback helps to

reassure and validate a person's overall competence: ("You're a great project manager and it's a pleasure working with you.") It's best to position your positive statements after the feedback, as described in Reverse the Position of the Positive Statements, below.

- **Use courteous language.** Avoid destructive labels (such as incompetent, impulsive, inept, or careless), which fuel negative feelings. Use "I" statements to help reduce defensiveness ("I notice when ..."). For more information, see Key #6: Extend Respect to Preserve Trust.

- **Focus on the behavior, not the person's character.** Make your comments specific to the situation (what, when, where, and how) by relating what you've heard or providing examples regarding the situa-

---

REVERSE THE POSITION
OF THE POSITIVE STATEMENTS

Positive messages are better received if they are offered after the "improvement information" (the feedback), rather than leading up to it. The receiver usually sniffs out a criticism in mid-air and wonders what nasty stuff is about to land right after it. He or she may totally discount the positive message, believing it's only a set-up for the letdown (or put-down).

By providing the "improvement information" first, followed by an acknowledgment of what's being done right, the receiver is much more likely to perceive the statement as truthful. This helps to focus your feedback on being improvement-oriented and helps prevent your comments from being perceived as a personal attack. When feedback concludes on a positive note, rather than a negative one, good feelings are conveyed, along with better receptivity for creating desired changes.

To some, it may seem that lacing feedback with positive comments is simply cushioning the blow from what usually comes next, the criticism. However, by expressing positive messages, you enhance the self-esteem of others by conveying appreciation for their contributions.

tion. Report facts, rather than why things happened the way they did, or what you think the person may have meant by such comments.

- **Discuss solutions.** Discuss solutions and emphasize how desired changes can improve the person's ability to meet future commitments. Focus only on what can be changed; don't waste time or drain your energy on things that cannot.

- **Encourage feedback in return.** This helps restore balance in relationship dynamics and provides an opportunity for those involved to express their perspectives.

- **Express your appreciation.** Express your appreciation for gaining a new understanding of the situation and your confidence that the solution under discussion will help improve future behavior.

- **Follow up after the session.** Ask whether they have any further questions or need anything clarified.

- **Evaluate the changes.** After the changes have been implemented, assess whether they're effective and creating the desired results. If not, other options will need to be explored.

HOLD THE SWEETENER!

One of our friends, Paula, works for a boss who pressed a sensitive button by asking her, "Honey, could you please get me a stapler in the supply cabinet"? With her intent to create constructive connections, Paula bit her tongue without snapping back a statement she might later regret—"Don't ever call me honey!"

She recognized that becoming contentious would have gotten in the way of a good connection. But Paula still wanted to let her boss know that she didn't want to be referred to in that manner. Instead, she tactfully replied, "I know you didn't mean anything derogatory by it, but I'm uncomfortable when you call me 'Honey.' Please call me Paula." It worked; he never again uttered the "H" word to her, and their working relationship remains sweet (without the syrup)!

A Step-by-Step Formula for Giving Feedback

Leading Statements	Action Step
I've been noticing that ...	Describe what the behavior is in specific and factual terms.
It's causing ...	Describe the impact of the behavior and the reasons for changing it. Give examples that illustrate the problem.
Pause for their feedback.	Provide an opportunity for the person to provide his or her perspectives.
I know this a difficult time. Or I know the report is time consuming. Or I know you have a lot on your plate right now.	Express empathy and acknowledge the challenges.
Let's look at our options for making this work better. Or I think it might work better if ...	Describe the change you want to see or discuss possible solutions
This change will ... or This way ...	Explain how the suggested changes will solve the problem or the benefits it will offer.
I appreciate your help on this and know this change will help improve _____.	Extend appreciation for making the desired changes, the value they bring, and the opportunity to gain a new understanding.
I am so impressed with your constant flow of great ideas. They have really made a difference in our operation and I value your commitment and dedication. *A sample statement for kids: I love you so much and am constantly amazed at your maturity and how well you manage all your responsibilities.*	Close with a statement that validates specifically who they are and what they do.

Following is an example of how to combine these steps to approach an employee whose behavior is in need of some feedback:

I'm concerned about a situation and want us to have a chance to talk about it. I've been noticing lately that you've missed some key meetings. It's causing some problems on the Jefferson account, because without you at our department meetings, we're missing key information. For instance, when you weren't at yesterday's briefing, we didn't have all the research data available that's necessary for us to move ahead. This is causing delays in the project, and the client is expecting us to be more responsive than we've been. (Pause for a response to gain more insight from their perspective.)

I know you've been working exceptionally hard, balancing the demanding needs of several of our clients. I think it might work better if you rearrange your schedule, or delegate some of your work, so you can be at these critical meetings. This way, everyone will be more productive, and we can keep all those folks at Jefferson happy.

I appreciate your help on meeting these commitments, as well as the wealth of wisdom and insights you bring to our business. You are such an essential part of our team and I really value your creativity. Thanks for the opportunity to learn more about your heavy time demands, and your concern about missing the meetings.

Manage the Specific Behavior You Want Changed

It's essential that you pinpoint the specific behavior you want changed. For instance, in a business situation, if you recognize that the difficulty is related to an employee's attitude, assess what it is about his attitude that needs improving. Is he answering the phone in a brusque way? Arriving late? Leaving early? Bad-mouthing other employees? Not being a good team player?

When you're clear on the desired behavior, be improvement-oriented and address the specific behavior so that actual improvements can be made:

- Describe the changes you want or expect.

- Help the person come up with solutions for making the desired changes. Ask questions to trigger his or her ideas; this enhances feelings of competency and includes the person in the solutions process: "How do you think you might improve your sales presentation?" "How do you think you could add more time to study during soccer season?"

- When the person gives you a commitment to a solution, repeat it back to them.

- Set a period of time during which you will evaluate the commitment and review its effectiveness.

Chances for creating desirable behavior improve when you stress how a behavior or their performance can be improved, rather than dwelling on and criticizing past performance.

Receiving Feedback: The Good, the Bad, and the Ugly

Receiving feedback is uncomfortable; yet, it's an important part of the connection dynamics that creates better relationships. The intent of feedback is to help improve something that's affecting a connection or performance. If it concerns others, it's a concern for you, so hunker down and listen up!

- Listen carefully to the person's description of your behavior and their recommendations.

- Restrain those defense mechanisms which are likely to flare up during the receiving side of feedback. Take some deep breaths to keep cool.

- Don't dismiss the feedback as irrelevant or unimportant. Take responsibility for the behavior. Acknowledge your willingness to learn more about the situation and remedy it.

- Be authentic with your responses. Perhaps you recognize that you haven't done such a good job at staying on task or keeping a commitment. Relate why that may be the case: "I assumed that because you were getting all the research for the report, that you had it all under control and didn't need anything else from me." Add "feeling" statements that support your behavior, such as "I'm embarrassed that I misread the situation."

- Communicate the changes in their behavior that may be needed to help you change: "In the future, please let me know that you want my help with the necessary documentation for reports."

- Paraphrase or summarize the feedback to make sure you've heard it correctly and understand its intent.

- Express your appreciation to the person for sharing feelings or information, and your willingness to change. Request that he or she continue providing you with feedback because it is so valuable for achieving workable solutions and maintaining positive connections.

HUNKER DOWN TO BUSINESS

While working as a civilian for the Marine Corps, I was "stationed" in an office in Washington, D.C. My colleague and I shared the same rank, but his work constantly required him to be in the field. Problems arose because we had to collaborate on projects together, but communication was sluggish between us. He rarely returned my phone calls or faxes resulting in delayed projects (we didn't have the luxury of e-mail back then).

In one situation, I urgently needed his input; without it, the project would not meet the required deadline. After leaving a flurry of messages, I finally heard from him. I addressed the challenges created by not being able to get his prompt feedback on matters and the need for his cooperation. I told him that if we couldn't get our projects better coordinated, we'd have to discuss the matter with the General. This was intended to demonstrate the need for better cooperation, not as a threat. However, he took it as a threat, and after I clarified how better communication between us would eliminate the need for the General's input, he listened. We outlined new procedures for working together and agreed to review them for effectiveness after they were established.

Had I not brought up the problems his behavior was causing, undoubtedly my aggravation and frustration would have increased, and productivity would have suffered, creating even more difficulties. By discussing our joint project expectations and the steps needed to resolve the impasse, he finally took action more regularly.

I was serious about arranging a meeting with the General, not as a power move but because sometimes we need the support of those who have a stake in outcomes or who can serve as facilitators to get us out of the trenches. Thankfully, I never had to call in the Big Guns. —A.S.

Understand BodySpeak:
It Goes Without Saying

It's not just what you say; it's what's conveyed that counts. While our words are powerful communicators, we also speak another language loud and clear—nonverbal communication. What we say, coupled with our tone of voice and body language, works together to create the image of how people see us. Words may be powerful, but research has demonstrated that our body language says it all!

Our body language reflects how we process information, as well as our feelings about the speaker and the subject under discussion. It quickly serves as an accurate barometer of our authentic feelings and corresponding emotional responses. While words can be edited and controlled, body language is the unedited version of what we believe to be true—it leaks out to tell the truth!

Your body always has something to say about connection—how comfortable you feel being with the person or discussing a particular topic. Be especially sensitive to the messages your body is conveying; it's communicating loud and clear! It says a lot, even when you're not saying a word.

The way we stand, how we move our arms and hands, how we position our heads, what our facial expressions express, and the way we walk, all send signals. Movements, posture, gestures, and spatial relationships all have nuances, but can be easily misinterpreted. For instance, arms folded across a person's chest is a classic sign of defensiveness or hostility; yet, it might simply indicate that someone is cold or just plain comfortable that way. A woman who nods during a meeting might be signaling agreement, or just that she's taking in the information, nonverbally saying, "I hear you."

Tune in to the body language of others. Decoding body language is a learned ability. Studies reveal that women are better at reading body language than men, but there are many factors involved for correct interpretation. We get a more accurate understanding of a person's body

language when viewed in a social and cultural context. For instance, our western culture encourages eye contact, while in some other cultures direct eye contact is a sign of disrespect.

Since the meaning of gestures varies widely across our global landscape, be sure to become knowledgeable about proper etiquette before you travel internationally. Check out www.culturegrams.com (1-800-528-6279) for their World Edition detailing international customs, courtesies, greetings, gestures, and more. Roger Axtell's book, Gestures—the Do's and Taboos of Body Language Around the World, is another excellent source for understanding global gestures. Identical gestures often mean entirely different things; what works in one country can get you arrested in another, so become familiar with cross-cultural communication to learn right from rude.

Words and movement combined together form the dialogue. If both verbal and nonverbal communication are in alignment, that strengthens our understanding. When they're not congruent, body language serves as the litmus test for truth and takes precedence over verbal communication. Our body language is a natural lie detector test!

JUST FACE IT!

About 75 percent of nonverbal communication relates to the face. Our facial expressions play a vital role in establishing relationships; we make judgments about people based on what we see in their faces. Facial expressions can say it all relative to our attitude and emotional state. Happiness, sadness, surprise, disgust, anger, and fear have universal expressions. We may speak different languages, but no translation is required for our nonverbal communication. Our initial impressions are usually long-lasting, so it's vital to put your best face forward!

What BodySpeak Might be Saying

Out-of-context body language can be easily misinterpreted, so the gestures discussed below may not be an accurate reflection of a person's true intent. It's still valuable to tune in to these signals because they might very well be speaking their truth:

- Crossing and uncrossing arms signal boredom; arms folded across the chest often accompany indifference or dislike.

- Rubbing the head might be a sign that someone is peeved (or maybe just a bad case of head lice!); rubbing the ear with the thumb and forefinger could show lack of interest or doubt.

- Hands and arms: Whether on hips, fingers pointing, clenched fists, or rapid arm and hand movements can convey anger and hostility (flailing arm and hand movements might also be cultural, so the context is important!)

- Signs of nervousness include: fidgeting; fiddling with fingers, jewelry, or clothing; excessive blinking or darting of eyes back and forth; and sucking, chewing, biting, or licking lips.

- Touching the neck while speaking can be a sign of deception or dishonesty.

- Foot twitching or tapping can be a sign of impatience as well as someone trying to conceal an attitude or information. When we try really hard not to show emotions in our faces, our energy can get pushed down and activate our feet. If you see a poker face, look under the table and check out their feet!

- People who are having difficulty making a decision might open and shut their hands repeatedly.

- Rocking back and forth is sometimes viewed as a sign of impatience or anxiousness to leave. This creates discomfort in others and distracts them from their focus, since it's challenging to carry on a conversation with a rocking horse!

- Picking at clothing, as if removing lint, signals opposition or disagreement.

About Face! Making Eye Contact

In Western culture, eye contact between the speaker and the listener is regarded favorably. Research has shown a definite link between eye contact and likeability. If people are really interested in what you're talking about, they'll look at you about 75 percent of the time, periodically glancing elsewhere. However, too much eye contact is unsettling, so making face contact is advised.

"Face time" means scanning your conversation partner's face for about two seconds and then the eyes for the same amount of time; gaze to the nose, then the mouth, then repeat the process. It may sound a little strange, but it's actually just a minimal shift of attention that helps to break a penetrating stare.

AM I READING YOU RIGHT?

If people are yawning, leaning back, avoiding eye contact, looking bored, glancing at their watches, or seem distracted in other ways, rather than wondering what they're thinking, inquire directly "Is there something that's a concern? This quickly confirms or denies the validity of their body language. Otherwise, you might jump to the wrong conclusions. Are they simply not interested or do they have valid reasons for being so distracted? Yawning? Are they tired, had a late night, or up half the night with a sick child? Looking at a watch? Are they out of time? Do they have another appointment? Or are they concerned that their watch may have stopped? When you go directly to the source, you can stop all that wondering and get it right.

Voice Tone, Tempo, and Quality

The sound of a voice can be music to our ears or grate on our nerves. We are judged by how we sound as much as what we say, all of which either enhances or detracts from how we're viewed. Sound is so powerful because it affects how we respond to others, as well as how they respond to us.

People who speak with a forceful voice, in a lower tone and a comfortable tempo, are often viewed as more powerful, confident, and believable. A soft voice is frustrating because we need to strain our ears. A wimpy or breathy voice is perceived as weak and fragile. A nasal tone or high-pitched voice is considered downright annoying! In a nationwide survey of 1,000 men and women, the characteristic about voices that annoyed and irritated people the most was a whining, complaining, or nagging tone. Negative words coupled with a negative tone produce a one-two punch that knocks us out of a ring of influence!

Positive tones reflect caring, concern, affection, enthusiasm, happiness, good nature, and a warm expression. Negative tones sound cold, tense, impatient, angry, rough, sad, sarcastic, defensive, blaming, abrupt, irritated, accusing, or anything else that creates a negative reaction in others. Voice tone also relates to the way something is said. Sarcasm, cynicism, criticism, pessimism, skepticism (and other negative "isms') are turn-offs and send out connection-crushing signals. "That was really brilliant!" can sound sarcastic, if the tone used reflects sarcasm versus an encouraging statement of reinforcement.

When your voice says one thing, but your words say another, the tone conveys your true feelings. Emotions have a way of leaking into our speech patterns. For instance, the tone conveying your authentic feelings, whether it's disappointment or anger, makes a difference in these statements: "Oh, it doesn't really matter," or "I'm not upset." People will believe the truth revealed by the tone, rather than the actual words spoken.

Some people aren't aware that their voices may be perceived as patroniz-ing, hostile, abrasive, or irritable, all of which can be very disconnecting. Our tone of voice can trigger an emotional reaction and prompt defen-

siveness. Since our attitudes are reflected in our voices, we need to monitor how we sound and the impact it creates on others.

It confuses people if our voices don't express the feeling associated with our intended meaning. For instance, if your intention is to show excitement, but your words are conveyed in a low-key, half-hearted, or monotonous tone, you won't sound genuine. You'll come across emotionally dead and unconvincing.

To make your voice sound more energetic, add more life to it! You might need to speed up the tempo. Avoid talking in a droning monotone or flat voice by emphasizing key words to punch up the rhythm. This helps keep listeners tuned in, not turned off.

Speaking clearly in a pleasant, resonant tone that is delivered with a comfortable tempo wins the interest and cooperation of people, and enhances your image as competent, caring, and confident.

Don't forget the power of a pause—it delivers results. A well-placed pause works wonders with attention-getting power to heighten interest, punch up a presentation, help others reach a decision, or make a sale.

Give Yourself a Hand!

Appropriate and meaningful hand gestures provide impact and add emphasis to reinforce a verbal message, whether you are talking about skyrocketing profits or plummeting performance. Observe the hand gestures of powerful communicators and how they contribute to their presence and message delivery; use them as "hand models."

Some people are uncomfortable using gestures and it shows through their awkward movements. If gestures don't come naturally, practice using them so you can make your points properly, without seeming contrived.

Make Every Move Count!

Research has revealed that people who make fewer hand and body gestures are perceived as more powerful, credible, and intelligent. People who are seen as leaders tend to move less and gesture less. This doesn't mean they're not animated, or stiff; their movements are more deliberate and purposeful. Research has also shown that if you want to create an impression of enthusiasm and drive, increase the use of meaningful gestures.

Position Yourself for Success

Our posture reflects both our self-regard as well as our emotional state. Slouching is often a sign of poor self-image or depression, so stand up! Sitting upright or standing and walking with your head up and shoulders squared back conveys self-confidence. People who project an image of leadership are often believed to be taller than they actually are—so strike a confident pose! Avoid stiff, wooden postures which make you appear uptight, cold, and distant; others may interpret you as difficult to talk with or unapproachable.

People perceived as leaders also use personal space to their advantage. They lean forward, extend their arms and legs, and take up more space, all conveying a "take charge" position.

When people are attentive and interested in what you're saying, or they like you, they tend to lean forward; turning away shows lack of interest or is a sign of hostility. When you're speaking to someone, be sure to turn your head along with your body to face them; turning just your head sends signals that you're keeping your distance. This body language tells others that you might not accept or like them.

Think Territory

We all have invisible "bubbles" around us and consider that personal space as our turf. How closely we position ourselves to others sends out signals regarding how comfortable we are, and whether others are comfortable within that same distance. In the U.S, the intimate distance zone extends out from a person to about 18 inches. If we're "space invaders" and step into another's zone, they may become intimidated,

distracted, or feel harassed. If it's too close for their comfort, they'll likely back away because you just burst their bubble!

It's important to preserve personal territory, especially when you want to influence others. The personal distance zone begins at the perimeter of the intimate zone, ranging from 18 inches to four feet. This zone provides a comfortable distance for many interactions and avoids entering sacred territory and feelings of intimidation. If you stand further away than four feet, others may interpret the extra distance as aloofness or snobbishness, or that you're shying away from closeness. Find the right comfort zone, as close as comfortably possible for making the right connections.

HUGS AND KISSES

People have different levels of comfort regarding touching. Expressive personalities tend to exhibit greater physical contact and like it; others are uncomfortable and offended by it. When congratulating others on some achievement or success, it's considered appropriate and customary to shake hands, or pat their back or arm; often, hugging is also acceptable.

While touching can have a very positive, connecting effect and promotes likeability, some find it objectionable. Since attitudes vary considerably, and with increased sensitivities (and lawsuits) regarding touching in the workplace, boundaries have become blurred. To be on the safe side, unless they're mutually agreeable, hugs and kisses might be better left to the chocolate manufacturers.

Are You Projecting a Connecting Image?

"There are four ways, and only four ways, in which we have contact with the world. We are evaluated and classified by these four contacts: what we do, how we look, what we say, and how we say it."

Dale Carnegie

Here's a quick checklist summarizing the main points of this Key:

- Are you making good eye contact? Do your eyes convey warmth and vitality?

- How close are you standing with your conversation companions? Stand within the range of the comfort zone for the interaction, as described above.

- Are you facing people when they speak?

- Do you greet people with a smile?

- Are your facial expressions congruent with your speech? Does your face show your interest in others?

- Does your body language match what you're saying?

- How's your posture? Stand and sit upright, leaning slightly toward others.

- Are you using the right type of gestures? Use open and expressive gestures without overdoing them or making them seem contrived.

- Do you nod your head while listening to encourage others to talk?

- Do you present yourself appropriately for the situation? Are you dressed right?

- How does your voice sound? Control your volume, pitch, and tone to suit the specific situation. Avoid speaking too fast, too slow, or too loud or soft, and aim for a good flow without sprinkling with filler words, "umms," "ers," or "ahs."

- Is your body language sending out all the right messages?

By understanding body language and the messages it sends, we enhance our chances of connecting with impact.

There's a lot to think about regarding how we come across to people. Monitoring how we relate to others and the messages we communicate both verbally and nonverbally ultimately determines how others rate our communication IQ.

Key #5:

Honor Communication Needs

"What a wonderful miracle, if only we could look through each other's eyes for an instant."

Henry David Thoreau

Given the plethora of personalities, perspectives, and needs, respecting communication differences is a top priority for peak-performing connections. When you get down to the very core of successful relationships, they include: meeting each other's needs; exchanging information about ideas, thoughts, and feelings; and relating well to one another. Communication is the currency of connection.

By bridging differences through increased awareness and adaptability, we increase our sensitivities (and hopefully our sensibilities) in our connections. Understanding communication differences helps us read people better, resulting in greater wisdom for strategically adapting to their needs and netting better results with less stress.

Sort Out Styles

Billions of people inhabit this gigantic planet of ours—each one an intriguing combination of unique gifts, talents, dreams, attitudes, motives, perceptions, personalities, and peccadilloes. When we mix and mingle together, our respective eclectic bundles of uniqueness can confuse, confound, frustrate, exasperate, and aggravate others; as well as delight, captivate, enchant, or energize them. By learning to understand some predictable "personality" patterns, we just might save our sanity when we're at our wit's end in dealing with those pesky peccadilloes!

Social scientists and psychologists have studied the rich diversity of human behavior for eons, dating as far back as Hippocrates (460-370 B.C.). Their research into how people respond to life events, and to one another, has helped to clarify and categorize distinctly different styles. The concept of behavioral styles, also called communication or social styles, has proven to be a useful tool for understanding the amazingly complex ways we think, act, and relate to people.

Many theories about behavioral styles have evolved over time, with four primary styles noted repeatedly and classified over the centuries with different names. Some researchers have further extracted and compartmentalized behavioral styles into even more complex categories.

We believe the four primary styles, each reflecting a unique pattern of personal energy, offer a simple tool for understanding differences, as well as offering guidelines for interpersonal interactions. As a result, we've given them names relative to the energy focus that is of paramount interest to each: Goal-Getters, Cooperators, Schmoozers, and Fact Aficionados.

While our individual energy patterns generally focus in one of the four areas, we may also express other behaviors borrowed or blended from the full spectrum of personal qualities. Of course, this is what makes us all so interesting, and why it's impossible to neatly compartmentalize humankind. However, defining behavioral styles does provide some useful clues in understanding one another and communicating effectively. A word of warning: No one style is better than another; each one has its respective strengths along with behaviors that may drive others a bit looney.

A Matter of Style ... a Spectrum of Patterns

"To effectively communicate, we must realize that we are all different in the way we perceive the world and use this understanding as a guide to our communication with others."

Anthony Robbins

Our primary behavioral style influences how we process life's events and interact with others—how we handle challenges, relate to our work environment, respond to rules or procedures, deal with conflict, and manage all the countless intricacies of interpersonal communication. Understanding the differences in social styles does more than help us sort out the perplexities and peculiarities of the people with whom we live, work, and encounter in our lives. It facilitates learning about their priorities, seeing situations from their perspective, and learning how to best communicate with them for building positive, productive relationships.

People with the same behavioral style relate to one another and situations in a similar pattern. As a result, they often see the world in much the same way. Developing rapport with people of a similar style is easier, especially those who give priority to the value of relationships, such as the Schmoozers and Cooperators.

Developing rapport with people whose styles are different from our own is often more challenging. Our reference points and priorities are different; we may wonder why others don't respond to us the way we might in the same situation. For instance, an extrovert with a light-hearted, fun-loving spirit might react with laughter and amusement at discovering a trail of toilet tissue attached to her shoe, while a more serious, introverted individual might react with anger or embarrassment. It's the same event, just an entirely different point of reference.

The entertaining extrovert might interpret that event this way: "I must have looked absolutely silly! Little did I know, as I was walking to the meeting, I was dragging a trail of toilet tissue behind me! How hysterical! People were laughing like crazy, knowing I was on my way

to the CEO's office. She got a chuckle out of it, too, and the unexpected episode gave us a chance to laugh a little before getting down to serious business. Life's little surprises show up in unpredictable ways as we blaze a trail behind us!"

A more serious soul might see it this way: "I am so embarrassed! I was trying to make such a good impression, and instead, must have looked absolutely ridiculous, traipsing toilet tissue behind me! People were laughing hysterically and I just wanted to bolt. My beet-red face was a telltale sign for sure and I felt totally flustered going into that meeting with all the VIPs staring and laughing at me. Everyone's still talking about how stupid I looked."

The same incident happened to both; yet their corresponding perception and responses to it created entirely different experiences. And so it goes with each of our responses to life's daily events and the people in them. We bring our attitudes with us and act accordingly. Since different styles respond to the same events in different ways, our cues are skewed! We might laugh hysterically at something because it strikes us funny; meanwhile, someone else thinks our laughter is way out of line, disrespectful, and definitely not funny!

By recognizing these different patterns and adapting how we relate to a person's style, we can dramatically increase our chances of getting along better and achieving our mutual goals. When we adapt our style to what works best for others, we're honoring their needs as well as reducing potential conflicts. This all works wonders in gaining trust and respect, and in forging dynamic relationships.

You've Got Style!

Circle the characteristics that best describe you most of the time, or in specific settings, such as at work:

C Relates personal feelings

F Problem solver

S Persuasive

C Easy-going

G Self-starter

C Dislikes conflict

G Impatient

S Generous

C Agreeable

F Quiet

G Quick-tempered

S Multi-tasker

C Peacemaker

G Achievement-driven

C Diplomatic

C Dependable

F Doesn't usually share personal feelings

C Calm temperament

G Results-oriented

S Emotionally expressive

C Empathetic

F Analytical

G Decisive

F Precise

G Demanding

S Focuses on the "big picture," not the details or obstacles related to it

G Strong-willed

F Detail-driven

F Logical

S Optimistic

S Energetic

F Serious

G Competitive

S Dislikes routine

F Perfectionist

G Efficient

S Spontaneous

S Charismatic

C Values personal relationships

C Loyal

F Solitary

S Nonstop idea-generator

G Assertive/ aggressive

C Supportive and helpful

F Organized

G Enjoys challenges

S Entertaining and fun-loving

F Conscientious

Now total up each of the qualities you circled and their corresponding letters. For instance, if you have more G's, you fall into the Goal-Getter profile. More C's than any other letter? You possess more of the traits of a Cooperator. We all have some traits from each category, and some traits are noted in more than one category, but you should see some kind of pattern.

GOAL-GETTERS

Profile: Goal-Getters are risk-takers and results-driven. They're independent thinkers, leaders, and visionaries. Goal-Getters are action-oriented and want results. They act fast and like others to make decisions quickly and perform their tasks as fast as they do. They love to compete, win, solve problems, tackle challenges, and be in control.

They want to know what the goals are, how they can save time to short-cut their achievement, and the options or alternatives for achieving results. They need freedom to select their goals and like to get things done their way and at their pace. Goal-Getters measure progress by the results they create and want to be appreciated for their capabilities.

They're not interested in minor details or small talk; they focus on results rather than relationships. When establishing rapport with Goal-Getters, praise their achievements, not their personal qualities. Be straightforward and assertive, and don't beat around the bush. Their mantra: "Give me the facts, get to the point, and get on with it!"

General traits of Goal-Getters:

- Achievement-driven
- Results-oriented
- Assertive/aggressive
- Competitive
- Self-confident
- Enjoy challenges
- Self-starters
- Intuitive
- Demanding
- Dominant
- Decisive

- Quick-tempered
- Efficient
- Pragmatic
- Risk-takers
- Strong-willed
- Impatient
- Visionaries
- Task-oriented
- Fast-paced
- Persistent

Their gifts: They see the vision and go for it with high-powered, nothing-can-stop-me performance.

Conflict style: With their strong wills and assertive or aggressive natures, Goal-Getters attempt to impose their thoughts and feelings on others. They're demanding and may overlook feelings and upset others with their sarcasm, insults, and impatience.

Avoid debating them since they can cut you to shreds with their quick verbal agility. They dislike sensitivity or signs of weakness, so stand your ground with them; they'll respect you more.

Motivation: Results, challenge, power, and credit for achievement.

Getting along with Goal-Getters:
- Be straightforward
- Be assertive and express self-confidence
- Speak clearly and at their rate of speed
- Be pragmatic, methodical, and more formal in your approach
- Use gestures and direct eye contact
- Show them how you'll get results
- Present facts, data, and statistics
- Be decisive and take action
- Keep your cool when they get demanding
- Focus on the need for cooperation

What they dislike: Small talk and being asked to do things that seem unreasonable, don't make sense, or get in the way of their goals.

Connecting tips for Goal-Getters: Ease up on your rigorous demands. Let go of some of your control. Laugh more. Listen to the ideas of others. Invest some time in building relationships. Focus on the adage, "Life is a journey, not just a destination."

COOPERATORS

Profile: Cooperators are steadfast, loyal, and love to be liked, appreciated, and validated. Relationships are a priority for them; they're supportive team players and prefer working with others.

Cooperators need information that explains reasons for doing things, along with detailed instructions, expectations, and an understanding of

their role in a project. They're slow in making decisions and sharing their opinions. Because they're relationship-driven, Cooperators like operating through group consensus. With their sensitive nature, it's important not to embarrass or disagree with them in public.

They prefer an informal and relaxed atmosphere. Cooperators are uncomfortable with change, so prepare them well in advance of any antic-ipated changes, emphasizing the factors that will remain the same. Reinforce their value and contributions, and your high regard for them as individuals.

General traits of Cooperators:

- Value personal relationships
- Relate personal feelings
- Agreeable
- Calm temperaments
- Easy-going
- Empathetic
- Dependable
- Diplomatic
- Supportive and helpful
- Good listeners
- Friendly and likeable
- Cautious
- Loyal
- Practical
- Peacemakers
- Don't like confrontation
- Accepting
- Uncomfortable with change

Their gifts: A calming influence providing loyal support and an easy-going, cooperative nature.

Conflict style: They dislike conflict and may stuff their feelings regarding issues, "giving in" to keep the peace and preserve the relationship. As a result, they may feel "put upon," but don't often openly complain.

Motivation: Appreciation, validation, camaraderie, and importance of relationships.

Relating to Cooperators:

- Allow ample time to listen to them
- Speak at a slower rate
- Approach them in a relaxed manner
- Show your feelings
- Validate them and their contributions
- Focus discussions
- Be patient and sensitive
- Show them how change is important and will improve their status
- Think in terms of "togetherness"; talk about how "Together we can work things out ... find a way ... reach the goal ... overcome the obstacle," and so on

What they dislike: Pressure and embarrassment.

Connecting tips for Cooperators: Speak up when you're upset. Your voice needs to be heard, too! Enjoy some spontaneity and the joy that springs from it. Don't belabor decision-making. Just do it.

SCHMOOZERS

Profile: Schmoozers are very sociable, well-liked, and excellent relation-ship- builders who absolutely thrive around people. They light up rooms with their dynamic nature and enjoy public recognition. They're sponta-neous and easily reveal their emotions. Schmoozers are inspired by encouragement, pep talks, and personal support.

Because of their high need for sociability, Schmoozers must have plenty of social contact and want to be included in events (even those they don't especially want to attend, but just want to know they've been invited!) They have lots to say and love to have people listen and share conversation with them. Schmoozers like unstructured environments and dislike routine or working in isolation. Because of their keen social sense, they know how to get people to work as a team. They're also intuitive about good timing and sensitive to body language.

Schmoozers are visionaries who see the big picture and would rather focus on it than on all the particulars of how to make it a reality. They can have a short memory for some details, and gloss over some of the important ones, including potential obstacles on the way to the big vision. Not surprisingly, they dislike paperwork, rules, and procedures.

They like excitement, variation, and flexibility, adapting well to changing circumstances. They get bored easily without stimulating projects or conversations to hold their attention. When a project no longer holds the same level of excitement, Schmoozers often turn their attention to something new or different and might shirk their responsibilities or tasks associated with it. Be on the alert for their tendency to exaggerate or over-generalize; they need to thoroughly check out the facts before making recommendations or proposals.

General traits of Schmoozers:

- Optimistic
- Charismatic
- Friendly
- Emotionally expressive
- Extroverts
- Ambitious
- Generous
- Competitive
- Intuitive
- Nonstop idea-generators
- Fast-moving
- Energetic
- Fun-loving
- Entertaining
- Persuasive
- Risk-takers
- Spontaneous
- Multi-taskers
- Visionaries
- Focus on the "big picture," not the details or obstacles to achieving it

Their gifts: An abundance of energy, enthusiasm, ideas, and proficiency in building positive relationships.

Conflict style: Watch out when Schmoozers get upset! Avoid getting hooked into their outbursts because they vent their feelings with gusto! Wait for them to calm down before discussing solutions, since they're not receptive to problem-solving until then.

Motivation: Admiration and recognition; need to feel loved and appreciated for their contributions.

Relating to Schmoozers:

- Move quickly
- Talk fast with vivid language and gestures
- Engage them in conversation and lots of small talk
- Share personal stories
- Approach with the "big picture" and the "vision"
- "Praise in public, criticize in private"
- Recognize them
- Be enthusiastic and energetic
- Use stories and colorful language
- Downplay routine; play up excitement
- When an agreement is reached, relate the discussion in a memo to document terms
- Give them an outline, timetable, or schedule because they may overestimate their own competence or the anticipated results from a project
- Show them how opportunities will provide a platform for them to "shine" or to raise their public recognition

What they dislike: Details, routine, rules, and procedures.

Connecting Tips for Schmoozers: Don't get distracted or add "more irons to the fire" before completing other assignments. Keep your commitments. Get more details to avoid jumping to conclusions or making generalizations. Stay on track and work with a system that manages your love for multi-tasking. Watch out for runaway emotions. Your effervescence (sometimes loud manner) can vex quieter, calmer spirits, so tone it down a notch or two, when in their presence.

STRENGTH IN VARIETY

In our seminars, we present an exercise that showcases the patterns of each style. Participants representing each of the four styles are grouped together and given the same task. We ask each group to offer solutions for cutting costs or increasing sales, and then to rank them in order of preference. The patterns of each style unfold much the same every time:

- The Goal-Getters may argue about the ranking of what will lead to the fastest and best results.

- The Cooperators love working as a team to get group consensus, but their combined list may not reflect anyone's true opinions.

- The Schmoozers have a jolly time in their corner, often sharing stories and sometimes getting sidetracked from the task at hand, but they sure do have fun!

- The Fact Aficionados, because they don't have access to all the facts, usually hesitate to come up with a recommendation.

FACT AFICIONADOS

Profile: Fact Aficionados thrive on details and information. They scout for information, not conversation. They are methodical perfectionists who don't commit to action until every detail is known. Fact Aficionados are careful researchers and need plenty of information before making decisions. After all, they believe no decision is better than a wrong one!

As a result, they compile a wealth of information and share it gladly when asked, but you may have to ask to get it (and be careful what you ask for!) They usually give out more information than other styles want or need.

Fact Aficionados like clearly defined tasks, consistency, stability, low risk, security, and tasks that require precision and planning, seeking practical ways to accomplish them. They have a strong need to do things right, "by the book," and follow rules.

Fact Aficionados dislike pep talks and too much small talk; they want to know the reasons why they should participate. They speak slowly, often in a monotone, with limited vocal or facial expression. Their eye contact is more indirect and body movements are minimal.

Fact Aficionados are task-masters, not relationship pros, and may feel awkward handling relationships. They are more reserved, even aloof in nature and don't typically radiate bushels of warmth. They may irritate others by their negativity, criticism, and need for so much information.

General traits of Fact Aficionados:

- Analytical
- Detail-driven
- Conscientious
- Organized
- Quiet
- Logical
- Slow to change
- Persistent
- Problem solvers
- Precise
- Perfectionists
- Responsible
- Serious
- Solitary
- Cautious
- Good listeners
- Don't usually share personal feelings

Their gifts: Precision, careful planning, providing a picture of reality, and looking for obstacles that could block success.

Conflict style: Fact Aficionados dislike conflict and tend to withdraw from undesirable or uncomfortable situations. They need time and space to think and respond relative to their relationships and problems. They tend to hold in their feelings and not share their ideas.

Motivation: Quality-conscious and a strong desire to be right.

Relating to Fact Aficionados:

- Be armed with facts and figures; provide documentation
- Go one step at a time and stick to the facts
- Be organized and precise in your explanations
- Be patient
- Use minimal body movement
- Slow down your rate of speaking
- Answer directly; don't beat around the bush
- Talk in terms of logic
- Emphasize what they're doing right, rather than finding fault
- Clarify responsibilities and approach them with step-by-step solutions; give them ample time to think about a situation before an important discussion or decision

What they dislike: People who don't meet deadlines or follow rules or regulations.

Connecting tips for Fact Aficionados: Evaluate the prime importance of "going by the book," sticking to the rules, or following inflexible policies in every circumstance. Life is not so black and white; others appreciate having their needs taken into consideration. Express your concerns in a caring way. Tune in to your feelings and express them more often, so others see your golden heart.

"Diversity: the art of thinking independently together."

Malcolm S. Forbes

Approach Others with Intent

Each style offers its own respective gifts, and we need them all! While we may have our challenges with different styles, each provides valuable strengths and plays a vital role in the business of living. Admittedly, if we all operated with the same style, we'd probably have an easier time getting along, but chaos would reign!

The world definitely needs the tapestry of gifts generated by each style (and recognizing these respective strengths is an excellent reference point when their behaviors might be driving us crazy!) Order flows best from the diversity and balance of energies, pace, and priorities available from each style.

One of the rich treasures offered by profiling styles is gaining "best practices" for enjoying higher quality, more productive relationships. Understanding and appreciating our differences guides us in greater awareness—whether we're negotiating contracts, making sales, supervising people, resolving conflicts, reaching agreements, improving productivity, or performing any of the other activities required to influence successful outcomes. By adapting our own style to better relate to the needs of others, we reduce our stress while achieving our goals with fewer hassles, snags, and opposition. Getting a view from the other person's vantage point gives us an insider's perspective into his or her needs and how best to satisfy them. Ultimately, giving others what they need is a valuable strategy that gets us what we want, too.

"No one can whistle a symphony.
It takes an orchestra to play it."

H.E. Lucock

What's Your Energy?

Two of the behavioral styles—Goal-Getters and Schmoozers—are expressive extroverts, and two—Cooperators and Fact Aficionados—are more reserved and introverted. The energetic Goal-Getters and Schmoozers boldly approach life and all the people they meet, while Cooperators and Fact Aficionados are more cautious and quiet with less revealing natures.

Extroverted styles do best approaching introverts gently, without overpowering them. Tone it down and let the introverts control the pace, volume, and content of the interaction. Avoid personal subjects unless they take the lead. Since extroverts like spunk, introverts are encouraged to stretch their boundaries of boldness in the presence of extroverts, and to not be afraid of adding a bit of flamboyance or a splash of panache.

Styles that are similar get a taste of their own medicine when interacting together, which presents a different set of challenges. With two introverts in the mix, one needs to take the lead to move beyond that awkward, uncomfortable feeling. With animated extroverts, both need to have time to share their perspectives, information, or stories (which they undoubtedly have in abundance!)

Where's Your Focus?

Another major distinction regarding behavioral styles is where people place their focus: tasks versus relationships. By being alert as to whether someone is task- or relationship-driven, and adapting to that preference, you're more prone to get their attention.

Goal-Getters and Fact Aficionados are task-oriented and place a priority on getting things done, tackling challenges, and solving problems. Keep tasks center stage when dealing with them. They usually prefer spending time focused on the best ways to handle tasks, rather than investing time in building or improving the quality of their relationships (except where required in pursuit of their goals!)

On the other hand, Schmoozers and Cooperators put a priority on relationships and have extensive networks of personal and professional contacts. These two types are best approached by focusing first on building a connection, relating to them and their interests, rather than "cutting to the chase" with the task at hand. Disregard the relationship and you're unlikely to win their affection, business, or attention!

DO YOU "C"
WHAT EACH STYLE WANTS?

Each style likes to be appreciated for its different strengths. Recognize each for what they value most and validate them for their special gifts:

- Carefulness—Fact Aficionados

- Contributions—Cooperators

- Cleverness—Schmoozers

- Capabilities—Goal-Getters

Adaptability = "Connect-ability"

A word of caution: With all this labeling going on, it's extremely important not to use behavioral styles as an excuse for being inflexible: "Sorry, I can't help it! Blame it on my behavioral style. That's just the way I am." The key to creating extraordinary connections is being flexible and adapting to the needs of others.

It also means pushing ourselves out of our comfort zones to make others more comfortable.

Understanding your style can help you capitalize on your strengths, monitor your weaknesses, and recognize and adapt to the differences in people, problem-solving, and the plethora of life's situations. Adaptability is one of connection's magic tricks; it's about the survival of the fittest. As in nature, creatures that are highly adaptable thrive and survive, like the ever-changing chameleon that changes colors to harmonize with its environment. The same is true for us humans in our choices to "adapt or die" (death isn't exactly the result, but a lack of effective social skills can kill your chances of success!)

Being adaptable doesn't mean you're pretending to be different; it means that you're consciously making choices to be more flexible, expressing the qualities that fit best into each situation. You're not losing yourself in the process; you're gaining stronger, more harmonious relationships that bring you greater cooperation, friendship, harmony, respect, and success.

"The path to greatness is along with others."

Baltasar Gracián, Spanish Priest

Gender Differences:
The Interplanetary Connection

Volumes have been written about men and women being from different planets. Although we may speak the same language, we have differences in priorities, internal processing, and behavior patterns. It's easy to misinterpret, misunderstand, or simply not get where the other is coming from. Since Earth is home for all of us, understanding some of these unique patterns helps to keep us all better connected, wherever on Earth we meet. Enhancing our ability to get along with "the other half" is our purpose for including this discussion here.

We tend to operate according to our own gender's communication rules or "gender codes" for a wide range of behaviors, such as how we show gratitude, take command, ask for assistance, and express emotion. Like our behavioral styles, one gender pattern isn't better than another; it's just different. Yet, these differences can cause friction and get in the way of clear, harmonious relationships.

While gender differences have been widely researched, and certain behaviors observed and labeled, it's never, ever appropriate to stereotype. Noting differences designed for increased understanding of male-female communication runs the risk of grossly oversimplifying behaviors and stereotyping them. (We want to make that especially clear, being the crystal-clear communicators we strive to be!)

Without question, each person is an individualized expression of uniqueness; gender-related patterns may or may not reflect any one person's specific patterns or style. Undoubtedly, all of us would passionately protest being squeezed into behaviors that don't speak our specific truth. Such predictability of patterns would surely take away the exquisite spice of life in our intriguing, ever-changing, and capricious universe!

The value in learning about some of these patterns, as with behavioral styles, is that they help de-mystify perplexing behaviors that might otherwise seem foreign and frustrating. By understanding these differences, we're better able to avoid some tricky communication cobwebs that can trap and entangle us in conflict, frustration, and confusion.

As with all of our communications, the more we understand the needs of others and adapt our communication patterns to them, the more successful we'll be in getting what we want and need. Earning one another's respect and trust, which is so fundamental to creating and keeping productive relationships, is no different between men and women.

The following are some of the differences noted by researchers regarding communication patterns of men and women. We offer caution as a caveat, not to apply these as gender stereotypes, but to let them serve as another guidance system for adapting to individual needs in the complex world of communication and connection. We offer a collection of the combined insights and wisdom of gender communication specialists John Gray, Ph.D.; Deborah Tannen, Ph.D.; Lillian Glass, Ph.D.; Suzette Haden Elgin, Ph.D.; and Kathleen Kelley Reardon, Ph.D.:

- Priorities: Women value the quality and richness of their relationships; they enjoy sharing and relating. Men place a high priority on tasks, getting results, and solving problems.

- Communication: Men talk to get specific information and to solve problems. Women talk to make a point, share feelings, give emotional support, reduce their stress, and gain clarity of choices.

- Conversational nuances: Women tend to notice the subtle nuances of interactions, of what and how something was said; men may not see them. Men interrupt more and allow fewer interruptions; they use less vocal inflection, allow more silence during conversation, use more command terms, and make fewer references to emotional states than women. Men tease and use more sarcasm, especially regarding sensitive issues, apologize less often, confront issues less frequently, and disclose less personal information than do women. Women use more words to express themselves and communicate more what's on their minds through stream-of-consciousness delivery.

- Body language: Nonverbal behavior varies between the sexes. Women tend to be more tuned in to body language and the tones expressed by others. Men may nod to show agreement, while women also nod as they process information. Men don't share as many facial expressions or reactions as women. Men frown or squint more when listening and don't provide as much eye contact, while women have more face-to-face contact. Men sit further away, fidget, shift their bodies, and lean back more when listening than do women.

- Problem-solving: Men like to have time to think about problems away from others. They may seek advice or help only when they've done whatever they can alone. Women tend to talk more about their problems; voicing their concerns reduces their stress about them. Men tend to jump in and offer advice to solve the problem, rather than discuss the concerns surrounding it. Women aren't necessarily seeking advice by talking about their problems; rather, talking provides an opportunity to sort out all the issues.

- Negotiation: According to Suzette Haden Elgin, Ph.D., author of The Gentle Art of Verbal Self-Defense at Work, "Most American men today define anything that involves negotiation as a game, at least temporarily, and they switch to game-playing behavior for the duration of the negotiation." Many American women don't apply this principle.

- Decision-making: Women tend to seek advice, input, and consensus from others. Men often like to make decisions independently.

- "Brag-ability": Men eagerly take credit for their achievements that demonstrate their competence and skill. Women tend to diminish their accomplishments, attributing their acquisition to team effort or luck.

- Assistance: Directions, anyone? Men tend to avoid seeking help and direction. Women are more likely to accept help, but ask for it indirectly.

- Confrontation: Men tend to be more straightforward. Women may "soften the blow" to protect feelings.

- World perspectives: Men are focused on the outer world; their small talk often revolves around topics related to business, sports, weather, and news. Women like to focus on the inner world of personal issues, of what's going on inside of others, and to share their inner worlds.

WHAT'S THE DIFFERENCE?

Brain scan research, conducted at the Indiana School of Medicine in Indianapolis, revealed significant differences in gender listening patterns. Most of the men showed activity exclusively in the left side of their brains, known as the temporal lobe, which is associated with listening and speech; the majority of women had activity in the temporal lobe on both sides of their brains. This research suggests that language processing is indeed different for males and females. According to researcher Joseph T. Lurito, "We don't know if the difference is because of the way we're raised, or if it's hard-wired in the brain."

Gender Differences at Work

"Human diversity makes tolerance more than a virtue; it makes it a requirement for survival."

Rene Dubos

In our professional relationships, following traditional gender stereotypes can be hazardous to careers, particularly for women. Prejudices still exist, even in our more enlightened era. Although many gender-related roles have changed in the workplace, some of the old stereotypes still haunt the hallways, boardrooms, and office suites. It's as important to break dysfunctional communication patterns as it is to break through glass ceilings.

According to Kathleen Kelly Reardon, Ph.D., a specialist in negotiation, persuasion, and interpersonal communication, the language habits of many men leading major organizations today "were developed when women were more clearly an out-group. There is a human tendency to treat members of out-groups as if they are all the same... A second tendency is to derogate outsiders." Some of the friction that occurs is not from intentional efforts to bring harm or insult, but is more a function of out-dated language habits that desperately need breaking.

What is considered to be professional behavior today is largely based on the male code of conduct. Even though it's been decades since women have joined the workforce to become career professionals, many have switched, mixed, and balanced their communication styles in order to gain acceptance and meet expectations. As a result, there's been a blending of male and female codes of conduct regarding acceptable or appropriate behavior and the expression of feelings at work. The challenge for both men and women is to work together to revise gender codes, relinquish stereotypes, and eliminate dysfunctional communication in the workplace.

Male and female work codes differ, and both bring important skills and proclivities to the workplace. According to Judy B. Rosener's research, published in the Harvard Business Review, women's communication patterns exhibit important leadership qualities such as encouraging participation, sharing power and information, enhancing the self-worth of others, and motivating others about their work. Women think in terms of equity and fair play, and prioritize the value of relationships. Men are more aggressive and direct, and think more in terms of results rather than what's fair.

The highly touted quality of teamwork is perceived differently by men and women. Men recognize the independent qualities, talents, and abilities of team members; everyone contributes to support one another, but each has a respective role to play. Men like to be in charge of their own tasks to get the desired results. Teamwork for women is more egalitarian and collaborative in nature—sharing responsibilities and tasks as members of the team, working together and even switching roles to achieve goals. Both men and women appreciate receiving public recognition of their achievements.

Building quality relationships in the world of business is a priority for women, and influences those they respect and trust. Men who don't take time to build relationships—who skip the "small talk," focus only on the bottom line, and don't show interest, appreciation, or concern—are less likely to gain the respect or trust of women. Men who wisely build connections will gain the support of women and their business, whether as a customer, client, or colleague. A valued connection can tip the scales in your favor when all things are equal and a choice must be made. Even if

you have a better product, the relationship that is the most grounded in relating to needs usually wins the contract or makes the sale.

The global workplace is changing and differences abound in communication styles. In the world of male-female communication, no single style or strategy is superior. It's vital that both men and women respect differences and adapt to the needs of one another for optimum function, creativity, and productivity.

This section focuses on increasing understanding of potentially different perspectives of men and women to enhance communication between them. With greater awareness, you can adapt how you relate to help make your relationships work better at work.

For men:

- Build considerate, caring, trusting, supportive, and respectful working relationships. Show your support through good communication and by making ongoing gestures of appreciation and consideration.

- When focusing intently on problem-solving (with a corresponding tendency to be totally absorbed in the process), be sure to monitor the needs of women and how you respond to them.

- Take time to listen and paraphrase what you've heard: "So what you're saying is ..."Women want to be heard, understood, and supported. The time you invest in listening will net you their increased respect and support.

- Give enough time for women to express their ideas. Avoid interrupting, finishing sentences, being sarcastic, lecturing, or changing the subject.

- Provide some feedback with periodic responses (such as "Oh," "Mmhhmm," and the like), instead of having words fall into dead silence. When speaking with women, provide good eye contact, show more emotional reaction in your face, and add more enthusiasm to your voice.

- Avoid fidgeting, frowning, and finger-pointing.

- Apologize immediately if you've made a mistake.

- Include more personal information in your conversations.

- Express support for emotions with empathy. Respond to the emotion being expressed: "That must have been frustrating." Or "It must be a big disappointment." Listening with empathy builds rapport and helps to gain women's trust and support. Avoid invalidating feelings, such as: "You shouldn't feel that way." Or "It's not such a big deal."

- Resist the temptation to give immediate advice or solve her problems. Show concern and support, and perhaps inquire how she's planning to proceed.

- Ask questions as a means of gathering more information to demonstrate your interest.

For women:

- Be firm, clear, and assertive in your communications, speaking up on matters that affect you, your work performance, and career. By redirecting communication dynamics, you become empowered to manage the perceptions of others with a corresponding positive impact on your own self-image.

- Give men advice only if it's solicited. Unsolicited advice might be viewed as insulting, especially if given in front of others. Use face-saving statements, such as "In case you didn't know ..." Or "You probably already know this ..."

- Avoid talking too much about problems; focus more on solutions. Get to the point quickly and address your main purpose. Don't complain unless you have a solution to offer. Stay calm and state the problem objectively, without accentuating the complaint with lots of emotion.

- Communicate without blaming. Complaints are often interpreted by men as blame. Express your concerns about the issue, then add a statement of appreciation for listening: "It feels good to talk about this and I really appreciate your listening."

- Be cautious about sharing your personal problems or feelings with men; share less personal information and keep small talk focused more on current events or topics of interest to them. Ask what men think, rather than how they feel.

- Minimize time being upset over situations. Accept differences that trigger conflicts, recognizing that the conflict is probably about an issue and not personal in nature.

- Take caution in expressing angry or negative feelings at work. Control negative emotions and find release for them outside the workplace. This means having to manage your heart, which requires suppression of anger and responding in ways deemed to be appropriate or professional. In the workplace, anger about an event is acceptable; expressing personal feelings is often misunderstood and misinterpreted, reinforcing negative images.

- If you ask for advice and disagree with a man's solution, don't invalidate it. Or, if you don't follow his suggestions, don't explain why you're not using them.

- Take credit for your achievements and focus on the results you achieved.

- Acknowledge and show appreciation for acts of consideration. Give encouragement rather than empathy, stated in an upbeat tone and focused on trust and confidence: "I trust everything is under control on the project." Or "You've got just what you need to close the deal."

- Create a commanding presence and keep attention. If others are carrying on side conversations while you're speaking, control the dynamics. Begin a sentence; then pause, while looking at those who are interrupting. Wait for them to stop talking, then continue.

- Don't apologize if you haven't made a mistake.

- Speak up when something is bothering you. State your concerns clearly and avoid playing mind-reading or guessing games.

- If you don't agree with something, don't nod your head in agreement just to be polite.

- Project your voice with authority, avoiding tones that are too high, breathy, or weak. Use fewer tentative statements such as "Maybe," or "I'm not sure." Avoid ending sentences with a rising pitch that make a statement sound like a question. These all convey less power, certainty, and authority.

Relating to Needs = Respecting Differences

*"The key elements in the art of working together are
how to deal with change, how to deal with conflict, and
how to reach our potential...the needs of the team are best met
when we meet the needs of individual persons."*

Max DePree

Getting along with others requires constant flexibility in adapting to their individual needs. Knowing that communication needs differ, enter each interaction with sensitivity as to what is likely to work best with them (and least likely to annoy or offend). When you treat people in ways that honor differences and relate to their needs and preferences, you demonstrate your concern as well as increase your chances for gaining their cooperation, acceptance of your ideas, and more of what you want.

While it is not always easy to adapt how you relate to what others need, you're more likely to get what you need when you do. In the complex world of interpersonal relationships, when you're tuned in to what is likely to work best with each person, and adjust how you communicate in response, you increase your effectiveness. Getting along is a continual process of discovering the individual behaviors required for relating best to each person, then bringing that wisdom into your interactions for enjoying the most positive, productive encounters (with the least amount of stress).

Key #6:

Extend Respect to Preserve Trust

*"Respect for self,
respect for others, and
responsibility for all your actions."*

The Dalai Lama's Instructions for Life

What a heavenly world it would be if earthlings all lived by these 3 R's! We get closer to a social Shangri-la by extending respect in everything we do and say. Respect is an attitude communicated through the words we choose, our tone of voice, our body language, and our demeanor.

These core connectors reflect the level of regard we have for ourselves and for others. How we conduct ourselves is pivotal in molding our reputation, and in shaping what people think about us and how they respond in turn.

Integrating Integrity

"There is no such thing as a minor lapse of integrity."

Tom Peters

Respect and trust are developed by making decisions that are consistent with good character—by doing the right thing when facing tough choices. When we set high standards for ourselves and work to maintain them, we act with integrity.

Integrity is accumulated as we pass through life's unending series of unexpected little tests and big temptations—whether, for example, we give back the extra money that the cashier doled out by mistake, return a lost wallet stuffed with cash, or make a choice that ultimately penalizes us financially but preserves the well-being of our employees. People witness how we handle life's ever-present "pop quizzes." When we pass each test with high-flying colors, we build ourselves excellent reputations, staking our claim on "taking the higher road."

ON PAR WITH INTEGRITY

After my morning presentation at a conference, the CEO of the corporation hosting the event invited me to join in a round of golf that afternoon with his senior VP and one of their vendors, Kent. As we played the course, Kent kept asking, "Do you mind if I move the ball a bit?" We gave him the green light since it didn't seem to matter much to us. But in fact, it did matter to the CEO, who confided in me later in the clubhouse: "Kent really showed his true colors today. While golf is just a game, I wonder if that cheating philosophy carries over to his clients. Now that I've seen him in this capacity, I question whether I would ever truly trust him again, thinking he just might be cheating us in our business." —A.S.

Integrity is the quality of being honest, sincere, and of sound moral principle; to be in unimpaired, perfect condition. To incorporate the components of integrity into your character, follow the standards listed below:

- Say what you mean
- Mean what you say
- Follow through
- Keep promises
- Act with high standards of behavior

Build a Reputation of Personal Responsibility

"You can't build your reputation on what you're going to do."

Henry Ford

Responsible behavior is reflected in everything we do—keeping our commitments, being on time, meeting our obligations, treating others with care and understanding, acting with dignity, being dependable, and treating property with respect. How well we uphold these building blocks of personal responsibility determine both our self-respect and our reputations. When people know we will do what is right, even though doing so might be difficult or unpopular, we win their respect and trust.

But trust is tenuous, forever dangling from a delicate thread over a precipice of faith. Just one misstep can sever that fragile thread instantly. Repairing a breech of trust is a difficult journey. Nagging doubts will plague those who once held you in high esteem and now question your credibility. The best way to avoid this grueling climb is to never act in less than honorable ways, ever.

Trust is a cycle. The more we act in trust-building ways, the more we are trusted. The degree of respect and trust we receive from others follows the universal law of "what goes around, comes around," either to help us or to hurt us. So, in every moment, think about what you want to receive back, and act accordingly, because both your character and your connections depend on the choices you make.

THE TECHS WE TOTALLY TRUST

We admit it; computer operation and repair skills aren't in the realm of our natural talents. We love our fancy systems when they work; we detest them when they fail (or when we fail to know what to do) because of the frustration and downtime they produce.

Arnold and I have many important connections in our respective businesses and we both agree that our computer technicians, Rob McCoy and Ray and Sally Strackbein, are business essentials! We respect, trust, and revere our techno-geniuses, not only for their mastery of technical skills, but for how commendably they respond to our sometimes-frazzled selves. When our computers have been attacked by viruses, worms, and other electronic vermin, Rob and the Strackbeins have saved our sanity, our precious files, and the day. They have hefty client lists, their expertise is internationally known, and their services are in demand as consultants, speakers, and trainers. Yet when our emergency calls go out, they call back promptly, wherever they are, and do whatever it takes to get our systems restored to peak efficiency. They do all of this and always more; we value their excellent service, wisdom, and guidance, and that gives us great comfort—in them we totally trust! —S.S.

Broken Promises = Broken Trust

"Hold yourself responsible for a higher standard than anybody else expects of you. Never excuse yourself."

Henry Ward Beecher

When a promise is made, either verbally or in writing, an agreement is created between the parties, with the expectation that it will be honored exactly according to the conditions specified. When it's not, a crisis in trust is created. We don't trust people who break their promises or those whose words and actions aren't congruent with one another.

For example:

- A manager says, "I have an open door policy, so stop by anytime." It's a well-intentioned statement. Yet time after time, when an employee does stop by to visit his manager's office, she's repeatedly inattentive, takes phone calls, and is not focused on her employee's

---

SERVING UP THE TRUTH

My son, Stephen, and I were on a ski trip with his friend, Danny, and Danny's father, Randy. We stopped at a restaurant in Bedford, Pennsylvania, and our boys were offered kids' menus, reserved for kids 10 and under. Since Danny had just turned 11, his dad asked for an adult menu because his son was now too old to order from the kids' menu. The waiter replied, "It's okay. You didn't have to mention your son's age. No one would know." Randy responded, "That's probably true, but Danny would know."

It was a small gesture, but it made a big impression on our sons about not getting away with things, even if others say it's okay. —A.S.

concerns. Her behavior contradicts her statement, and her actions demonstrate that she doesn't truly mean what she says.

- A company says, "We want you to be 100 percent satisfied with your purchases." Yet if you're not satisfied and contact the customer service department, you have to jump through hoops to get your money back.

- Your teen knows he's never allowed to drive with more than two other passengers. Yet you find out that half the basketball team went to the after-game party in his car.

Even if we have every intention of keeping our commitments, our reliability is called into question if we don't, unless we have a very credible explanation. However, if too many excuses or reasons are given as to why

---

GETTING TO THE CORE OF THE CREDIBILITY QUOTIENT

Your credibility is always on the line with every connection. People assess whether to venture into or sustain a relationship with you on the basis of your credibility quotient—

how much faith and trust they have in your ability to maintain their trust. Their responses are often influenced by these core questions:

1. Do you care about me and what I need?

2. Do I have every reason to believe you?

3. Are you a person of integrity?

Your credibility quotient is crucial to gaining and keeping viable, trustworthy connections. It's a critical factor in the formula for your success.

---

a promise can't be kept, that too will rust away trust. We preserve trust by constantly demonstrating that we mean what we say and our actions prove it. People can count on us to honor whatever agreement we've made; if for some reason we can't, they would rather hear the truth than a boatload of excuses. In this era of rampant trust-busting, honesty is a precious quality.

Any time our expectations clash with reality, we're in for a rude awakening. It makes us mad when we expect quality craftsmanship and get sloppy performance; when we expect friends to show up on time and they don't; when we purchase a product and it doesn't perform as advertised; when fraud and deception are revealed; and when people say they will do something and don't follow through.

We build and preserve trust in our relationships by matching or exceeding expectations, or by finding a satisfactory solution to remedy the situation when we can't keep a commitment. Whether our connection is with a business, institution, or individual, preserving trust is a constant showcasing of integrity for keeping relationships on solid, well-connected ground.

DON'T KEEP 'EM WAITING

People place high importance on punctuality, keeping to scheduled times for appointments and meetings. Making people wait is a good way to make them mad; we all have better things to do with our time than wait for others to make time for us. Show respect by honoring time commitments.

MAGIC CARD TRICKS

Sandy and I created our Charisma Cards™ a few years ago as a tool to reinforce many of the skills we discuss in our workshops—improving communications, increasing confidence, strengthening relationships, and building a powerful presence.

One day, after a customer service training session at which I spoke about the importance of being responsive and reliable, the client ordered a set of our cards. I sent her a deck immediately. Barbara loved the cards, but called to report that the plastic case in which they were enclosed was damaged. I told her I'd send her another case right away, and carefully wrapped it in bubble wrap and shipped it out that same day. The case cost about 30 cents; the postage and shipping material, about $3.

As soon as she received it, Barbara called to report that the second case, too, had arrived cracked. This was most unusual; gorillas must have been crushing those packages! I apologized for the inconvenience and immediately sent her several new decks, along with five extra boxes, all cushioned carefully. I even paid extra for next day delivery. Fortunately, the package arrived intact and she was delighted (I was thrilled)!

The end result was a happy client who was impressed with the service she received, and the fact that she had gotten more than she expected. More importantly, the incident reinforced the "walking my talk" message I had presented to her staff earlier that week. The actual cost incurred for the 30-cent box? About $30. However, it was worth every penny, and I considered it to be an investment in trust. —A.S.

Rudeness Wrecks Relationships

"You cannot do a kindness too soon, for you never know how soon it will be too late."

Ralph Waldo Emerson

The time to extend the most courtesy and respect is when you probably feel the least like doing so—when others act in awful ways that fly in the face of common courtesy. More often than not, being courteous in spite of someone else's bad behavior cultivates the right atmosphere for more productive communications. When people are really riled up over things, they may forget their manners (assuming they have them and are just choosing not to use them!). With emotions surging, they focus on venting their frustration, perhaps lacing it with free-flowing venom.

Extending kindness, courtesy, and consideration usually gets people down off their high horses, unless you're dealing with some forms of prickly behavior. See Key #8, Handle Prickly People with Care, for specific techniques that work best in those situations. Calming energy serves as a counter force for reining in animosity and aggravation.

Most people feel less threatened and reactive when treated with respect. Mind your own heart and the hearts of others. Express your feelings and concerns and get them off your chest, without denying the dignity and respect of others. Don't create new problems by being rude; instead, focus on solving problems and moving beyond anger and hurt to construct better, not bitter, feelings. Don't resort to humiliating others, even if you think you'll never see them again. Nasty words and actions have a way of backfiring and hurting you instead.

Where Are Your Manners!!?

*"The way you see people is the way you treat them and
the way you treat them is what they become."*

Goethe

Research from a number of sources has revealed that manners are increasingly missing in action, with uncivil behavior on the rise, leaving people feeling angry, irritated, and disrespected. A survey conducted by Public Agenda, called Aggravating Circumstances—A Status Report on Rudeness in America, revealed that more than one-third of the 2,013 people questioned thought about moving to some kinder, gentler place! Getting along with people requires extending courtesy. Civility matters.

We bring a whole list of expectations into our relationships, particularly in reference to how others treat us. If our greeting or parting statements (such as "Hello!" "Good morning!" or "Good-bye") are ignored, we may get confused, angry, or even outraged. We expect an exchange of these customary social graces; they acknowledge our very presence. We may interpret their absence as disrespectful, wondering why we've been overlooked or made to feel invisible.

For instance, if we pass someone in the hall and are not acknowledged by them, our brain might kick into the "wonder" gear: "Why wouldn't he say 'hello'? What's wrong with him? Is he really that busy to just ignore me? What nerve! Did I do something wrong? Was it something I said earlier? Am I invisible?" In reality, the person might just be absorbed in faraway thoughts; however, even such little things left unspoken can trigger wild imaginings, big misunderstandings, and a loss of respect, so mind your manners, for lots of good reasons including to keep you "out of hot water" or on the "outs."

Phone courtesy (or lack thereof) is another area that is striking a discordant chord with many today. Telephone technology has plugged people in to having immediate access to others, and that ability is infringing on having uninterrupted or quality connections with them. Here are a few telephone taboos:

- Not returning calls
- Taking and making unnecessary calls during meetings and social occasions
- Abruptly putting callers on hold
- Interrupting a conversation to take a call
- Multi-tasking when on the phone (such as eating, simultaneously talking to others not intended to be part of a three-way conversation, or carrying on different phone conversations with multiple phones)

When your attention is diverted or you're focused on other conversations, people get the clear impression that you do not consider them to be as important because your priorities are obviously elsewhere. Direct your attention to those you're with, refrain from making or taking calls unless they're urgent, and be sure to return phone calls as a sign of courtesy— all of which win high approval ratings.

WHEN SERVICE SUCKS

If you're feeling miffed about the unpleasant attitude of a service provider, whether exhibited by a salesperson, medical professional, receptionist, or computer technician, remember that there may be a valid reason underlying their behavior. Although you certainly have the option of withholding your empathy or understanding, you might not if you knew there was something beyond their rudeness that was desperately driving their distress: they might be overworked and taking a double shift, their children might be sick, efforts to care for an ailing spouse or parent might be taking their toll, or a family member might have just passed on. Instead of lashing out in indignation, simply asking, "Is there something you're concerned about?" might reveal an answer that opens a heart for some compassion to flow. Even if it doesn't, you may have just extended some badly needed TLC.

Rudeness Wrecks the Workplace

Rude behavior, and failing to demonstrate concern and regard for others, is a problem for many organizations. It hurts productivity, job commitment, job retention, and the health and well-being of employees. Researchers studying workplace aggression and rudeness are finding its frequency is increasing and taking a toll on employees:

- A University of North Carolina (UNC) study called Workplace Incivility: The Target's Eye View surveyed 1,400 workers and revealed that both men and women equally reported being targets of discourteous and insensitive behavior. The majority of the instigators were men, and they were three times more likely to be of higher rank than their targets:

  - 52 percent said they lost work time worrying about the incidents of rudeness

  - 46 percent considered changing jobs (12 percent actually did quit)

  - 37 percent reported that they felt less committed to their company

  - 22 percent deliberately cut back their efforts

- Research from the University of Michigan revealed that 71 percent of 1,100 workers had experienced condescending remarks or other rude behavior at work during a five-year period.

- In another UNC study, 1,601respondents were asked whether they believed rudeness, backstabbing, poor communication, and incivility existed in the workplace. Eighty-nine percent said "yes." The same group was asked whether they themselves were uncivil, rude, negative, or talked behind others' backs: 99 percent said "no." Obviously, this shows how people disconnect their own negative behavior as compared to others. Either people don't acknowledge or admit their negative communication, or they are clueless.

As encounters with uncivil behavior rises, so do symptoms of anxiety and depression; those who don't do or say anything about their mistreatment have the worst mental health. Two out of three workers who "resisted"

demeaning treatment experienced retaliation, either work-related (given less-favorable duties, denied promotions) or social ostracism.

Executives have the responsibility of creating a culture of civility, but it's everyone's responsibility to treat others with respect. Some executives and managers are simply baffled by what they can or should do to stop the behavior. If you serve in a leadership position, emphasize the need for respect and courtesy in all communications with colleagues and customers. Establish written policies against abuse and enforce them, letting employees know that disrespectful behavior of any type will not be tolerated. Avoid speaking disparagingly to staff, which sets a standard of acceptable behavior for lower-level supervisors to imitate. Above all, model respectful behavior in all your interactions to show employees that extending respect is always a priority.

UNINTENTIONAL RUDENESS

For people who unintentionally irritate others with their rude behavior, but who truly want to get along, often letting them know how it's affecting your work solves the problem. For instance, if they are conducting personal conversations around your door or cubicle, telling them that the noise is affecting your concentration might give them a new awareness (they may have been so wrapped up in conversation, they didn't realize the impact of their behavior on you). Many people simply do not know they are being rude. While you may be uncomfortable talking about your concerns, if you don't provide feedback, others won't know how their actions are affecting you or your work performance.

TOP 10
ACTS OF RUDENESS

1. Talking about someone behind his or her back

2. Interrupting others when they are speaking or working

3. Flaunting status or authority; acting in a condescending manner

4. Belittling someone's opinion to others

5. Failing to return phone calls or respond to memos

6. Giving others the silent treatment

7. Insults, yelling, and shouting

8. Verbal forms of sexual harassment

9. Staring, dirty looks, or other negative eye contact

10. Intentionally damning with faint praise

Source: Joel H Neuman, director of the Center for Applied Management at the State University of New York at New Paltz

Exude Positive Energy

"The true measure of an individual is how he treats a person who can do him absolutely no good."

Ann Landers

We usually receive back the same type of energy that we give out. It's the Golden Rule in action, so it's to your advantage to send out the same energy you want to receive. If you huff and puff or rant and rave, don't be surprised if dragons start breathing fire your way!

By exuding positive energy even in the face of negativity, we increase our chances of being treated with greater respect and courtesy. Of course, there are never any guarantees regarding how people may respond; but when we take the lead, others often follow. They notice the positive forces at work—the calming energy is sometimes enough to shift their highly charged behavior. However, while one person's positive energy has a soothing effect on the field of interaction, it still may not sufficiently deflect someone else's pulsating, emotional currents. Some people are positively determined to unleash their emotions, one way or another, and absolutely nothing can stop them!

The bottom line: positive energy rarely has a negative effect on people, except possibly driving some crazy, since you're not engaging in their energy-draining game of Outburst.

KEEP THE CONNECTION CURRENTS POSITIVE

- Focus on actions that create positive connections
- Listen and acknowledge the ideas being expressed
- Look at situations from the viewpoint of others
- Avoid stereotyping
- Remember the benefits that flow from positive connections and your desire to enjoy them

---

The Right Words Reap Results

"Words can destroy. What we call each other ultimately becomes what we think of each other, and it matters."

Jeanne Kirkpatrick

Words take just seconds to say, yet some echo for a lifetime and far beyond. The words we choose and how they're conveyed contain massive power that can build, strengthen, or destroy relationships. Any offensive ones might instantly wipe out a connection for a time or possibly forever. The right words work wonders.

What pours forth from our mouths can enhance or alienate our connections. Certain trigger words or phrases can incite reactions with damaging consequences. Any communication that reflects a lack of respect is verbal garbage and causes rotten connections!

Be wary of the language you choose and how you phrase your statements. Used properly, your words can encourage cooperation and compliance, both at work and at home.

For example, people get angry when they feel controlled or ordered to do something: "You have to do your homework now!" "You have to take inventory." "You have to contact the supervisor." Hackles go up with "you have to" commands, even if "you have to" is implied ("Clean the basement now!").

Re-phrase orders or commands as requests. A question conveys the ability to make a choice and reverberates on a level of cooperation. By using courtesy rather than a command, you gain cooperation and respect. "How about ...?" and "Would you ...?" work wonders, serving as suggestions rather than commands:

- *How about we try it this way and see how it works?*
- *How about labeling work assignments in order of priority?*
- *Would you give me a draft of the document by tomorrow so we can review it before the meeting?*

Command style: *"You have to rework this report because it's missing the benefits section."*

Cooperative style: *"Good job on such a detailed report! Would you just add a section on benefits?"*

When choice isn't an option, communicate requirements with courtesy. Other phrases that work well include:

- *I'd appreciate it if you would ... .*
- *Perhaps you might ...*
- *I would prefer ...*
- *May I suggest ...?*

These create and keep more cooperative connections and reduce conflict and clashes.

Kick "But" From Your Lingo

Our "buts" get in the way of acknowledging the merits of someone's work, the good they've done, or what they want. What type of reaction do you get when you make these statements?

- *You had good intentions, but didn't follow through on them.*
- *You've offered some good suggestions, but I'm afraid we can't use them.*
- *You included some good material, but ...*
- *Sir, I understand, but ...*
- *You're trying hard, but ...* (Obviously not hard enough!)

"But" starts the defenses rolling and blocks solutions. It also discounts the effort put forth and squashes self-esteem: "You obviously put time into the proposal, but ..." A string of not-good-enough thoughts often surface to eat away at the receiver's self-regard. These type of statements often trigger a conditioned response, signaling the expectation of bad news to follow.

NO BARKING ALLOWED!

Barking orders doesn't create cooperation; respect does. A professor of management science at Ohio State University studied management decisions in 376 situations. He found that when explanations for the work request were not offered, workers ignored the boss' orders about two-thirds of the time. However, when the bosses explained the reasons behind their decisions and asked for the employee's suggestions, they received 100 percent compliance. It pays to provide reasons for requests!

The word "but" also implies an excuse, something that can't be delivered, such as "We want to give our customers excellent service, but I can't do what you're asking." Meanwhile, the customer's frustration or anger is triggered, as he or she wonders, "Why not?"

Build a Bridge with "And"

On the other hand, "and" serves as a connector. No buts about it, "and" works to gain cooperation and the receiver's acceptance of the feedback:

- *I was unexpectedly interrupted and now I'm back on your request!*

- *We had all of your information and my computer crashed. Now I'm in the process of retrieving the file and can assist you without further delay.*

- *Your report card looks very good and by putting in some extra time in those additional assignments, I bet you'll also be able to bring that social studies grade up, too.*

- *I liked the way you added such a colorful description to the ad layout and by changing the background color, it should be an Addy award winner!*

The Power of a Single Word

Sometimes, just changing one word can help make the recipient more likely to understand and accept what you have to say. Here are a few examples:

- Avoid "never" or "always" coupled with "you" statements, such as, "You never listen to instructions." Together they sound accusatory, ruffling feathers and activating defenses. A better choice is to use "sometimes": "I notice that you sometimes seem confused about instructions." This speaks the truth more accurately and maintains respect. It also prevents "the accused" from pulling out specific scenarios to fire back demonstrating they "don't always" do it that way!

- "Should" (as in "You should have done it this way") implies blame or shame and conveys feelings of doing something wrong. Instead, substitute "might": "Next time, you might ask customers if they would appreciate information about assembly instructions."

- When phrasing requests, use "Would you ..." rather than "Could you ..." It's more direct, with less "wiggle room" for others to slip away from your requests.

> ### IT'S A GUY THING
>
> To gain and keep the respect of women, avoid calling females, "Honey," "Sugar," or any other sweet-named thing (unless you're related or they approve). Men, don't refer to women as "gals" or assign the term "my girl" to your assistant. Avoid telling sexist jokes (especially if you want women to like you!)

Avoid Connection Crushers

"Sticks and stones can break my bones,
but words can break my heart."

Robert Fulghum

When verbal garbage gets dumped, it causes a cesspool of negative reactions. Put-downs, sarcasm, accusations, and other verbal barbs stir up energy as egos jockey for respect. Verbal attacks usually deploy self-defense mechanisms and obliterate positive connections.

Certain words or phrases block connections cold, while at the same time making us steaming mad. They kick up a whirlwind of emotion, just like in weather patterns when cold and warm conditions combine to form a tornado! Connection-Crushing Communication usually brings out the beast, rather than the best in others. This includes:

- Blaming and accusations:

  - *If you hadn't screwed up, we wouldn't be in this mess!*

  - *How could you ever ...?*

- Sarcastic remarks

- Profanity

- Discriminatory remarks or insults about age, gender, ethnicity, religion, or sexual orientation

- Denial statements:

  - *It can't be that terrible!*

  - *You're telling a bunch of lies!*

  - *You shouldn't say those things.*

  - *You're wrong!*

  - *That's not true.*

  - *I don't believe you.*

- Name-calling, put-downs, and anything that makes someone else feel inferior or stupid:
  - *I told you so!*
  - *How many times have I told you (or gone over this)?*
  - *What an absolutely stupid thing to say!*
  - *I can't believe how unprofessional you looked!*
  - *What an idiot! How could you do such a thing?*
  - *Can't you ever do anything right?*
- Ultimatums and threats:
  - *If you don't, then ...*
  - *You better—or else!*
- Demands:
  - *Do it now!*
  - *Do as I say!*
  - *That's the end of it. I don't want to hear another word!*
- Gross generalizations and exaggerations:
  - *You never do what I ask!*
  - *You always say that!*
  - *Everything is always such a crisis with you.*
  - *All you ever do is complain!*
  - *You're always late!*
  - *I've told you a million times to clean up your room!*
  - *Why don't you ever ...?*
- Emotionally loaded responses:
  - *Here we go again!*
  - *Oh, brother, I can't believe you!*
  - *I know exactly what you're thinking!*

- *That's not how it happened!*
- Impatient remarks:
  - *Not now!*
  - *Keep it short.*
  - *Hurry up!*

Especially for parents: Unfortunately, well-meaning parents who swear they will never use certain dreaded phrases on their own children (which they hated to hear as kids themselves) nonetheless often repeat the same disheartening statements. These are passed down like verbal DNA, only to get on the nerves of their own kids. Here's a sampling:

- *How many times do I have to tell you ...?*
- *If you do that one more time, I'm going to ...*
- *What did I just say?*
- *When I was your age, I always ...* (Beware! If you use this phrase, just watch their eyes roll!)

Most of these responses either escalate the friction or discourage communication, causing resistance, resentment, and reactivity. Although it might be very tempting to litter your language with "zappers," it's better to refrain from engaging in any verbal artillery. Verbal blows cause massive damage to relationships and crush your chances for keeping quality connections. To create good connections, make a commitment to consistently choose your words wisely.

Don't Go to Extremes

Extreme statements (never, always, everyone, all, everything) are exaggerations and are bound to trigger extreme reactions; they're unfair and accusatory. The attacked instantly begin scrolling through their experiences, recalling when their actions proved otherwise, and hurl back the facts in self-defense. Unfair judgments generally fire up defenses!

Focus on the desired action by requesting information: "When can I expect the final report?" Ask questions such as, "What needs to happen

on Tuesday evenings?" instead of blasting accusations: "You never remember to take the trash out!" Nudging with a simple one-word reminder ("Trash!") also makes the point. Nudge rather than nag!

When inflammatory, extreme remarks are unfairly lobbed your way, reverse them with a question that refutes their unfair claim. For example, you've been accused of never being on time, but you know that statement is simply not true. It's fair to repeat the statement as a means of discounting its validity, "I'm never on time?" Spoken in a dubious tone with facial expressions to match your disbelief makes the point. This repositions you in a fair light and demonstrates that you do indeed act responsibly; your actions speak louder than words.

CONNECTION-CRUSHING COMMUNICATION CRUSHES COUPLES

Psychologists at the University of Washington videotaped disagreements of 124 couples who had been married for fewer than nine months. In tracking the couples, the research revealed that those who expressed connection-crushing communication in just the first three minutes of a disagreement (such as blaming or using name-calling statements like "You're lazy and never do anything around the house") were more likely to get divorced. The researchers concluded that the words, gestures, and emotions expressed during conflicts are critical factors in predicting the probability of divorce or marital stability.

Make "No Way!" Go Away

Some language slams the door cold on possibilities, without a glimmer of hope of either expressing our perspectives or satisfying needs:

- *No way!*
- *No can do!*
- *Couldn't do that.*
- *There's nothing I can do.*
- *It's your problem.*
- *It's not company policy.*

These statements create adversarial relationships, pitting our requests and desires against a greater authority. To keep the door open to future possibilities, speak in a positive frame of reference, or state the conditions that must be met to make the recipient's wishes a reality. Think first of whether his or her wishes might be granted. Is it a definite "No!" or is there a way to make it work? Consider the conditions that would make the request possible.

For example, you need to have a report finished by close of business, but your assistant wants to leave early. Instead of issuing a definite refusal ("No, you can't leave early!"), think about it—does it really matter, as long as the report is finished first? In this case, "Yes, you can leave this afternoon, as long as the report is done," is music to your assistant's ears.

By considering the conditions for making wishes a reality, you gain greater cooperation and respect. "As soon as," "as long as," and "right after" are statements that keep the flow of possibilities open and prevent doors from slamming on desires.

Really Watch Out for This One!

Pay attention to the intended meanings laced with "If you really" statements. They're loaded with assumptions, serving as bait that someone expects to hook you with and start an argument, such as "If you really

cared about ... " or "If you really wanted ..." Usual responses to these inflammatory remarks include:

- *What makes you think I don't really care about ...?*
- *Why do you think I don't really want ...?*
- *Where did you get that idea?*

These responses create a no-win, "gotcha!" argument. The ball is now in your challenger's court, and they're perfectly positioned for rattling on endlessly about whatever they think supports their argument.

There are two strategies for neutralizing such an attack. One way is to respond using a "When" question:

- *When did you start thinking that I didn't care?*
- *When did you get the idea that I wasn't concerned about the proposal?*
- *When did you feel the project didn't matter to me?*

Responding to such attacks with a "when" question takes you out of a defensive posture and poses a specific question back to them. Now, they must address a specific matter rather than cloaking their intentions with a vague accusation.

The second way to neutralize "if you really" statements, is to respond with a firm "Of course" statement, followed by a positive comment that runs counter to their assumption:

> *Of course, the proposal is a great concern to me. In fact, when I met with our client yesterday, I got another idea I'd like for us to include in it.*

Suzette Haden Elgin, Ph.D., author of The Gentle Art of Verbal Self-Defense at Work, suggests that when responding this way, make a swift change of subject without pausing, and do not make eye contact with the attacker.

Both of these responses send messages that you're not taking their bait and have no interest in playing their game.

WHEN YOU CAN'T MAKE IT BETTER, OFFER A TRIP TO FANTASY LAND

Even though people get frustrated when they can't get what they want, it's sometimes still beyond our ability to provide the services or things they desire. On the other hand, the act of acknowledging their desires lets them know that you understand their frustration and wish you had it in your power to do something about it.

Whether it's a disappointed or angry customer, or someone else with a big wish list, simply repeat their desires back to them: "I wish I could ... get you a seat on that flight ... give you a full refund ... put you in the Presidential suite ... buy you that Jaguar." The very fact that they've been heard often works its magic!

In some cases, especially with kids, you might want to put their wishes into writing and read it back to them. "Let's see if I have everything on your list. You want ..." This makes it obvious you've heard their hearts' desires, without promising that those wishes will be granted.

Honor Ideas

People need to feel they're being heard and their opinions are being honored. When ideas are discredited, it crushes feelings of capability and creates bad connections. No one likes having their ideas invalidated.

Criticizing or negating ideas can be deadly because it violates a person's need for respect. Think in terms of honoring both egos and ideas. For instance, "That's a really dumb idea!" gets personal; a face-saving alternative that avoids personal attacks would be, "That idea would cost an extra $50,000 which isn't in our budget." This focuses the issue on dollars, not egos.

Resistance sets up polarities—the more you resist, the more others push back and hold firm in their positions. Likewise, the greater the acceptance you express, the more flexibility they will feel, since you've honored their need to be heard and respected. You don't have to like their ideas, you just need to hear and respect their thoughts.

Some responses instantly evoke antagonism, contempt, or animosity, all putting respect in jeopardy:

- *Do you really know what you're saying?*
- *Oh no, that would never work!*
- *Do you know what a stupid idea that would be?*
- *You can't really want that!*
- *You can't be serious!*
- *You're crazy! You want what?*
- *Don't be crazy ... ridiculous ... stupid ... !*
- *You don't know what you're talking about!*

WE ALL HAVE OUR REASONS

Diplomacy is essential for maintaining respect. When you ask people to express their thoughts or feelings about a specific matter, it shows your willingness to hear them rather than discredit them. Asking the question, "Why do you feel that way?" frequently gets to the heart of the matter. Here are a few variations:

- I have a different opinion, and I'd like to hear why you see the situation that way.

- We obviously see this from two different perspectives and I'd like to know your thinking on it.

- Please tell me why you see it that way.

- Although I disagree with your conclusion, I'd appreciate hearing your insights about this issue.

Pump Up Your Persuasive Powers

The art of persuasion is the ability to gain trust. It's cultivated when someone believes you're honestly communicating with them, and that you understand their needs. This is influenced by a complex combination of factors, including how they judge your credibility, character, attitude, appearance, choice of words, body language, and other aspects of your demeanor.

Gaining the confidence and trust of others, whether in a personal or professional situation, sometimes takes some convincing. Some skeptics are reluctant to trust anyone and that's always a big barrier to forming productive connections. Trust is usually withheld until people gain the evidence they need to put their trust in another; only then will their doubts subside. Your job as a conscious connector is to build confidence in others and provide them with just the reasons they need to trust what you say and do. To properly position a connection for mutual benefit and success involves the gentle art of persuasion.

Persuasion is the act of influencing a person, by appealing to his or her reason or emotion, into taking a certain course of action. Although the choice has the appearance of being made independently, it is in fact being influenced by your powers of persuasion. Persuasive prowess can be a significant influence, valuable in both personal and professional arenas. To increase your ability to influence others, learn to design persuasive messages that target people's needs, beginning with answering any questions they might have about how a particular request, product, service, policy, or new course of action will make a difference.

The art of persuasion and influence is different from manipulation, which has strong ties to control, pressure, and dominance. While manipulation sows the bitter seeds of resentment, defensiveness, and distrust, persuasion enhances the decision-making process and gains the cooperation of others willingly; you are simply introducing them to the value and corresponding benefits of making a particular choice. True persuasive power is the ability to demonstrate to others how certain decisions satisfy their needs and are in their own best interests.

The following steps are helpful for influencing the outcomes you want, as well as satisfying the needs of others. By preparing for encounters in the ring of influence, you'll powerfully perform with persuasive prowess!

Persuasive Prowess

1. Target your messages to what others want or need. By focusing on what they want or need, you connect to their concerns directly. Do they want to ...

- Improve relationships with friends and family?
- Make more business contacts?
- Build new friendships?
- Manage or save time?
- Manage or save money?
- Reduce stress?
- Impress others?
- Build a rewarding career?
- Become financially secure?
- Enhance their self-image?
- Gain more skills?
- Improve their health?
- Achieve maximum performance?
- Gain recognition and acceptance?
- Enjoy an adventurous life?
- Ensure safety for themselves and others?
- Increase profits?
- Enhance cooperation and morale?
- Maximize productivity?
- Simplify procedures?
- Achieve financial independence?

When you're clear on what needs someone wants to satisfy, you gain clarity on how to focus your "selling points." For instance, if a couple is shopping for a car for their family with an expressed need primarily for safety, you would direct their search to the corresponding safety features and reinforce the value they provide. Or, for a woman who wants to lose weight and is considering joining a health club, she is more likely to be motivated to take action based upon how that membership will contribute to her appearance, self-image, and good feelings. When you talk the language of what others need, you're communicating with them in ways that build respect, trust and connection.

HEED NEEDS

In addition to speaking about successful interpersonal dynamics, I also create strategic communication plans for organizations. An effective communications plan requires a thorough assessment of the firm's needs and how to reach its target audiences with key messages about its products, services, or issues. Developing that key message into a "hook," something that catches the interest of those you most want to reach, is vital if you want them to invest their time and energy to learn how your product or service might satisfy their needs. Poorly crafted messages will miss the mark because the needs of the target audiences weren't properly addressed. Precious resources, yours and theirs, are wasted in the process.

The same is true in our personal interactions—enduring connections focus on satisfying needs. People want sound answers to their perennial questions, "Why should I care?" and "What's in it for me?" Invest your efforts and energy toward their needs—the currency of connection. When your messages are laser sharp and focused on what people need, you produce a powerhouse of motivational energy that nets the results you want and they benefit from them. —S.S.

2. Communicate clearly to accelerate the other person's understanding:

- How does my message accommodate their needs, interests, and values?

- What questions might they have at this point?

- Am I articulate and using the right words?

- Is my language descriptive?

- Have I provided examples or stories to improve understanding?

- What other information might they need?

3. Inspire the other person's confidence by providing evidence and showing enthusiasm:

- Provide information that is relevant to their needs.

- Document information from reliable sources.

- Provide information that helps them understand the solution or the problem.

- Demonstrate enthusiasm to make your statements compelling.

4. Enhance retention: Think of what you want others to remember about your message. Ask yourself, "How can I make it unforgettable?" Ask them for their reactions to your ideas.

5. Request an action: Ask the other person to take the desired action. It may seem obvious to you, if you've gone through all the steps and they appear ready to say "Yes." Yet it requires following through with them to obtain their signature, check, credit card, consent to the terms, or whatever else is desired.

The proof of your persuasive power is whether it prompts people to respond in the way you want. Did they buy your product or service? Agree to sponsor the charity event? Sign the petition? Accept your invitation to go out? Take action in the direction of your desires?

RELIABLE SOURCES FOR BUILDING CONFIDENCE

Confidence levels increase when claims are supported by additional sources, such as:

- Advice from experts in the appropriate field

- Annual reports

- Articles

- Trade or professional association materials

- Industry publications

- Media reviews

- Professional guidelines

- Competitive shopping

- Price guides

- Other people they trust

Strategically Think It Through

"The key to all motivation is desire, and the master key to creating desire is responsiveness to the needs, desires, and interests of the people you would lead."

John R. Noe

At the beginning of any project, proposal, or other venture or activity, a little strategic planning can vastly improve your chances of successfully achieving your desired objective. Careful planning enables you to accurately assess the needs of the project and helps you obtain the necessary resources. More importantly, a strategic overview provides you with

TRUST-BUILDING TACTICS

To influence others, we need to establish an atmosphere of trust. With scams, corporate scandals, and reports of some 80 percent of people lying on their resumes, it's small wonder we are increasingly skeptical and suspicious.

One of the biggest hurdles I have as a speaker is persuading people to hire me. To increase my chances, I do whatever I can to build trust. For example, one association president who was considering me as a speaker told me that he had been "burned" in the past by another speaker. The speaker had talked ad nauseum about his capabilities, and in fact, sounded most convincing, so he was hired, but didn't deliver on all his promises.

Knowing the president's trust level was low, I offered to do a number of things to gain his trust. I offered to meet with him and a few of his key staff to present a 15-minute demo. I was honest, telling them that hopefully I would be the right speaker for their needs, but that they would be the best judge of that. This calmed the president's fears, and he appreciated the fact that I wasn't pushing him into anything.

After the demo, I provided him with a list of my last 100 speaking clients and their phone numbers. Many speakers give just two or three such references, but I thought more "evidence" from other executives and meeting planners would be more convincing. I gave him copies of my books, and even invited him to attend a luncheon speech I was giving that week. Furthermore, every time he contacted me, I promptly returned his call, and when he requested any information, I got it to him immediately. No one else went to this much effort to develop trust and build a relationship, and it all paid off. I got the job, but more importantly, I had created an enduring connection. —A.S.

a critical communication framework for the project, which reveals the most important factors to be considered, most vital messages to deliver, and other factors critical to its success. To flesh out your plan, ask yourself the following questions:

Who?

- Who will benefit?
- Who can help or make contributions?
- Who must I sell on this idea?
- Who can help me get additional resources?
- Who might resist, find fault, or try to stop me?

What?

- What is the first step?
- What is the best way?
- What do I need in the way of additional resources?
- What techniques or methods can I use?
- What will make them take action?
- What are the alternatives?
- What difference does it make?

Where?

- Where should I start?
- Where am I likely to find resistance?
- Where should I plant seeds to make this idea grow?
- Where does this idea work best?
- Where can I go for inspiration?

When?

- When should I introduce the plan or idea?
- When might the ideas be best implemented?
- When should we revise our strategy?

Why?

- Why should they buy this idea?
- Why is this way better?
- Why might resistance be so strong?

How?

- How can we improve on the idea?
- How can we test the waters?
- How can I persuade the centers of influence?

A CHILLING EXPERIENCE

Right out of college, I worked for a major appliance manufacturer as a consumer specialist, training their sales and marketing reps in product sales. To instill firsthand knowledge of the quality of the appliances, part of the training included taking apart washers, dryers, dishwashers, and disposers. I was totally convinced as to their durability and continued purchasing the company's equipment long after I left. For years, the appliances worked liked a charm, just as I had eagerly promoted during my employment with the manufacturer.

When we were remodeling our kitchen and needed to purchase a new refrigerator, it was a no-brainer. My former employer had recently purchased another appliance line that included refrigerators, so although their name wasn't yet on the product, I knew what I wanted. I went to the showroom to ask a few questions, opened the refrigerator door, slammed a few drawers, and felt totally comfortable in selecting a refrigerator from my old trusted employer.

(Continued on next page)

(Continued from last page)

While we were away, our new refrigerator was delivered and installed by our kitchen contractor. Upon our return, when we loaded up the food, we immediately learned of a major design flaw. When the door was opened, bottles and other items stored on a door shelf would sometimes fall off. I could see immediately that this wasn't going to work; living with the prospect of bottles and jars smashing to the floor for the next 15 to 20 years just wasn't a good option.

Customer service calls were still being handled by the other appliance manufacturer. When I reached them, the customer representative began by chiding me for not doing a better job of selecting the features I wanted in my refrigerator! In retrospect, I guess I had taken some things for granted, such as assuming that my ketchup and other condiments would stay put. Thinking a little cold cash would satisfy my frustrations, she first offered me $70 toward the purchase of a different refrigerator, then upped it to $100; but that wouldn't solve the problem—the other models had the same design flaw. What I really wanted was less resistance, a different brand, and a talk with the customer service supervisor since this rep was leaving me out in the cold. She finally agreed to connect me with her supervisor.

The supervisor listened to my predicament and offered her apologies. She then put me on hold for two minutes, and came back with the offer of a full refund. Next, she told me what to expect and when, and followed up with several phone calls and emails to make sure the situation had been resolved to my complete satisfaction. Her committed efforts to ensure my complete satisfaction had both warmed my customer service heart and restored my total trust. —S.S.

Don't Rust Your Trust!

"The time is always right to do what is right."

Martin Luther King, Jr.

As individuals, our character is always showcased in what we say and do. Even organizations have "characters" that are revealed to us by their behavior. Because trust and respect is essential in preserving integrity in every relationship, it's crucial to do everything you can to build and protect it. Be clear about the qualities you want to project and the values you want to uphold, and always act in accord.

Evaluate the impact of every anticipated action, whether large or small; it all matters and adds up to create pleasure or pain for yourself and others. Trust is golden; losing it tarnishes and taints both your reputation and your self-image. Don't rust your trust! Doing so is hazardous to healthy relationships. Stepping on a rusty nail infected with bacteria can cause tetanus, a disease commonly called lockjaw. Likewise, stepping on someone's trust may cause a similar response—locking up jaws and zipping lips when trust is pierced.

Deception, fraud, broken promises, and other forms of distrust are destructive elements that cause ruined reputations, spoiled relationships, and lost opportunities. While some people do indeed get away with their wrongdoings, at least for a time, the rust can turn their own dreams to dust. In addition, consequences from a breech of trust ripple outward with multiple effects on families, organizations, communities, and even whole nations. True success is built on honorable actions—a treasured collection of character-rich qualities that construct quality-rich relationships that don't turn sour, tarnish, or wear out over time.

FROM WORN-OUT TO WOWED

Getting your car serviced often requires an act of trust. Stories abound with people getting ripped off by repair shops, paying for unnecessary parts and huge labor bills. I've recently been to several dealers; each one promised me something, but never delivered. My personal experience reinforced all the nightmare stories. One shop promised that my car would be ready by noon. High noon and no car. Then they said it would be ready by 5:00 p.m.—but it wasn't. Two days later, my car was ready, but still not fixed right! Even though the mechanic was nice and I liked him, he had lost my trust.

So I took my car to another dealer. They did everything right. The service supervisor told me it would be ready by 5:00 p.m., but called at noon to let me know it was ready (wow!). They had also done the unexpected—washed and vacuumed my car (another wow!) They had exceeded my expectations and restored my trust. Obviously, this dealership offered more than "smile" training. They realized that keeping promises builds solid business relationships and keeps customers coming back.

Everything being equal, people deal with people they like and trust. Everything being unequal, people still deal with people they like and trust. —A.S.

SOME THINGS CAN'T BE FIXED

When people act rude, don't keep their promises, or discount the needs of others, we lose respect for them. It's very hard to mend broken trust or repair respect. Sometimes, the damage is permanent and can never be made right or whole, ever again.

Bridge
Connection Chasms

"The real winners in life are the people who look at every situation with an expectation that they can make it work or make it better."

Barbara Pletcher

- One of your friends is a graphic designer and has complained recently that his business is in a slump, causing him financial strain. Since your company needs some promotional materials, you extend a goodwill gesture and give him the design project. However, you're shocked when he submits lackluster layouts. When you address your concerns with him he gets defensive and says you're being "too picky." Now your friendship is being strained.

- Your sister-in-law drops by with her toddler twins on a Saturday morning to see what you're doing. When you tell her that you're going to be gardening she remarks, "Perfect! Since you'll be home anyway, I'll leave the boys with you so I can run out for a few hours. They're driving me crazy. Hope you don't mind! Be back around 3:00. You're great, Sis!" Now you're angry because she just ruined your plans and you feel "put upon."

- You've arrived at a new resort, anticipating a week-long vacation in an island paradise. The trouble is, their brochure boasted of a beautiful beach that actually is about six beach blankets wide, their entertainment facilities are not yet fully operational, and your whole family is now both disappointed and upset. Payment for the entire week was required in advance but you're dissatisfied and steamed about misleading advertising.

- You're putting the final touches on a report that's due in a few hours when an office colleague bursts in from down the hall, stewing over her latest problems with her boss. You value her friendship but this is becoming an unwelcome routine, draining you of your time, energy, and productivity.

- You rented a spacious mountain retreat to accommodate your relatives for a family reunion with the understanding that everyone would pay their fair share. Halfway through the week, two of your cousins have a fight and one leaves without paying his share of the rent. After you return home, you call him to request the balance of payment, but he refuses to pay since he was only there half the week. He sees it one way and you see it another. It doesn't seem right or fair.

Life presents us with an ongoing series of situations that can strain our relationships and tug and pull apart our connections. Getting along with people is a life-long endeavor. But conflict is a natural part of life, with the potential to arise when we face resistance, pressure, change, or inter-action. It brings up uncomfortable feelings because we often don't know how to relate to situations which we see as threatening to our well-being. Whenever friction arises from unmet or competing needs, wants, and values, a gap occurs, creating a "connection chasm." Whether a small fissure or a gaping gulf, chasms cause frustration, discomfort, separation, and angst.

Our judgments, assumptions, frustrations, annoyances, misunderstand-ings, expectations, suspicions, opposing perspectives, and more can all spark conflict, an inevitable part of life's interactions. When a connection chasm forms, anger, whether mild or wild, can result. Yet our anger doesn't have to eat us up, pollute the atmosphere, or ruin our relation-ships. In fact, it's often because we don't deal with the discomfort chasms create that we continue to be distressed, drained, and disconnected by them.

The desire to have your needs met and your intention to connect can bring you to the edge of your resourcefulness. Fortunately, when connections go awry and a bundle of emotions are brewing, there are ways to navigate over troubled water and get things back on track. By making wise choices and choosing the desired direction in the inevitable twists and turns of your interactions, you become empowered to manage conflicts rather than be ensnared in them.

Although conflict is often avoided, it is inevitable. By seeing conflict as a natural part of life, it simply shows where a relationship needs attention. With this perspective, it can be seen as a change agent for creating and maintaining dynamic, purposeful relationships.

CHASMS IN YOUR CONNECTIONS?

Frequent causes of connection chasms include:

Criticism and condemnation
Hanging on and hard-heartedness
Aggravations and assumptions
Self-righteousness and stubbornness
Misunderstandings and mind games

Clear Connection "Cobwebs"

Cobwebs pop up everywhere; their sticky strands hang in unkempt, messy places, growing more prolific unless swept away. Cobwebs can also grow in our connections; without careful tending, people get trapped in messy relationships that grow worse over time unless they, too, are tidied up.

Eventually it's bound to happen—a connection cobweb develops. We find ourselves entangled in a sticky situation from something that was said or done, perhaps caused by a misunderstanding, a difference of opinion, or an outburst of anger. Cobwebs grow at work, in families, among neighbors, between best friends, in business transactions, and even at centers of spiritual enlightenment. If we don't sweep them away, they'll keep us stuck in feelings we don't want to have, draining our collective energy, creativity, and well-being.

How do you know you're caught in the cobwebs? You feel it (usually everyone involved feels it, too, even if it's swept under the proverbial carpet). Connections get cockeyed, good feelings disappear, and the atmosphere becomes heavy and often putrid. You're definitely out of "The Connection Zone"!

Whenever you notice a connection cobweb, sweep it away with your determination to maintain a well-tended relationship. Remember, you choose how long to hang on to an incident, a grudge, a hurtful remark, or whatever is causing the discomfort or distance.

When upset by the actions of others, call on the wisdom of this statement, which helps you sort out your options: "I choose how to feel and act when people don't do what I want them to do, or treat me the way I like." You have a whole universe of possibilities as to how you can respond. This statement brings your focus back to help you respond in ways congruent with your positive intention.

Do your part to restore the connection. In doing so, you may first need to dust off a rather bruised ego and make it mind its own business so you can proceed with your intention to meet the needs of others as best you can. Your ego might fight you on this one, since it opts for the path of winning at all costs! However, this is not about winning, but about creating respectful, caring relationships.

In a nanosecond, you can make a choice to restore a connection, get rid of bad feelings, dump a bad attitude ... or whatever else is causing distress. In every situation, you always have a choice as to what you think and do regarding the connections you want and the actions needed to create them.

DON'T GET DISCONNECTED

Like a disruption of phone service preventing good connections between parties, a wide range of actions and attitudes can cause people to disconnect, preventing clear communication. Some of the behaviors that foster disconnections are represented in the DISCONNECT acronym:

Disrespectful and deceptive

Impatient

Selfish

Critical

Oppressive

Need to be right

Neglectful

Easily outraged

Careless

Thoughtless

Speak Your Truth

*"While you may have difficulty defining your
own sense of authenticity, you are acutely aware
when you are not being true to yourself."*

Gary Simmons, The I of the Storm

When some people are peeved, it's unmistakable; they let you know their feelings in no uncertain terms, and they "tell it like it is." At the other end of the spectrum are those who repress, swallow, and stuff their feelings because of the discomfort they produce. Holding back powerful feelings breeds resentment and sabotages authentic relationships, which must be based on emotional integrity.

People remain silent about situations that upset them, refusing to express their anger for many reasons, including wanting to avoid an unfavorable image, being labeled a troublemaker, admitting their unhappiness with a person or situation, or their discomfort with conflict itself. They may decide that some trivial matters just aren't worth sacrificing their relationships, making a scene, or rocking the boat (although that boat is already riding over troubled water!).

But the drawbacks of suppressing your anger can add up. Over time, irritations or issues fester, and the pent-up energy from stuffed feelings can make you resentful and bitter. Not speaking your truth in alignment with your needs and values is destructive to emotional integrity and healthy relationships. And keeping silent on issues that concern you is particularly harmful to long-term relationships. It takes an enormous amount of emotional and physical energy to keep powerful feelings stuffed inside where they silently brew.

Repressed anger doesn't go away; it simmers for awhile and usually finds an outlet, sometimes "out of the blue" from the slightest provocation. Its wrath can escalate into verbal abuse, sarcasm, irritability, temper tantrums, overreactions to minor annoyances, or even physical assaults on people or property. It can produce headaches, ulcers, heart disease, hypertension, rashes, digestive disorders, and many other maladies. Over time, repressing feelings deadens the ability to feel much emotion of any kind, including the joy of living.

Speaking your truth enlightens those who may be clueless about what you want and need or what may be missing in the relationship. They also

WHEN LIPS ARE ZIPPED

While silence can be golden, dealing with people who are regular clams and rarely talk or share their feelings can be exasperating. Without their feedback, you end up wondering and second-guessing their thoughts, which, of course, is very dangerous. You might construe their silence as indifference or assume that they're judging you. But their lack of expression doesn't necessarily mean they don't care. They might care very much but are unable to verbalize their feelings, perhaps stemming from a protective mechanism they learned long ago that is now actually detrimental to their relationships.

While some with zipped lips are fearful of expressing their opinions and sharing their truth, others may use silence as a way to manipulate or intimidate you. Their sense of power comes from their ability to make you squirm and keep you guessing. While you might want to extract their inner thoughts, you can't demand clams to open up and speak.

With clams, stay calm (because you may be tempted to scream!). Ask them open-ended questions that cannot be answered with a simple "yes," "maybe," or "no." Then wait patiently for their reply. Avoid drilling them. Be warm and make them feel comfortable in order to improve the chances that they'll open up and speak their truth.

learn about your limits, the boundaries of what you consider acceptable and unacceptable behavior, how a situation affects you, and where they "crossed the line." When you don't express your boundaries, others may think their actions were acceptable to you.

By bringing matters out into the open, you provide a platform to learn more about the other person's point of view and their needs. Through honest communication, you talk about the issues that are in the way of connecting you. This dialogue helps to resolve the accumulated tension surrounding a situation, clarifies needs, and desirable future behavior. Sharing your authentic feelings builds and strengthens integrity, harmony, and healthy relationships.

A FRAMEWORK
FOR EASING FRUSTRATION

"Not everything that is faced can be changed, but nothing can be changed until it is faced."

Source unknown

Situations will arise when we need to tell people that certain behaviors are creating problems. Thanks to the work of Thomas Gordon, his three-part message is a handy framework for expressing concerns and alleviating tension for stressed-out souls. In addition, it informs others about the impact of their behavior and its effects:

- *When you do X...* (Name the behavior, using *"When"* rather than *"If"*)

- *I feel Y...* (How does the behavior make you feel?)

- *Because of Z.* (What's the consequence of the behavior?)

  When we're with Mike and Alicia and you ignore me, I get angry because it seems your focus is totally on them. It makes me feel excluded and nearly invisible.

This can also be supported with facts or statistics.
For example:

- *When you don't get sales figures to me on time, I feel frustrated because we can't issue commission checks on schedule.*

- *When you don't update me on the status of the QualityCrest project, I feel embarrassed when the CEO mentions new details about it and I'm expected to have the latest information but don't.*

Resolve Complaints

"An open ear is the only believable sign of an open heart."

David Augsburger

The word "complaint" is loaded with negative connotations. But in fact, complaining does offer an opportunity to set things right. According to Sandra Crowe, fellow speaker, friend, and author of Since Strangling Isn't an Option, "Every complaint is a hidden request. How the complaint is handled is a bigger issue than what is wrong." Sometimes that hidden request isn't so hidden, but rather is expressed quite vehemently. What others want is for you to make it right, make it better, and replace their feelings of frustration with satisfaction.

When people don't get what they want or expect, they can express their aggravation ranging from mild to wild. Don't waste your time defending why you can't do something. Instead, invest your time and energy in finding solutions to make it right or better. Explanations don't solve problems; they sound like excuses. Frustrated, disappointed, or angry people aren't satisfied by reasons; they want to be heard and they want solutions.

If people dump their aggravation on you, arguing just adds fuel to their fire (or ire!) and they're more likely to react aggressively. The situation may not be your fault, but they're ticked or peeved and want answers rather than an argument. Their anger or irritation is a strident call for assistance.

Arguing is the wrong approach because it activates resistance and escalates their exasperation. People may become abusive when their upset isn't being validated, raising their voices to make sure you hear them loud and clear! Without acknowledgment, they might rattle on because you don't seem to "get it." When people are irritated or angry, acknowledging their frazzled feelings eases their pain. By doing what you can to make it right or better, you help to restore their composure and confidence that you'll provide the needed support and assistance.

Answer the Call for Help!

> *"Discussion is an exchange of knowledge;*
> *argument an exchange of emotion."*
>
> Robert Quillen

When someone brings you a complaint, agree with what you can. Agreement is a form of empathy and shows that you understand their feelings or concerns, usually reducing the intensity of their reaction. Seek agreement regarding the things you can. Avoid arguing because it's likely to escalate anger:

- *You're right, ma'am. The lines are exceptionally long today.*

- *You're right, sometimes I don't put away the laundry.*

- *You're right, sometimes I do procrastinate.*

Listen. Let them air their grievances. When people know they've been heard, the high-velocity energy surrounding an issue is often miraculously diffused.

Smooth ruffled feathers. Continue adding balm to their frustrated souls with an apology. Apologies help reduce angst by acknowledging the situation, and showing your concern for the problems it's provoked. Along with the apology, you can also name the factors responsible for the difficulty— not as excuses, but to clarify what contributed to the problem: "I'm so sorry you've had to wait. This horrendous hailstorm caused cancellations in so many flights today and we've been working double shifts to handle all the additional passengers." This might even evoke a sympathetic response, but don't count on it—doling out sympathy is difficult when perturbed.

Move into action: when someone's been wronged, they want it made right, pronto! By taking immediate positive action, you're demonstrating concern for their plight and doing something about it. Think about what might improve the situation to make it right for them. Would it help if you found a replacement? Gave them a full refund? Offered something for free? Provided an alternative? Took it to a higher level of authority? For

example: "I'm booking you on the next flight, scheduled at 2:00 p.m. I'm also giving you a voucher for lunch. Once again, I appreciate your understanding and your patience. It's been quite a day!"

Ask yourself the following questions to expedite a successful and satisfactory resolution:

- What is really needed here right now?
- How might I provide that?"
- How can I help?
- What else might help?
- What other needs are important to this person?

Master Emotional Control

"We are being judged by a new yardstick: not just how smart we are, or by our training and expertise, but also how well we handle ourselves and each other."

Daniel Goleman, Working with Emotional Intelligence

Being in control of your emotions puts you in charge of your destiny and increases the trust and respect you earn from others. Mastering emotional control gives you power—when you "lose it," you lose your power, too.

Whether we're conscious of it or not, we decide every instant how to respond to the events of life, whether it's an insult hurled our way, a rude gesture, or an embroiling conflict. While other people or situations may aggravate, irritate, instigate, frustrate, disappoint, or dishearten us, ultimately we choose what to feel and how to respond. We're completely in charge of our emotional responses. No one makes us feel anything; we do it to ourselves. It's our own thoughts that make us cross or keep us calm and centered.

When we feed ourselves anger-arousing thoughts, it activates a feedback loop, circulating more anger—all dependent on what we tell ourselves. If you think or say, "He's acting like an idiot! He makes me so angry!" your body will respond to your verbal cues and kick the body's defense mechanisms into high gear. Our thoughts and feelings create mental and emotional states which influence how we relate to situations and the people in them.

Our anger buttons might go on alert when a certain word is spoken, a particular tone of voice is used, or an eyebrow is raised in displeasure. Countless things activate anger based on how we believe others should be thinking, behaving, or feeling. When people behave in ways that conflict with what we want, need, or value, our anger heats up. For a more detailed discussion about how we measure the behavior of others, see Check Out Your "Rule Book" later in this chapter.

Anger isn't a "bad" emotion. However, it produces bad feelings if not effectively managed. It leaves behind a trail of bitter feelings with powerfully destructive consequences, such as fueling hostility, resentment, and a desire for revenge. Recognize and acknowledge angry feelings as signals for exploring wants and needs. Anger is a natural human emotion that is experienced by everyone; it can be safely expressed without being aggressive or obnoxious.

Avoid heated discussions. When we feel pressured, stressed, or threatened, effective communication is often compromised. We may talk faster, speak at a higher frequency, or interrupt or rattle on as a means of dominating the conversation. These behaviors put others on red alert and they're more likely to strike a defensive stance, with less willingness to listen or negotiate with us.

Uncontrolled or poorly managed anger prevents us from extending compassion and understanding. Instead, we might become indignant, scathing, rejecting, ridiculing, criticizing, punishing, abusive, vengeful, or raging. All of these responses have their price; we hurt ourselves and others, often ending up with severed connections. By mismanaging anger, we risk losing the respect and trust of others.

Anger patterns are habits. Over time, we develop fairly predictable patterns of behavior when we're frustrated, irritated, or in conflict. Our "hot buttons" are triggered by a stimulus that sets them in motion; they've been pressed for so long, and our reactions have become so automatic, that we've forgotten what provides the energy that sets them off. We then react on impulse, forgetting that we have choices. When we don't take charge of our emotions, we climb aboard an emotional roller-coaster—and risk hurting others by our jerky behavior!

You don't have to ride through life stuck on a track circling back to the same ol' predictable patterns. Get off that track by consciously choosing desired responses that help to sustain good connections. Anger contains a powerful energy with the potential to suck away any awareness of choices. It can whoosh away all good sense. If you feel yourself sucked into its energy, return to the thought that you do have a choice, and you can choose a different response. Making the right decision in that split nanosecond of time is a decisive step toward mastery.

By making brain-powered choices about how to handle and express your emotions, you're managing your responses with every interaction—whether it's handling an irate customer, dealing with disgruntled staff, managing an out-of-control supervisor, or a defiant child. Taking charge of your emotions is empowering; it puts you in the driver's seat. Ultimately, your responses determine the quality of your connections and the degree of respect and trust you receive.

"Between stimulus and response, there is a space.
In that space lies our freedom and power to choose our response.
In our response lies our growth and freedom."

Victor Frankl, Man's Search for Meaning

What to Do When Your Temperature's Rising

"Patience is never more important than
when you're on the verge of losing it."

Source unknown

Venting anger by raging, shouting, and yelling actually heats up the atmosphere and causes more rather than less anger. It also prolongs the duration of angry feelings and hinders your ability to understand the issues at hand. With intense emotions riding high, feuding parties put a priority on wanting to be heard rather than seeking to understand what's at issue. This prevents meaningful dialogue to sort out issues and find solutions.

When emotions heat up, switch to "cool-down" self-talk. This sends different messages to your brain, reducing the intensity of emotional reactions. It helps by changing your physiological responses and corresponding emotional state; thinking "cool" brings down your internal emotional thermostat:

- I use my energy for solving problems.
- Stay cool ... I'm keeping my cool.
- I keep focused on solutions.
- We can work this out.
- I can handle this calmly.
- My intention is to create connection.

*"When you live in reaction, you give your power away.
Then you get to experience what you gave your power to."*

N. Smith

Watch Out for Mind Games!

We are limited by our inability to see everything (although some people never seem to miss a thing!). We may get glimpses of a situation and so we "fill in the gaps" of what we don't know, with missing pieces supplied by our thoughts, beliefs, and impressions—our assumptions. We may witness a certain behavior but not what motivated it, and jump to conclusions in our attempts to put 2 + 2 together.

Mind-reading is hazardous to connections because our presumptions often conjure up false information. Assumptions about what people are thinking, feeling, or doing can lead us into dangerous waters:

- *I know exactly what you're thinking!*
- *I know she's disappointed in me.*
- *He's trying to cover up for blowing it!*
- *Oh, I know he won't mind.*

You may think you can read a person like a book and know exactly what they're thinking. Your assumptions might be based solely on a gesture, a sigh, a comment, or perhaps even total silence. Those cues might lead to the correct conclusion, but unless you confirm their accuracy, there's a real danger that you're mind-reading! Your deduction could be totally off-base, resulting in your needlessly withdrawing trust, getting defensive, or driving people around you crazy—simply because you misread them or the situation.

Danger! Avoid getting trapped by assumptions—that you know what people want, that you can make a decision for them, or that they know what you mean. This holds especially true for our closest relationships, for those with whom we think it's easy to get inside their heads and know their every thought. However, we never can know for sure. In long-term relationships, we may tend to avoid vital questioning for fear of rocking the boat, making waves, or bringing up sensitive issues—thereby missing the mark entirely.

In any situation, instead of relying on assumptions, ask for more information. When we get the facts, we're much less likely to draw connection-crushing conclusions.

By collecting more data, you increase your understanding and help avert potential arguments:

- *I want to make sure I understand the situation completely. Can you please review the matter once more?*

- *I'm not totally clear on your ideas and want to make sure I get the whole picture. Please tell me again.*

- *Give me more specifics so we can make this work.*

JUMPING TO CONCLUSIONS CAN BE COSTLY

Stereotypes are pre-packaged judgments that can lead us straight into trouble; they're errors in judgment with costly consequences. A female purchasing agent who attended one of my seminars shared her story of how she had been cast in a stereotype.

Christina had researched the product line she wanted to buy, along with the vendor who could supply it. She asked her male assistant to schedule the meeting with the sales representative, convinced he could offer exactly what she wanted. Christina also invited her assistant to attend the meeting to learn more about the new product.

During the meeting, the sales rep devoted his attention almost exclusively to the enthusiastic assistant, assuming he was the decision-maker, rarely directing his comments to the female executive. Recognizing the sales rep had brought his stereotypes to the meeting, Christina smiled and left without giving him the order. The sales rep entered the meeting with a ready buyer, but lost the deal because of a costly error in judgment. —A.S.

Observe when your mind starts second-guessing others. Note your observations, bypass mind-reading, and question the source directly: "I noticed you were looking at your watch. Are we running late?" "I noticed you haven't been talking much. Are you bothered by something I said?" Concocting fantasies can cost us connections. Probe for the truth.

OH, THEY WON'T MIND!

If you think something won't matter to someone and they won't mind, think again! Check it out to be absolutely sure. Some "little things" can become BIG issues if not checked out first with those involved. For instance ...

- A friend gets angry because you invited someone else to join the two of you for dinner. You may be thinking, "the more the merrier!" while "three's a crowd" is on her mind.

- You accept a work assignment, thinking it will help lighten the load of an overworked colleague, while he's steamed that you "had the nerve" to be so presumptive.

- You inadvertently plant an azalea bush just a tad over your neighbor's property line. You think they'll be thrilled at your beautification project. Instead, they're furious that you dug up their land without asking them first. They erect a fence to make the point that you overstepped your boundaries, as well as to make darn sure you'll never do anything so thoughtless again.

Your motives may have been quite innocent and well-intentioned, but if you didn't consult the person beforehand, they may consider your actions to be bold, impulsive, thoughtless, or something totally different than your truth.

Since we all see situations differently, ask for the opinions of those involved, so you don't end up stepping on toes, bruising egos, or bashing feelings. If you act on impulse and realize later that you've neglected to consult with others first, bring your concerns to their immediate attention. Explain your views of the situation, apologize for not getting their feedback first, explore acceptable reparations, and take remedial action.

Mend Misunderstandings

It takes two to tango and two to tangle! "You do this..." "I think that ..." "I say this ..." "You think that ..." Cha-cha-cha! The dance of misunderstanding creates a series of missteps, of misinterpreting motives or actions. More than toes get stepped on when dancing to this confusing rhythm—so can good feelings and the connections created by them.

Because the events in our lives are colored by the meaning we give them, we may misinterpret someone's motives, miscalculate situations, and overlook what is needed. We may not understand why somebody is making "a big deal" out of something, because what it means to them does make a difference, while to us it is "no big deal." Likewise, other people may not understand why something is "a big deal" to us. It matters because of the meaning we give it.

You may know exactly why you did what you did, but if it's a mystery to others, confusion can quickly turn to chaos. Be willing to make the first move to sort out the confusion and help people better understand your decisions or your actions. Give them a chance to air their concerns and explain the situation from their perspective. Seek solutions for getting connections back on track.

FAR FROM BEING UNDERSTOOD

Sometimes, my clients are in a rush and forget to provide me with some of the details. One of my clients contacted me to speak before a group of government officials from Mongolia. It seemed pretty straightforward, except for one critical detail—he didn't tell me that the audience couldn't speak English! He believed that I spoke Chinese, and I automatically assumed that he would arrange for a translator. It wasn't until the morning of the presentation that I learned of the major misunderstanding; so, my motivational speech was composed entirely of nonverbal gestures and drawings! A.S.

WHAT'S YOUR BEEF?

When a beef is brewing, don't stew over it. Turn "What's your beef?" into "The relief of B.E.A.F.!" Bring out the BEAF by creating opportunities to:

Be heard

Explain needs

Air grievances

Find solutions

Don't let a beef simmer too long! There's too much at stake (or steak). Otherwise, you just might be the one that gets cooked!

Misunderstandings can be detrimental to trust in relationships as well as the bottom line in business. For instance, customers confused about a company's return policy can become irate if they misunderstood its guidelines. If mishandled, they'll feel betrayed and take their business elsewhere, potentially spreading some lethal commentary along the way, creating a network of animosity and ill will.

Always apologize if you've made a mistake, or misunderstood or overlooked a situation. It's not the right time to preserve your ego, at the expense of severing a connection. When in doubt, these seven magical words can turn around any situation: "I am sorry. I made a mistake." Make them genuine and mean it. If misunderstandings are frequent, try to determine what might be causing them. Make a habit of regularly sharing perspectives to enhance understanding as well as to clarify policies or procedures.

Let Go of Labels

*"It is only by knowing what to let go of, that you know
more clearly what to hold on to."*

Maggie Bedrosian, Love It or Lose It: Living Clutter-Free Forever

How do we judge thee? Let us count the ways! We judge people on the basis of what we think is true about them. Our thoughts, however, are subjective, influenced not only by past experience, but also by vague rumors, gossip, and the opinions of others. We absorb this information—filtering it through the lens of our own expectations, feelings, interests, needs, values, prejudices, and attitudes—and combine it to form a judgment about the person.

This process is how our mind understands people, putting them in frameworks that make sense to us: "Mary isn't doing much of anything today, and she seems distracted. Maybe she's tired, or worried about something." Problems arise when the judgments become rigid, and we attach too much significance to them. Instead of judging Mary's behavior, we make a judgement about Mary's character: "Mary isn't doing much of anything today, and she seems distracted. How lazy can you get?"

When repeated difficulties with the person "confirm" our judgment, we program ourselves to expect only certain behaviors. We tend to slap an invisible label on him or her, such as Grouch, Hothead, or Jerk. Once we have affixed the label, it colors our reactions with every exchange: "Watch out! Here comes Mr. Volcano! Wonder what he'll explode about today?" or "Oh, oh! Wanda the Whiner will be at the meeting this afternoon. I can always count on her to throw a wrench into my ideas."

When we label someone, we begin discounting any information that goes against the label. Often, we're not even aware of these labels, but they can dramatically color our responses to the person. We project past memories of their behavior onto our future expectations, and anticipate trouble. Although their behavior may truly be causing us problems, attaching labels only exacerbates the issue. They're stuck with our labels, and we're stuck in negative patterns of response that doom any possibility of authenticity or growth the relationship might have had.

Parents get into the labeling act, too, perhaps as a way to explain or justify a child's behavior to others or even to garner a little sympathy for themselves for dealing with their child's perplexing or vexing actions. They assign labels such as "Our wild child," "Our willful one," or "My shy little girl." Parents also attach labels to their offspring for "star" behavior: "Our smart one" or "The athletic one," which can affect the self-esteem of other children in a family, who may internalize the message that they do not measure up to their "star" sibling. Labels stick, and children often respond by trying to live up (or down) to them, or by justifying their actions as a result of a label.

Our judgments put people in boxes and we may dismiss their behaviors, tune them out, or not give them enough credit or a fair chance. Labeling can get in the way; we might ignore the person we labeled, even if he or she truly does have a valid concern or is absolutely right, as in the classic fable, The Boy Who Cried Wolf (who everybody ignored because of his earlier misbehavior even when he really did see the wolf).

One of the challenges of responding to difficult people is breaking free from how we see and judge them. When we remove the labels, we're no longer restricted to seeing them in confining roles. By meeting them fresh with each encounter, we don't drag along our accumulated shared history. Therefore, greet each encounter with an open mind that is free of labels. Closed minds close off options.

What's Wrong With "Being Right"?

Standing firm on the hallowed grounds of "rightness" is a dead-wrong approach for connecting with others. It smacks of arrogance and alienates. The need to "be right" gets in the way of winning the acceptance, appreciation, and respect of others—qualities critical to caring connections, customer satisfaction, and harmony everywhere. Whenever you need to be right, you make others wrong in the process with a polarizing effect, and that pushes people away.

If you find yourself playing the "Right and Wrong Game," get out immediately! Remind yourself what you could lose by winning. Naturally, you want your beliefs to be validated by others, but not at the price of alienating them. It boils down to this: "being right" jeopardizes your connections. Would the loss of your colleague or comrade truly be worth a momentary victory in a ridiculous battle of egos?

Giving up the need to be right doesn't mean giving up your preferences and perspectives. Rather, it means letting go of demanding that others must or should see things your way. It's respectfully disagreeing, but not demanding that others conform to your beliefs. You strengthen your relationships with a willingness to accept and respect differences.

A steadfast insistence on "being right" can throw you steadily off course with people and the direction you want to head. "Being right" can be expensive, costing you clients, customers, credibility, and connection; it's definitely the wrong approach if you want to keep valued relationships. Instead of "being right," do what is right for the integrity of the relationship and demonstrating your intention for creating good connections.

A SALE THAT WENT DOWN THE DRAIN

Rick and I had just purchased a house in the Virginia suburbs and were now eager to sell our home in Maryland. A buyer soon appeared who, as part of the terms of the contract, wanted the washer and gas dryer to convey with the house. However, we had just purchased the laundry equipment and, since our new home didn't have either, we wanted to take them with us. So we held our ground.

Ultimately, that firm stance made us lose the sale and turned out to be a costly decision, since another buyer didn't show up until several months later. That was painful enough, but when we learned that our new neighborhood didn't even have gas, we realized how "sticking to our guns" turned out to be a most ironic lesson. Focus on outcomes, not positions. —S.S.

Check Out Your "Rule Book"

"Sometimes people treat us the way they do not because of the way they are, but because of the way we are."

Sam Horn

We each have an invisible edition of our personal "rule book" deeply ingrained in our brains. These guidelines define our expectations and desires of how others should treat us; what we believe is right, fair, and just; and how the world and its people should behave.

We judge people by our book. We have rules about being courteous, extending appreciation, acknowledging work, honoring time, demonstrating concern, being compassionate, delivering service, and the degree of effort required for projects. We have rules about how fast people should return phone calls and e-mails, reply to requests, respond with answers, handle problems, pitch in on projects, and most importantly, what people generally should do and what they shouldn't. The rules all serve as our invisible code of conduct with expectations of reciprocal exchange, or else!

Observe your own rules in action whenever you become frustrated, irritated, or annoyed with a customer, coworker, friend, or loved one. Not knowing how important something is to you, they may have just bumped up against one of your RULEs:

> **R**estrictive
>
> **U**nknown
>
> **L**ife
>
> **E**xpectations

People play by their own rules (and RULEs) and may not be familiar with yours. In fact, they may be totally clueless! Even if they know yours, it doesn't mean they'll abide by them (as every parent knows only too well!). In any case, when someone breaks your "rules," your expectations start generating a steady stream of reasons to penalize or disconnect from the "violator." Imposing your expectations on others only adds to your aggravation and creates or widens a chasm.

Rules at Work

Whether whispered around water coolers, voiced over the phone, or overheard at meetings, the following comments are sure signs that people are either puzzled, peeved, or both, and that someone's "rules" have been violated:

- Who does she think she is, butting into the copy machine line?
- Everyone should do his or her share of work!
- It's not my job! They should (replace the coffee pot ... pick up their own stuff ... make their own arrangements).
- She's been here long enough and should know what to do, without me having to be so specific.
- They've been through the training and shouldn't have to be told how to do something again.
- They should have followed my recommendations!

Examine your rules as they arise. Don't waste your time collecting "evidence" of violations; invest it in creating good connections.

DEFENSIVE IN DYSFUNCTION LAND

When people know they're being judged, they become much more selective in how they communicate. They may not say what needs to be said, or they may say what they don't mean or perhaps even what shouldn't be said at all. Fear stops the flow of good communication, fueling defensiveness and disconnection, which leads to dysfunction. —??

NO TRESPASSING!

*No trespassing allowed
under penalty of withdrawal
of one or more of the following:
Loyalty, affection, attention, respect,
trust, love, friendship, and business.*

Do you live by the "No trespassing" rule listed above? Sometimes we're not even aware of our own rules until something or someone treads on our sacred turf. But consciously or not, we give out "invisible citations" for violations at work, at home, and everywhere. These citations manifest themselves in the form of private judgments we make against the "violators":

- *I can't believe she would do such a thing!*

- *How dare they!*

- *They should know we don't do that around here!*

- *Why on Earth did he do that?*

Remind yourself that people operate from their own rules. Many irritating things in life are often petty. Rise above them or risk losing a valuable connection.

Pinpoint Problems

"The problem is not that there are problems. The problem is expecting otherwise and thinking that having problems is a problem."

Theodore Rubin

When a problem arises, what exactly is causing it? Sometimes, it's obvious. At other times, something is undeniably in the air and the atmosphere is heating up, creating tension and short fuses, yet you're unable to put your finger on its cause.

If the problem isn't clearly identified, unravel the mystery. Get to the bottom of it with some probing "who, what, where, why, when, and how" questions, which will provide you with valuable data for defining the specific nature of the situation:

- Who's involved?
- What's going on?
- Where does it happen?
- When does it happen?
- Why does it seem to happen?
- How does it happen?
- How frequently does it happen?
- How do you feel about it?

Examples:

- When does the problem occur? During peak hours? Weekends? Right before the annual meeting.
- What is causing it? We don't have enough support to handle all the extra work before the annual meeting.
- What actions could improve the situation? We can hire a temporary employee.
- Who can help alleviate the problem? The accounting department can review the budget again.

Evaluate your responses to help understand and devise possible solutions. Once you're clear on the specific nature of the problem, focus your energy on finding solutions and ask others for their ideas. Deal with one problem at a time. There might be multiple concerns, but stick to handling one at a time to reduce stress and tension.

THINK U-S-A FOR FINDING SOLUTIONS

Understand the problem: Describe the predicament to those involved in it. Once you clearly identify the situation, you'll have more information to help resolve it.

Size up the situation: How is it affecting you? The staff? The work environment? Productivity? Morale? Customers? Your family?

Ask for ideas and offer your solutions: Explore options together to create mutually acceptable solutions. It may not be possible to provide exactly what everyone wants, but asking people directly often reveals the real issues and helps to reach a satisfactory solution or agreement.

Ask for ideas:

- *What do you suggest?*
- *What would you do?*
- *What would it take to make you happy?*

Offer your solutions:

- *What if ... ?*
- *Here are your options.*
- *Which would you rather have, this ... or ...?*
- *Have you tried ...?*

Clarify What You Want

"Influencing people is the art of letting them have your way."

Source unknown

When you're clear on what you want, it's easier to stay on track to move closer to your desired goals. Clear objectives are less likely to get derailed. In each interaction, asking yourself "What do I want?" provides a centering point for clarifying your purpose and the choices you make. It serves as a lightning rod regarding desired outcomes, so your time and energy are creatively channeled into reaching those results.

By knowing your bottom line, you've got a litmus test for every choice. You know when you can be flexible and agreeable, and when the issue is non-negotiable. As a result, you feel more confident approaching each interaction, knowing what's most important to you. Whether going into an interview, performance review, client negotiation, or family meeting, you know where to draw your "line in the sand." You're clear on your objectives and you make choices to keep moving toward them. Mindful of your purpose, you approach the situation with greater flexibility and focus on the subject at hand.

Without clarity of purpose, it's easy to get sidetracked, caught up in issues, and get derailed along the way. Our egos and emotions then drive us away from our connection-conscious value system. But when our goals are kept firmly in mind, we are able to stay focused and separate the facts from the feelings, laying the groundwork for effective negotiations.

Let the question, "What do I want?" serve as a mantra, an automatic response that's called upon with every conflict, concern, interaction, or issue, and constantly kept at the forefront of your thoughts. With the objective of creating and keeping positive relationships, you'll negotiate for what you want in fair and reasonable ways. Continually monitor your thoughts and actions so they're working toward satisfactory solutions, as well as maintaining the integrity of your value system.

Focus on What Others Need

"It's a luxury to be understood."

Ralph Waldo Emerson

"But you just don't understand!" A customer is at her wit's end because she doesn't think the customer service department understands all of her aggravations. Or your assistant is furious that you won't grant him the requested leave after he's put in extra hours on a project. Or your teenager pleads for reviewing her case after being grounded.

Not feeling understood is exasperating, especially when you've clearly stated your case and the situation seems so obvious. Feeling understood supports a fundamental universal desire to be fully heard, discuss our needs, air our grievances, and explain why something is important to us.

In an ideal world, mutual respect and understanding flow freely, given to and received from everyone in our professional and personal relationships. In the real world, you're guaranteed interactions with an ongoing cast of characters who inevitably will not respond in expected or desirable ways. This is exactly when it is critical to do the thing that is most difficult at the time: seek to understand the other person first.

Seeking to understand the needs of others first shows you've put their needs and concerns as your number one priority. It demonstrates your willingness to keep their needs at the forefront, validate the meaning and value they represent, and find ways to satisfy them. This honors their perspectives, demonstrates your sincere concern, maintains openness, strengthens connections, and puts you in a positive light.

When you seek to understand what others want or need first, they listen better and longer and become more receptive to your needs. Understanding what they want pays off in greater acceptance, cooperation, and their willingness to negotiate—all pivotal components in reaching a compromise or agreement. You gain their respect and each of you is more likely to obtain what you desire.

With a need to know:

1. **Ask questions.** First, ask broad-based, indirect questions to make people feel comfortable talking about what's important to them, such as "Can we talk about this?" or "How is this affecting you?" Next, get more direct with specific questions to nail their needs: "What do you think will make this work for you?" or "What do you think is fair?"

2. **Let them voice their concerns.** Listen without interrupting. Often, all others want is a chance to state their case. Invite them to talk about their concerns by saying, "Tell me more." This demonstrates your interest in what they have to say as well as "getting to the bottom" of an issue, which is sometimes masked by a trivial complaint or other concern. The question, "Is there anything else?" also gives them an opportunity to bring up other matters of equal or greater concern.

3. **Show acceptance.** You don't have to like what others may want or give it to them, but showing that you accept their position eliminates much of their resistance.

   When acceptance is conveyed, a person's worth is validated and his or her dignity remains intact. A willingness to fully listen in the face of disagreement and intense emotions takes courage, strength, and a compelling desire to seek understanding. Other people have a right to their opinions, conclusions, and feelings even though they may differ from your own: "Your points do make sense, although I see the situation differently." "Now I understand why you feel that way." Letting them know that they have been heard provides the platform to springboard solutions.

4. **Don't dig in your heels.** Insisting on having your way has a polarizing effect; the more resistance, the greater the friction. Look for areas of agreement to reduce defensiveness and demonstrate your desire to resolve the conflict: "While I agree with you regarding ... I still believe this will work better for the team." "I'm in total agreement with you on the importance of taking action. Where we differ is in how we should respond."

5. **State your perspectives briefly and brainstorm solutions.**
"I can understand that you feel you've got too much to handle right now. If we both review everything that needs to get done this week and think of some ways for prioritizing tasks, that should reduce some of the stress." "My number one priority is your safety. Now that I understand what's been happening, let's see how we can figure out some safer solutions." See the next section on Brainstorm Solutions for specific tips.

"We may not always see eye to eye. We can try to see heart to heart."

Sam Levenson

SEE IT DIFFERENTLY

When you look at a situation from the perspective of how others see it, you get a different picture, which can provide a pivotal shift:

- What are their concerns?

- What do they need?

- What are their expectations?

- What are their reasons for wanting to hold firm?

- What is needed for them to feel satisfied and achieve resolution?

A new perspective with fresh insight can be a beacon filled with new possibilities.

Gaining understanding regarding the perspectives of associates, customers, clients, or adversaries has a bottom line bonus—studies show they're less likely to retaliate or initiate lawsuits!

Be a Masterful Negotiator

"It's easier for people to see it your way if you first see it their way."

Jack Kaine

More negotiations break down because of animosity between parties or objections about the situation, rather than differences over issues. The tips listed below will help to cultivate a positive environment for reaching agreements and keep negotiations on a productive (and hopefully civil) level:

1. Help define how people see the situation. Show them what's in it for them and the value they'll receive from your proposed solution.

2. Demonstrate your desire to find acceptable solutions and that your intentions are honorable.

3. Set the stage for success. Establish your interest up front for productive negotiations. Demonstrating goodwill minimizes defensiveness: "I know we'll be able to reach a workable solution." This creates a more relaxed atmosphere, puts people at ease, and minimizes stressful interactions.

4. Anticipate objections in advance, if possible, and formulate options.

5. Reflect shared values and areas of common interest. Use language that reflects their values and what's important to them.

6. If some change will be required, make it easier for them to accept by showing how the modifications will extend or expand their personal interests or self-image.

7. Highlight undesirable outcomes or alternatives as a contrast to more viable options: "We could choose to do it that way, but then you wouldn't be able to..."

8. Focus on mutual interests, not fixed positions. Stay flexible, focusing on reaching mutually acceptable agreements about what's really at stake. For instance, is it about taking a particular training course at a busy time of year, or gaining important skills at a more convenient time? Is it about negotiating for an increased budget for your department, or about doing your best job for the company?

9. If there's any confusion about which option to choose, offer two choices to help generate a decision.

10. If an impasse is reached, restate your interests in a different way. Know in advance about your "walk-away" options—your bottom-line.

When you know what you want and learn more about what others want, work toward win-win solutions. Negotiate for what you want and be fair and reasonable with others, too.

CONSIDER THE "O'S"

In any problem situation, evaluate the obstacles, objections, and options in order to reach an agreement:

- What are the **O**bstacles to resolving the situation?

- What are the participants' **O**bjections?

- What options are available to **O**vercome the **O**bstacles and **O**bjections?

WHEN SILENCE IS GOLDEN

We often need some time to think about what we really want or need. During conflict or negotiations, a period of silence is a powerful tool for percolating priorities and the real truth of what is desired. It clears the clutter of information overload and offers an oasis of quietude for making choices. It's a useful negotiation tool; keeping silent under pressure is often seen as a sign of strength and shows that you mean business.

People may be uncomfortable with the silence, yet a pause from all the information processing often creates a climate for closure. Avoid the temptation to fill up silence with conversation. Give others a chance to focus on what they want.

Brainstorm Solutions

"Just remember: People tend to resist that which is forced upon them.
People tend to support that which they help to create."

Vince Pfaff

In a conflict, you want something and another person wants something else. Your needs are on the line. You're as intent on getting what you want, as they are on satisfying their needs. When positions are deadlocked, it's time to break out all the brilliant brain power!

Brainstorming is a powerful problem-solving strategy that opens up a dazzling array of new possibilities. Tapping your creative brainpower opens up viable alternatives to reach mutually agreeable solutions in what once seemed to be a problem-plagued, limited landscape.

Follow the steps listed below to effectively brainstorm:

- Write down everything that might help to correct or improve a troubling situation. Do not evaluate the ideas as you're writing them down or fixate on any one possible option. Sometimes the ideas that seem the craziest at first glance often turn out to offer real solutions.

- Ask those interested in reaching a satisfactory decision for their ideas. Gather a broad range of options for review.

- Consider which options seem to provide some useful solutions, looking at each one's strengths and weaknesses. What would be gained? What would be lost?

- Choose the option likeliest to lead to a favorable and satisfactory result. A wise choice meets your needs and is viewed as fair by everyone involved.

- Implement the option and determine a date to evaluate its effectiveness.

OFFER A CHOICE

When flexibility is an option, providing a choice honors the needs of others and whisks you right out of a potential battleground. When you're willing, this puts the ball in their court and gives them buy-in power. Whether you're dealing with a teenager, disgruntled customer, or colleague, when they're involved in the decision-making process and can choose between options, they become responsible for the outcomes they experience. If they're unhappy with the result, they made the choice and are responsible for experiencing its consequences:

- *There are two ways we can handle this matter. You choose.*

- *The dishes need to be washed this evening. You choose—right after dinner, or after you finish your homework.*

- *You make the choice.*

When your respect others' opinions, they're more likely to respect your requests. Offering choices accelerates action. In the case of parenting, it reduces or eliminates nagging!

Choose Your Options
for Handling Difficult Situations

We have the power to choose what we do when situations are difficult and connections fray. Knowing that we always have choices gives us the power to take control. Throughout our lives, we'll mix and mingle with plenty of people—the outraged and the obstinate, the belligerent and the bothersome, the annoying and the agitated, the rude and the ruthless, and other people who press our buttons.

Basically, we have three choices for handling difficult situations with people:

1. **Accept it.** Sometimes we must surrender to what is, because nothing we can do will ever be able to change it. With an attitude of making a situation work as best as you can and releasing any related negativity, you're better able to manage it. Sometimes accepting things as they are without our ability to change them is hard to swallow; yet continually butting our heads against walls in frustration hurts, too!

    Remember what is possible to change and what is not:

    -   You cannot change a person's perspective. You cannot change how anyone else sees a situation even after you've clearly outlined your reasons. Your perspectives and rationalizations may seem obvious to you, especially after all the hard evidence you've presented to make your case. You may find yourself at your wit's end, wondering why they don't get it. It's frustrating when you want others to see it your way and they don't. It's not within your power to change how someone else sees a situation, even with the most brilliant and convincing case.

    -   You cannot change a person's behavior. You can request a change of behavior, but you cannot make a person act differently. Their choices may frustrate your needs, but it's the best they can do with their interests at stake and level of problem-solving skills. They have their reasons and their beliefs; their assumptions and attitudes simply fuel their actions. People will usually only change when they believe a new behavior is in their own best interest.

- You cannot change another person's feelings. It does no good to tell others how they should feel. You may not see the reasons for them to feel a certain way, but their feelings are their truth. If they feel it, it's real to them.

2. **Change your behavior.** You can change your way of thinking about people and how you respond to them. Taking responsibility for your responses dramatically influences your interpersonal dynamics. You claim more personal power when you give up trying to change things outside of your control. If you're not happy with how people treat you or the outcomes that result, you can change what you do and say to transform the energy surrounding negative dynamics. Remember to also communicate empowering messages to yourself about your capabilities and personal worth.

3. **Get out.** Some situations or relationships are so destructive and energy-draining that leaving becomes the best option for your head, heart, and stress level. Be clear whether the time is right for you to go. Leaving may be your best choice, but determine whether you'd be leaving behind something you might regret later. For instance, if you find your job unbearable, getting out might be your preferred choice but it may not be in your financial best interests to resign quite yet. If you're physically in danger, the choice is clear—your safety is a number one priority.

A PLANE MESS

I had flown from a conference in Reno to the Denver airport and just missed my connecting flight. An earlier hailstorm had severely damaged more than two dozen planes and they were grounded for repairs. This was wreaking havoc for passengers and agents alike. Lines were long and tempers were flaring throughout the airport. I could see the ticket agents were obviously taking on the frustrations of passengers and doing their best to re-book flights.

Adding to my irritation was fear that I might not get back home in time to catch a plane the next day for Spain. After an hour of waiting in line to get re-booked, I finally got to the ticket counter and chose to connect instead of complain. I asked the agent how she was doing handling all the upset passengers. She confided to me that it was challenging and said that most of the agents were now working double shifts, a 16-hour stint, to handle the extra passenger load. That's all I needed to hear to get an instantly fresh perspective. She certainly didn't need me unloading my aggravation to add to her overload. I acknowledged her commitment to doing her best and told her I appreciated her assistance.

Although I was unhappy about the long delay, it was one of those things that couldn't be changed and required an attitude adjustment on my part. While thousands of us were indeed being inconvenienced, my perspective shifted when I focused on those tired souls handling the excruciating long delays. —S.S.

Refuse to Stay Stuck

*"Each difficult moment has the potential to open my eyes
and open my heart."*

Myla Kabat-Zinn

When suffering unfair or undeserved treatment, bitterness, hostility, and resentment can clog connections. By holding on to these negative emotions, you actually become bound to those involved by giving them the power to control your feelings. When this happens, it is you, not they, who become shackled to your list of "unforgiveables." In fact, they might not even realize that their actions or words are causing you anguish.

Whatever their cause, bad feelings become the glue binding you to an uncomfortable, awkward, or unbearable connection. These feelings usually endure unless they're brought to closure and you choose to let them go. This is true even if you may never see the other person again; bad feelings usually persist and the connection remains full of static. The invisible energy continues sending out negative currents that can also seep their way into your other relationships.

By constructively handling the fallout from conflicts, hurt, and broken trust, you're taking responsibility for creating better connections. You, rather than your emotions, are then running the show.

The purpose of forgiveness is "for giving" up resentment, anger, or feelings of separation. It's something you do for yourself—give up attachments to negative energy that otherwise only end up draining you. Unforgiveness hardens into rock-like resentment, a roadblock making the going rough on the path to forgiveness. Forgiveness frees the pathway for better connections; it can be a long haul, but the payoff is a lighter load.

When you are willing to let go of the negative debris that's clogging up a relationship, you perform heart surgery of sorts. Forgiving others is not a sign that you're willing to tolerate unacceptable behavior or excuse their actions. Forgiveness doesn't mean you'll allow others to continue hurtful

behaviors. It's an act of will and determination, an operation necessary to extract the injustices in order to open your heart again. Reconnecting to the offending party or parties may not always be desired. However, by severing the constrictive bond, your reward is freedom from bondage.

Saying "I forgive you" without truly feeling forgiveness is not enough. We don't forgive because we're "supposed to." Real forgiveness melts away resentment, hurt, and anger so that you can move beyond it, without remaining stuck in the past. You set your own timetable for releasing the resentment; the quicker you can, the less hurt you'll endure. No amount of thrashing or rehashing the situation can alter whatever resulted and wastes your energy. Use your energy to rebuild instead.

When you find yourself wanting to let go of a heart-wrenching experience, but having a hard time doing so, seeking support from a friend, therapist, spiritual counselor, or others can lighten your load. Guidance and support can also come through insights and words of wisdom from other sources—such as reading books that inspire you, give you courage, offer hope, shed new light, lift your spirits, and remind you of what you want most. Draw on your reserves of resiliency, of your choice to break free and bounce back.

Taking positive action has a restorative effect. Consider the options that best serve your needs. Release the past and any related negative energy that's draining you. Refuse to stay stuck.

"HEY! WE'RE ON THE SAME SIDE!"

When there's disagreement about how to achieve desired objectives and both sides are holding firm, Sam Horn, brilliant speaker, friend, and author, suggests using this unifying statement: "We're on the same side." Sometimes, we hold to our positions so tightly, we lose sight of our objective. It serves as a reminder that we're not so far apart on what we both want, and by getting a renewed perspective we can shortcut our combined stress, reach a quicker solution, and meet in the middle instead of opposing sides.

BREAKING THROUGH THE BARRIERS

Spend some time objectively assessing an energy-draining situation and how it might be possible to break through the barriers:

- What do you believe caused or is causing the clogged connection?

- How do you now act around the person who is part of the situation? How do they act around you?

- What problems is the situation causing? What might result if the situation continues or even worsens?

- What is stopping you from seeking resolution?

- What are options for resolving it?

- What might you be willing to do to restore the connection?

- When might you be ready to move forward on those possibilities?

- What will happen if you don't move forward? Are you willing to accept those consequences?

Build Bridges Over Connection Chasms

"What a world this would be if we just built bridges instead of walls."

Carlos Ramirez

We foster good relationships by building bridges to understanding. Sometimes, we must make the first move to reach out and build that bridge, in accordance with our total commitment to keeping our connections in good repair. If we wait for others to take the initiative, it may never happen; we'd then be permanently caught up in a connection chasm. Building a bridge offers both sides an opportunity to straddle differences to meet in the middle and span into a new land of understanding.

Instructions: How to Build a Bridge

1. First, build a foundation of respect and trust by discussing the interests of others and what they want and need.

2. Next, construct the bridge across common ground, of what you both want and what will serve your mutual needs.

3. Finally, discuss your interests and what is important to you.

Ideally, the bridge is built with flexibility and an understanding of mutual needs; then, we're more likely to meet in the middle to successfully cross the chasm. However, it takes a lot of energy for us to let go of our entrenched positions and seek common ground together. We may get so caught up in our issues (a colleague says something that humiliates us, someone else takes credit for our idea, neighbors have a "falling out" over a fence) that we forget what's at stake. We may disconnect from others for countless transgressions, but not seeking to repair a relationship will cost us dearly in fractured feelings and broken connections.

It's a difficult journey to rid ourselves of the "sludge" (all the negative baggage we're often so slow to discard) and get to a place of wisdom. When we can, it works wonders. Doing so may not actually change the desired outcome, and we may not get everything we want, but responding with insight and perception makes a big difference to our own personal experience—and to the experience of others, as well.

When we banish our judgments, we're better able to get a clearer picture of what's good in others or what truly matters in a particular situation; this shift in perspective will reinforce an atmosphere of trust, support, and cooperation. When others are unyielding and hold fast to their positions by refusing your attempts at reconciliation or resolution, recognize that some people simply are unwilling to let go for reasons you may not know. Continue to demonstrate your commitment to reaching a workable solution or repairing the rift.

If your bridge-building efforts should fail, and others don't make an effort to resolve the differences, you've at least demonstrated your desire to do so. Even though you've done your best, exhausting all possibilities for bridging the gap, the other person still holds on and won't let it go or move beyond it. At this point, it's important to remember that you cannot change either the attitudes or feelings of others—it may take time for their minds to work it through and their hearts to open; the minds and hearts of others often are not synchronized with our own. The reality is that sometimes there's nothing else we can do to restore a connection, except hope for and visualize its restoration in the future. Bridges collapse from too much weight carried across them; inflexible, rigid positions are a heavy load to bear.

No matter that others refuse to budge; by choosing to transform your own experience and accepting the situation for what it is, you've done everything within your power to bridge the chasm. In these circumstances, be sure to keep the bridge in good repair so that others may cross whenever they're ready. Extending forgiveness and compassion is the mightiest connector (and may take all your might!) and holds the greatest promise for restoring connections. For mending broken connections, forgiveness is always the most powerful glue in your bridge-building kit.

> *"He who cannot forgive others destroys the bridge over which he himself must pass."*
>
> George Herbe

Handle Prickly People With Care

The Prickly Patch—Where Getting Along is a Thorny Challenge

Prickly People are those who express behaviors that get under your skin, on your nerves, or irritate, annoy, or enrage you. Their behaviors make getting along a challenge and create obstacles for constructive connections.

There is no greater test in the art and skill of getting along than interacting with Prickly People, those thorny creatures whose irritating, nasty, tiresome behaviors can wreak havoc with your spirit and destroy your peace of mind. They appear everywhere—in the next cubicle, at the customer service counter, or even sitting across the dinner table, perhaps pummeling you with insults or exasperating you with other obnoxious behavior.

Although you may be filled with disgust and despair, you're still not sure what to do. You would like to get along, make things work better, and preserve your self-respect; neither do you want to complicate things by creating more conflict or hurt feelings. However, their actions or attitudes (or both) are unacceptable, disrespectful, hurtful, and stressing you out.

Any of the following situations sound familiar?

- As an eager team member, you gladly shared your ideas for the client proposal, and the majority of your strategies made the final cut. When the team leader submitted the proposal, the boss was impressed with your team's creativity. The problem is, your name was left off. And this isn't the first time you haven't gotten the credit you deserved from the team leader.

- One of your co-workers is a fiery hothead. She spews her wrath over the slightest frustration and loves to blame you and others in your department for her mistakes. She moderates her behavior when the managers are nearby, but an atmosphere of irritation and anger has settled over the rest of the staff.

- Your neighbor's favorite hobby is working the grapevine. She delights in getting the latest scoop about everyone—from couples to kids. She's a one-stop rumor shop who has spread damaging false information, hurting your family and your friends with her "grapes of wrath" antics.

- A colleague discounts your ideas and believes it's always "his way or the highway." He disgraces you in meetings and makes sarcastic remarks occasionally to others about your competence.

- Your mother-in-law doesn't agree with the way you're raising your kids. Whatever you do isn't "good enough" or in agreement with her suggestions. Every time she visits you're a nervous wreck, wondering whether she's making a judgment or about to send one your way.

Prickly People are thorny rascals who come in quite a collection of challenging styles—from hostile, hot-tempered, and verbally abusive to sarcastic, sneaky, and intimidating (as well as a multitude of other difficult-to-deal-with, disconnecting variations). They can poke, jab, and aggravate us to no end and put our connecting power to the test! We may wonder why they're in our face, going for our backs, or getting under our skin. Rather than enjoying enduring connections with them, we may see them as connections to be endured. They create problems instead of pleasure; some cause trouble unknowingly, while others seem to gain pleasure from their intentional malice.

Prickly People pop up everywhere. They might work with us, live near us, or even live with us. We may attend classes with them, serve on the same committee, worship together, or play on the same team. They might be our customers, clients, supervisor, partner, or CEO. They come in all shapes, sizes, colors, ages, and degrees of irritation and outrage. They're part of life; no doubt we will encounter, interact, and need to deal with them at the worst or most inconvenient times.

While we may be tempted to ignore or avoid confrontation with people we consider to be difficult, it's important to manage them in constructive ways for a number of reasons. In our personal relationships, ignoring prickly behaviors takes a toll on our physical, mental, and emotional well-being and splinters connections, both in that moment and over time. But these behaviors do much more than get on our nerves—they can zap our energy, exhaust us, shut us down, and even provoke our own difficult behavior in response. The longer prickly behavior goes unchecked, the more well-worn the pattern becomes, wearing us out at every turn.

At work, ignoring prickly behavior can be costly in terms of increased stress levels and conflict; this in turn affects job satisfaction and retention, and affects our fellow employees in the same ways, with a multiplier effect on decreased productivity, lost time, and crushed creativity. Difficult behavior also ripples beyond to directly affect customers and clients, rubbing them the wrong way and creating negative impressions with bottom line impact.

In our remote-controlled era, how tidy life would be if we could instantly turn off the irritation, frustration, or other kinds of upset caused by others. However, since we don't have remote controls to change people's behavior, adjustments can only be made within ourselves. This requires the willingness to absorb new information and a new perspective, some of which you might (probably!) want to resist or reject altogether.

Wherever you bear the brunt of someone's prickly behavior, you may be tempted to slap a label of "difficult" on him or her, especially when the bothersome behavior becomes frequent or even predictable. However, labeling the person rather than the behavior can be harmful for everyone involved; for a discussion on the problems associated with labeling people, see the section on Prickly Profiles on page 321 in this chapter. We invite you to read this entire chapter for pumping up your "get along power" with Pricklies.

A Prickly Person is a Matter of Personal Perspective

"We don't see things as they are, we see them as we are."

Anais Nin

While most people don't describe themselves as "difficult" (although some actually find pleasure in doing so!) difficult behavior can nonetheless come from anyone, anytime, anywhere; we all have the capacity to express it. What constitutes difficult or prickly behavior is very subjective, shaped by our personal perceptions. We each define individually what annoys or frustrates us; it's our own perception as to what causes our negative reaction.

For instance, a person may irritate us incessantly, while someone else gets along with him just fine. Likewise, we may have an easygoing relationship with someone else's Prickly Person. It's a matter of perspective that determines what behaviors we consider to be difficult, and how well we manage them when they surface. Like beauty, a Prickly Person is in the eye of the beholder. A person becomes prickly to us when they push one or more of our buttons, derail our desires, put up barriers to our goals, or have agendas different from our own.

It's an interesting revelation that everyone is eventually somebody's "Prickly Person." "Who, me?" you might ask. Probably so. Even if you typically go out of your way to get along and have excellent interpersonal skills, some situations arise that simply get the best of you and bring out a bit of the beast, transforming you into someone else's thorn!

We usually don't see ourselves as the problem, or understand how we might be contributing or causing the difficulty. When we get angry and frustrated, our emotions can provoke our own prickly behaviors, which irritate others. Our behaviors might actually be triggering reactions in others, who see us as the troublemakers.

To avoid being a thorn, it's valuable to regularly monitor how people respond to you. Do they appear intimidated? Do they avoid talking to you? Do you get a regular stream of defensive reactions? Do people stop talking when you're around? These are often telltale signs signaling their discomfort and the desire to avoid contact with you. Some thorny behaviors that quickly earn the label of "difficult" include being easily riled, argumentative, impatient, unreliable, critical, inattentive, harassing, and verbally abusive, as well as behaviors such as interrupting others, spending more time talking than listening, and blaming others. Keep in mind that prickly behavior can range from wild to mild and all the way to idle, since another annoying variation is more mild-mannered but nonetheless irritating: being lazy or slow to respond. If an honest self-assessment reveals that you have any of these behaviors, they can be disruptive to building and sustaining productive relationships.

If people aren't connecting with us, our behavior may be making connection difficult. People judge us by what they see and believe to be true about us—but their perceptions can change. When we change what we say and what we do, they notice the difference and respond to us differently as a result. With getting along as a goal, taking personal responsibility for our connections is critical to our success—as is making any necessary behavior modifications to enhance the quality and quantity of our relationships.

Degrees of Difficulty

Difficult behavior is provoked for different reasons and with varying degrees of frequency and intensity. Some prickly behavior isn't intended with malice. Actually, people are sometimes unaware that their behavior is causing problems for others and wonder why life just seems to be problematic for them. We have divided prickly behavior into three categories to differentiate different manifestations of difficult behaviors:

- **Stress-related (temporary).** Occasionally, people may exhibit prickly behaviors as coping reactions to some of life's stresses. These are considered within the range of normal responses to stressful events, albeit not pleasant or engaging ones. When people are at their wit's ends because their needs aren't being met, or they're in a crisis situation, or when life presents them with unexpected, distressful obstacles, it can bring out their "prickles." Their reactions may even be out of character for them, but they reach a breaking or a boiling point, and resort to prickly behavior as a coping mechanism.

  For example, any of the following situations would boost your stress levels: You've just arrived for your sister's wedding, and your luggage is lost ... a computer virus zaps your system and you've got a critical report due the next day, but the computer tech can't fix the problem ... you've had a tough quarter, sales continue to decline, and your job is on the line ... your colleague feels he's been upstaged and starts some juicy rumors about you ... your friend didn't back you up at work like she promised, leaving you to fight the battle alone. Or major life stressors may take you to the edge—you're going through divorce, your son's on drugs, you've been diagnosed with cancer, and you just lost your job. When stress becomes unbearable, people often act out their frustrations in unpleasant ways. Fortunately, as the stress level subsides or becomes more manageable, the prickly behavior does, too.

- **Bad chemistry.** In some cases, prickly behavior may manifest as a result of "bad chemistry" between two people who are not on the same wavelength and far from the Connection Zone. More than likely, both are exasperated by their frequently plagued or thwarted interactions. They may be "oil and water," rub each another the wrong way, set off each other's "buttons," or be a total mismatch of energy and interests. Each may get along fine with others, but the two of them together is definitely not "get along" territory. For a more detailed discussion of the dynamics of a prickly relationship, see "Prickly Ponderings" on page 315 in this chapter.

- **Persistent.** Persistently prickly people may have well-known reputations for being chronically difficult and stirring up trouble, whether at the office, at home, elsewhere, or maybe even everywhere. They may have psychological, personality, or biological disorders that inhibit their expression of better behaviors and prevent them from learning how to behave more agreeably. Their abusive, obnoxious behavior is destructive to their relationships, and often with corresponding impact on the health and well-being of those who regularly interact with them. Since they are not interested in getting along, the Persistently Prickly are especially challenging to handle.

The handling of Prickly People requires caution, special knowledge, and constant vigilance. Strategies and tips for managing your interactions and ongoing relationships with them are discussed throughout the remaining sections of this chapter.

Close Encounters with the Prickly Kind: Save Your Energy!

Since prickly behaviors pop up everywhere, we're constantly faced with making decisions about handling them, sometimes in an instant. It's a matter of picking our battles as well as honing our ability to immediately filter the event and determine how we'll respond. In other words, is it really worth making something into an issue? Is losing your peace of mind worth the price? Often, with the smaller skirmishes, it is decidedly not. Life's aggravations and irritations can rattle us, but making them into "a big deal" is not only costly to our connections—it's costly to our health and well-being, as well.

We might encounter a nasty taxi driver, a waiter with an attitude who dishes out more than fast fare, a speedy motorist who gestures rudely, or an opinionated uncle we only see at weddings and funerals. In situations

where the connection is short-lived, the stakes are low, you have little or no interest in maintaining the relationship, or you only interact with them occasionally, a good choice is to let it go, if you want to preserve your precious energy. Pick peace or pay the price.

Save yourself valuable energy by not getting riled by trivial matters. Sweating the small stuff may even escalate into big problems if you meet the wrong person at the wrong time. Playing real-life games of Trivial Pursuit—as illustrated by road-ragers, parking lot vigilantes, and other hotheads who take small matters to deadly extremes—can wreak potentially tragic consequences for themselves and others. How much better it is to put things in perspective and let go of the small affronts, minor disputes, and unintentional "slings and arrows" that mean nothing at the end of the day.

When the stakes are higher and a relationship is important to you, addressing prickly behavior that gets in the way of good connections is a necessary step. Otherwise, the ongoing friction will continue to drain your energy, and put a major strain on the relationship. See Key # 7: Bridge Connection Chasms, for more information on handling these vexing interactions.

When something rubs you the wrong way, give it the test:

- Is it a matter worth pursuing, or more of a trivial pursuit?
- Is it likely to continue? Does it matter to you whether it does?
- Would addressing the situation actually hold promise for lasting change?
- Is it an intentional aggravation? Is someone purposely trying to "get your goat," or is it an annoying behavior that just gets on your nerves, without any ill-will intended?
- Are you willing to let it go? What might be the consequences if you do?
- What would be gained by pursuing it?

> *"We make our decisions, and then*
> *our decisions turn around and make us."*
>
> F.W. Boreham

The Persistently Prickly

If you interact with Persistently Prickly people regularly, they're prone to cause you chronic wear and tear on your psyche as well as your relationship. They typically lack constructive interpersonal skills to positively influence and motivate people, instead using tactics that are counterproductive. People with poor communication and interpersonal skills often have lives that are littered with fractured friendships, workplace woes, and chronic stress. As a result, developing healthy, harmonious relationships isn't their forte; dysfunctional relationships become their norm.

The Persistent Pricklies aren't focused on getting along with you because their chief concern is satisfying their own needs rather than the needs of others. Their difficult behavior "rewards" them by enabling them to stir up reactions in other people, giving them a sense of power and control. In a distorted way, their difficult behavior is a desperate attempt to prove something to themselves and boost their feelings of self-worth.

Because the Persistent Pricklies cause chronic wear and tear on you and the relationship, getting along with them is a great challenge. Like the multi-layered artichoke, all thorns and prickles on the outside, when you peel them away, voila, there's the heart! You have to treat these thorny characters like that problematic vegetable by getting underneath all the prickly actions and demeanor (as difficult as that can sometimes be) to reveal the heart within. The real trick for maneuvering your way through encounters with the Persistently Prickly is to remember that their hearts are there, just more troublesome to access. Sometimes their thorny, protective shield simply won't permit entry.

Since they're all decked out in those irritating thorns, Pricklies are likely to become a source of stress, perhaps even high-intensity, off-the-charts stress. Dealing with them is challenging, especially because the tried-and-true techniques that typically work well with others may not be as effective or work at all with the Persistently Prickly, which further adds to your frustration.

To deal with persistently prickly behavior, you must follow winning game strategies. When you understand the game they're playing, you can then

use the appropriate strategies to position yourself to achieve your goals, reduce your stress, and preserve your self-respect—always a winning combination! It's not a game of one-upsmanship; it's played for personal, social, or professional survival.

When all parties are motivated to create win-win situations (as is usually the case, even with people who exhibit more "normal" ranges of difficult behavior), the winning strategy in the game of "Getting Along" focuses on fairness and cooperation. With the Persistently Prickly, however, the rules are modified because their motivations are different.

Because some Pricklies don't make getting along a priority, and they don't have much compassion about how their behavior affects others, they ignore rules based on cooperation and fairness; getting along or being fair isn't part of their game plan. Although they seem tough on the inside, in reality they play their prickly games out of fear—deep down, they worry about not having enough attention, enough wisdom, enough recognition, enough power. On a deeper level, they yearn to plug up the needy spaces inside themselves, which drive them to plot masterful strategies to net the prizes they seek. Unfortunately, the tactics they use are ineffective and don't fulfill their inner desires.

When you understand what lies beneath their behaviors, as well as strategies for dealing with them, you gain access to some inside plays. You avoid getting trapped in a losing position, and you score some big points for holding your ground and not getting sacked under foul conditions.

Gain a New Picture of "The Prickly Patch"

What's behind all those barbs? How do you gain a new perspective of those who frequent the Prickly Patch, all filled with thorns that puncture relationships and poke holes in connections? By looking beyond their disconnecting dynamics and focusing on what's driving their difficult behavior—in effect, by deciding to explore their world from another level. It's like tuning in to a "discovery channel" for revealing new insights and adventures in human behavior.

What might you learn by seeing beyond their angry, nasty, frustrating, or rude behavior? That chronically difficult behavior is usually driven by fear, low self-worth, and feelings of not being "enough." Those who are weighted down by this burden often use poor strategies to gain a sense of power and control, lifting that heavy weight off their shoulders and pumping them up—but knocking others down. By messing with the minds and hearts of other people, Pricklies get reactions that often provide them with a warped sense of power and control at the expense of their victims.

It may come as a surprise, but people who tend to hang out in the Prickly Patch want the same things we all want: to feel good about who they are and what they do, as well as to be loved and valued by others. Sadly, some of the methods they have learned along life's path—abuse, sabotage, intimidation, and other forms of malice—are counterproductive, and toxic to building trustworthy and reliable relationships. Since trust is what builds enduring connections and makes them thrive, those who choose to act in ways that erode trust will be distanced from the very things they desire.

When people are persistently prickly, their acting out is a reflection of what's going on inside them. While something you said or did may set them off, their behavior has little to do with you; instead, it indicates insecurities within them. This doesn't excuse their behavior, but it may give you a handle on relating to them and a better understanding of the

dynamics at work. However, this is hard to remember when they're up to their thorny tricks!

It makes a dramatic difference to look with compassion at a person exhibiting difficult behavior, enabling you to see that they may not have the internal resources to act in a more appropriate way. When you're able to change viewpoints—from believing that "They make my life difficult," to understanding that "They make reckless or misguided choices," you gain a more holistic look at the root cause. It's a pivotal shift because the new perspective demonstrates that it's not about you, even though the anguish they cause affects you. This helps you redirect your energy toward seeking ways to better support and manage yourself, instead of condemning them and compromising your peace of mind.

If you can curb your sense of outrage (which is tough when someone is in your face and their thorns are sticking in your side!), and look beyond their prickly behavior, you might be able to view them from a new perspective. Underneath their shenanigans is a desire for acceptance, even if their behavior is to the contrary. They just haven't learned effective strategies for getting what they want.

By seeing them differently, you strengthen your resolve to not let their unacceptable behaviors get the best of you, and to find constructive ways to manage them. This doesn't excuse their conduct or eliminate your aggravation or angst. Their actions are definitely misguided and sometimes far beyond understanding, but when you can see them in this light, you stand a greater chance of not taking their outrageous actions so personally.

With a commitment to create the most productive relationships even in difficult circumstances, being willing to shift your focus can dramatically change the dramas played out in the Prickly Patch.

Positive Strategies for Managing Prickly Behavior

Getting a more global perspective about what's at the core of the prickles is valuable, but what can you do to handle them, manage your own reactions, and get unstuck from their drain on your energy?

While prickly personalities often need a humongous heaping of TLC (tender loving care), what you need is self-protection and an assortment of useful strategies for handling them—whether the Prickly Person is a wisecracking member of your team, a nanny with an attitude, an insulting supervisor, an employee with a perpetual short fuse, the chairperson who constantly interrupts, or the bully who coaches your daughter's soccer team.

Handling prickly behavior involves establishing what outcomes you want from the relationship and focusing on achieving those results by expressing your rights, needs, concerns, and ideas in appropriate ways. It means choosing wisdom rather than revenge, and focusing on connection rather than contention. You always have a choice about how to respond to anyone, at anytime. Even though we can't control all the events and situations that befall us, we can control our responses to them.

From the know-it-all neighbor to the chronically complaining colleague, you always have a choice about how to react to prickly behavior. Since you are responsible for how you respond—even when people don't do what you want them to do or treat you the way you'd like to be treated—you have the power to direct your experiences. How you handle each interaction determines whether you create bigger problems or reduce or even eliminate them entirely.

Your response does make a difference in the outcome of the interaction, so it's important to consider the probable consequences of your choice. One way to look at this question is to try to determine what you have to gain or lose with each choice you make. Raging back at someone who vents hostility at you, or blaming them for the headaches and frustrations they cause, won't facilitate communication and cooperation.

Instead, take the time (beforehand if possible) to calculate how they will react to your response. Will your becoming explosive, vindictive, or rattling off a chain of expletives actually create the outcomes you desire? More likely, these behaviors will escalate the degree of difficulty, or even ratchet up the intensity a notch or two. Before reacting instinctively to the Prickly Person's misbehavior, determine which response will help you obtain your outcome.

The most difficult step involves doing the only thing you can ever do to contend with problematic people: change your way of thinking about and responding to them. Changing your way of thinking and reacting can dramatically transform the field of interaction. By assuming control of your responses, and eliminating any impossible desire to control others, you gain more power.

You manage prickly behavior best by managing yourself, using assertive strategies to pump up your power in dealing with them. Over time, when Pricklies recognize the change in the pattern, their behavior may change, too. Unfortunately though, there are never any guarantees in how people will ultimately respond, even with the most intense wishful thinking!

Prickly People are perplexing. Their misbehavior causes us anguish, often with gut-wrenching and heart-pounding intensity. However, when we have greater awareness as to why a behavior upsets us, it helps diffuse its draining energy. Instead of getting caught up in the same relationship dynamics, we can focus on managing both ourselves and the prickly behavior. This requires us to disrupt and replace our ineffective patterns with new ones. By modifying our internal and external language patterns, body language, and emotions, we gain greater freedom from all the agony and distress.

Research has proven that taking positive action in a negative situation can actually reduce your fear and anxiety. Even if your new response doesn't change how the Prickly Person responds (and it may not), you gain greater confidence in your ability to manage yourself in challenging interactions.

The first step in taking action is to gain awareness of what's causing the energy-draining dynamics. To get to the heart of the matter, identify just

PRICKLY PONDERINGS

To gain a better understanding of some of the personal dynamics associated with prickly behavior, ask yourself the following:

- Which behaviors specifically upset me or cause me to react?

- How do I respond to them?

- What might I be doing that may be reinforcing these behaviors?

- How is the person being served by their behavior?

- What do I really want or need from the person that I'm not getting (such as appreciation for my work, understanding my perspectives, or communicating with respect)?

- Does this behavior remind me of other energy-draining relationships I've had and is it repeating those same or similar dynamics?

- What are some of the judgments I've made or continue to make about this person?

- What is within my power to control in this situation?

- What are the things that are beyond my control?

- What steps can I take to make the relationship work better, and am I willing to take them?

- If the negative behavior continues to be unacceptable, unproductive, and energy-draining, what are my options?

how you feel you're being attacked, manipulated, or being forced to cope with a difficult behavior. Clarify the exact nature of the behavior that's upsetting you; be specific, not subjective. If the person is rude, how is he or she rude? Does he or she interrupt you? Have bad manners? Swear at you? Curtly reject your suggestions? By understanding what they are doing to press your buttons, and observing how you respond, you acquire valuable insights. As you recognize these dynamics and change how you respond in turn, the drama can lose its draining punch.

The following sections will help you learn specific strategies for masterfully managing yourself, and dealing effectively with Prickly People. Doing so may actually improve how they respond to you. Hopefully, you'll find yourself wonderfully free of (or at least with less intense) headaches, heartache, and a pile of prickles!

Handle with Care

Here are some general sanity-saving strategies for handling jabs, stabs, and other prickly behavior. More specific strategies are listed in the profiles of prickly behaviors featured later in this chapter:

- **Approach the situation from a problem-solving perspective.** Focusing on ways to improve the situation itself, rather than trying to remedy its consequent emotional wear-and-tear, puts your attention on creating solutions.

- **Explore how you might be playing the role of a victim.** Since we're creatures of habits, we fall into predictable patterns. Observe how you might be playing into any prickly behavior. What triggers or perpetuates the problem behavior? For instance, if you become the target of a verbal sharpshooter's high-velocity put-down, rising to the bait fuels their fire. When they dish it out, if you get hooked into responding in kind or trying to outdo them, you've won a starring role in their personal drama. Ask yourself, "How do I play into this behavior? What am I doing that might be feeding it?"

- **Change responses that aren't getting the desired results.** By not rising to someone's bait, what happens? The game (let's call it Time to Terrorize Tamika) ends when you no longer react to their ridicule or insults. Many Pricklies delight in squeezing reactions from their victims by belittling, humiliating, or embarrassing them—their payoff is in making others feel or look bad so they can feel superior. If you don't play, the game is usually over and Pricklies will likely find other victims to torment.

- **Establish and maintain clear boundaries.** If anyone behaves in ways that are not fair, courteous, or right, it is your duty to let them know when he or she crosses the line of acceptable behavior. However, people may be unintentionally encroaching upon your boundaries; they certainly won't even know they exist, unless they understand what they are. Normally, if people overstep your boundaries, they will respect them when you tell them tactfully. See Speak Your Truth on page 258 in Key #7: Bridge Connection Chasms. On the other hand, Prickly People may intentionally test you to see, in effect, if and where you "mark your turf." They are deterred by your firmness and standing your ground. They usually leave the people alone who won't let them get away with their misbehavior, so don't tolerate their mistreatment.

There are a number of first-line strategies to use to let Prickly People know when they've gone too far. One is to give them a blank stare, the "Look"—a silent, expressionless stare (made famous by many parents) that says they've crossed the line. Another potent expression is a scowl of utter disgust, complete with a raised upper lip, squinty eyes, open mouth, and wrinkled nose (a look that says it all!). You can also respond verbally to make it clear that they're out of line: "Excuse me, what did you just say?" Additional effective responses are listed in various strategies highlighted in the Prickly Profiles section of this chapter.

- **Plan positive responses.** How can you develop a positive response to a negative situation? Plan your responses in advance to maintain your self-respect and satisfy your needs without abusing or violating the self-respect of others. Giving a positive response means that you express your rights, needs, concerns, and ideas, in appropriate ways, while engaging in assertive, not aggressive behaviors (except, where bullies are concerned, as a last resort). This means voicing your needs without violating the rights and needs of others.

- **Decide what you will say and do (or not say and do)!** Planning a new response in advance of repetitive, thorny problems, as

described in more detail throughout this chapter, can help you nip problems in the bud and minimize negative relationship dynamics. Look at your options and decide which responses will create the most positive outcomes. Decide what you will say (or not say) and what you will do (or not do) to create those desirable results.

- **Constantly visualize your new ways of responding.** Get clear on what actions you can and will take. Then, draw on your courage and fortitude to follow through. Play out your desired responses repeatedly in your mind, "rehearsing" how you will respond to the person or people involved when you encounter them. For more information on using visualization to help change behaviors, see Call on Your Courage: See Yourself as Brave on page 42 in Key # 1: Cultivate Confidence, The Cornerstone of Connection.

- **Project confidence through your body language, tone of voice, and choice of words.** Adjust anything that might be sending out signals of negativity, defensiveness, or weakness. Maintain eye contact. See the section on body language throughout Key #2: Rev Up Rapport, and projecting confidence throughout Key #1: Cultivate Confidence: The Cornerstone of Connection.

- **To neutralize your instinctive reactions to prickly behavior, observe your thoughts and emotions.** If you automatically expect difficulty, you'll be on the lookout for it and ready to catch Pricklies at their game no matter how they behave. Meet each interaction fresh, and focus on reaching solutions and desired outcomes, such as repeating to yourself "I want to talk about this calmly and rationally."

- **Use positive self-talk to reinforce your determination to create desired outcomes.** Repeat messages such as "I am committed to working with this person in a positive way." "I can handle this." "I am a strong, confident, capable person, and I can handle this." Avoid negative inner dialogue that demonizes the person, escalates your emotions, or fills you with dread or feelings of helplessness: "Why me?" "Why do I always have to deal with this impossible person!"

- **Focus on your breathing.** Deep breathing from your diaphragm helps to disengage your body's automatic fight-or-flight response and gives you a critical moment of calm during which to make choices that create better outcomes. A sense of calm is vital to dealing rationally with situations that activate anger. Tuning in to your breathing, rather than fueling anger-provoking thoughts, enables you to focus on producing productive responses. Slow down your rate of speech to remain rational rather than reactive.

- **Keep your cool!** The more you react to them, the less influence you have over the situation. Maintain your personal power. Remember that you're in control of your responses. See the section on Master Emotional Control on page 265 in Key #7: Bridge Connection Chasms.

- **Each time a difficult behavior arises, use assertive strategies.** If you find yourself back in the same old situation again, remember your new approach. Conviction will keep you strong; it's easy to fall back into old habits, especially when your buttons are being pushed. Refocus on your new plan of response. What will you say? How do you want to act for the best outcomes? Then do your absolute, determined best to follow through in creating those results.

- **Seek support.** Remember that you don't have to go it alone in your quest for getting along. Talk to a friend or seek the support of other trusted individuals. If the difficult relationship is at work, a supervisor or your company's human resources department may be able to offer assistance. Dealing with difficult behaviors is stressful and can impact your physical, mental, and emotional health. Professional guidance, counseling, and other support systems can safely guide you through challenging situations as well as providing much-needed relief.

WHEN IT'S ROUGH ON THE OUTSIDE...

EXPLORE TO THE CORE

Getting beyond the angry, nasty, or rude isn't easy. Holding to the belief that there's a universal desire for connection keeps me focused on seeing beyond the ornery, obnoxious, or out-of-control appearances. I've had my share of opportunities to test this belief system in real-life encounters with some pesky personalities (and this is when the enduring connection becomes somewhat of an endurance test!)

I once worked with a graphic designer (we'll call her Glenda), who held a very powerful position in terms of getting the organization's materials designed and printed. Unfortunately, Glenda always seemed to have a chip on her shoulder and an ongoing need to gripe. She was well-known by the entire staff for her bad attitude, and people chronically complained about her complaining!

Glenda had a reputation for delaying projects if you were on her "bad side"—a side you didn't ever want to be on. Because I was responsible for volumes of printed material and committed to doing my best, I made it a priority to get along with Glenda in the best way possible. This was not without obstacles. Her scowling face, sarcasm, and negativity were big barriers, but I was determined to break through them to secure a good working relationship.

I had to "walk my talk" to keep our relationship on an even keel. Whenever I had to visit her department, I'd take a deep breath and review my positive intention to create a good relationship. My goal was to drill down beyond her dismal demeanor to reveal her diamond qualities that were there, just hidden away.

Initially, I received a chilly reception, but each time I greeted her with a smile and added a few splashes of humor. She was a frowner, so I was determined to see even the slightest sliver of a smile across her face. Little by little, the reception became warmer, and her heavy heart seemed to lighten. With my determined intention to look beyond what I saw on the outside, and to focus on what I knew was there on the inside, we eventually got along quite well and enjoyed a very productive working relationship. —S.S.

Prickly Profiles: A Colorful Cast of Connection-Crushing Characters

A colorful array of prickly behaviors pops up in plenty of places, often with fairly predictable MO's (modus operandi or ways of operating). These connection-crushing qualities are hazardous to be around and put relationships at risk. Taking a peek into their prickly plays can help you understand what's probably prompting those prickles; once you know their exact game, it's easier to implement winning plays. Approaching prickly behaviors strategically helps you score in the game of getting along, especially under foul conditions.

For the purpose of profiling and identifying connection-crushing patterns, we've named some of the more classic behaviors exhibited by Prickly People. We do so with this caveat—that you label the behavior, not the person! Labeling the behavior helps you understand underlying motives and manage interactions more strategically. Labeling the person sets you up to expect only negative behavior from them. Use the labels only to identify and understand; then let the label go, so it doesn't continue to color your responses. For a further discussion on the negative effects of labeling people, see Let Go of Labels on page 274 in Key #7: Bridge Connection Chasms.

Although it's not possible to lump all prickly behavior into one huge pile of prickles, the following profiles describe some of their more universally known maneuvers. In addition, these are the types that are asked about most often by participants attending our programs.

Some of these behaviors overlap. For instance, someone expressing Bully behaviors can also spew like a Volcano, attack like a Barbed Bomber, or hog the floor like a Monopolizer Maniac. Remember to focus on managing the specific behavior rather than affixing a permanent label.

Back-Attackers and Buzzer Bees

Back-attackers, also known as back-stabbers, might seem easy-going, even complacent, with a "don't worry" attitude—but don't let them deceive you. At heart they're double-dealing hypocrites with sabotage in mind. Their strategy is to be nice to your face and act like your best friend, lulling you into a false sense of security that tricks you into revealing information you really don't want them to have. They fish for some morsels of ammunition to fire back when you're unsuspecting; then they attack behind your back, bad-mouthing or implicating you. They may lie and deny their involvement, even by pointing fingers at others as the source of their malicious mischief.

Back-attackers may oppose some action you've taken and try to outwit you in order to gain control over the issue. You may have done something that irked them, so you become their "target" practice.

By calling them on their game, you take away their satisfaction with their own cleverness and prevent them from exulting in their sense of power (false though it may be). When dealing with them, be vigilant and watch your back!

Tips for Handling Back-Attackers

Take action to stop back-attacking behaviors from recurring with these strategies:

- Gather your evidence with concrete examples, if possible, of exactly what was said, to whom, and other specifics related to the incident. You'll stand on much firmer ground with facts rather than just hearsay.

- Whether you can document the situation or must rely on rumors or other reports, discuss the remarks openly with them. Use a calm, gentle tone and ask them to specify whatever accusations they've made: "Britney, I'd appreciate you clearing up some confusion. It's come to my attention that you said (describe the content). Please tell me what you mean."

- Give them a graceful exit. If they deny their actions (and they probably will), let it go by saying, "Oh, I'm glad to hear that the information given to me was an exaggeration and you didn't mean it as criticism." This also serves as a subtle warning that you're on to their games. Don't argue if they deny their intent to harm.

- Tell them the behavior you expect in the future. "Next time, let me know exactly how you feel before discussing this with anyone else."

- If you actually did make a mistake in accusing them of the particular behavior or incident, apologize. Providing an apology is a sign of strength, not weakness.

GETTING ALONG MEANS HAVING TO SAY YOU'RE SORRY

If a hurtful remark should ever roll off your tongue, flow out of your mouth, and end up hurting someone's feelings, make amends as quickly as possible to repair the damage. Extend a sincere apology with more than just "I'm sorry." Tell the wronged party exactly why you're sorry for what you did and how you regret hurting them, so they know you have accepted responsibility for your misjudgment.

Give them an opportunity to air their feelings and listen so they know they've been heard and you understand what that experience caused them. Even with your gestures to make amends, they may not be willing to forgive you right away; it's important to respect their need for some time to heal from the verbal wounding or from the feeling of betrayal.

Sincere apologies are courageous acts for restoring broken connections.

Variation: Buzzer Bees

Buzzer Bees love the buzz and they pollinate it everywhere! Their behavior is poisonous to good morale. They gossip about others, pick up the buzz, and pass it quickly through the grapevine, often distorting the truth. They love getting private information, then using it to embarrass others, as well as delivering bad news (especially when it's negative) under the pretext of "helping." Buzzer Bees have a special way of twisting information and fingering the blame on others.

Since they're masters at working the grapevine, avoid talking about Buzzer Bees behind their backs. Before confronting them with their misdeeds, get the facts: What was said? To whom? How it was said, and when? If you become a target, let them know you're aware of their involvement by approaching them with the information. Request that in the future they tell you directly whenever something negative is circulating (as described in the section on Back Attackers).

When a Buzzer Bee approaches, it's best to keep out of the rumor mill by clearly stating your desire to steer clear:

- *I don't think this is a very appropriate subject for us to talk about.*

- *I'm not interested in talking about that and I don't think (Name of Target) would appreciate it either.*

> *"Gossip is nothing more than mouth-to-mouth recitation."*
>
> Source unknown

Barb Bombers

Barb Bombers get juiced by using others as players in their favorite pastime, the game of "You're It!" They fire off verbal bullets of sarcasm and insults. While some sarcasm is innocent and not intended to hurt, it often has a vicious component. Bombers' assaults might stem from their feeling unappreciated, unacknowledged, or uncomfortable talking about what's bothering them. Sarcasm is a form of passive-aggressive behavior that masks anger underneath a layer of humor, directed toward their target. They may poke at your sensitive spots as part of their "good-natured ribbing," which isn't at all funny.

Sometimes victims of these attacks (and bystanders) laugh or smile in response—but often uneasily because they're unclear as to the Bomber's intent. The classic response is for the Victim to act as if nothing hurtful, negative, or sarcastic has been said. If he or she responds to the jab, the Bomber may say, "Oh, I was just joking. Can't you take a joke? Don't be so sensitive!"

A comeback that shows you're on to the Bomber's game: *"Truthfully, it really wasn't funny and didn't make me laugh."*

Here's another sound bite from a Barb Bomber in action:

You: *"Maybe it's my imagination, but it seems that some of the remarks you made during my presentation were sarcastic. Was there something I said that bothered you?"*

Bomber: *"Oh, c'mon! Where's your sense of humor?"*

You: *"I enjoy a good joke, too, but that sure seemed like an insult. It didn't feel very funny and didn't come across that way. I'd appreciate you not doing that anymore."*

Tips for Handling Barb Bombers

- Don't laugh at their remarks when either you or others have been attacked, which encourages repetition. Don't put up with put-downs!

- Ask them to repeat their remark: "Excuse me, what did you say?" Bombers don't expect their victims to ask them to repeat their sarcasm or insults. It puts them on the defensive and they're less likely to attack you in the future.

- Recognize the intent to harm; don't make excuses for the behavior. If the Bomber knows of a special sensitivity and "goes for the jugular," respond by saying, "I'm surprised you'd make such hurtful comments about that, especially knowing how I feel."

- If there is some truth to any part of the statement, respond to the presumption or implied statement, not the insult:

  Bomber: "Your presentation sure got results yesterday. I heard the XYZ account exec snored through half of it!"

  You: "It got results alright. While their account exec was dozing off, XYZ's buyer was totally alert and called in their approval to proceed with the order this morning."

- Question the Bomber's intention. Ask directly for an explanation:

  - *What did you mean?*

  - *Why would you say that?*

  - *Could you please explain?*

  - *What is it about (name the issue or subject) that you don't like?*

  Direct questions force the Bomber to make specific comments—probing for the truth usually makes them feel uncomfortable because they're being called upon to own up to their insults.

- Turn the tables. Deflect the jab: "Are you having such a horrible, no-good day that you're taking your frustrations out on me?" "Do you get your kicks trying to make people feel bad?"

- Humor can be an effective antidote. It shows that you're up to their tests in jest! Using self-deprecating humor or having some quick comebacks on hand makes you laugh instead of squirm and throws them an unexpected curve. Some insults can be exaggerated, taken to extremes, and used to your advantage. Prepare for a likely attack on a perceived target (such as your height, weight, or hair loss) with some appropriate comeback or self-deprecating remarks. When you prove to be an impermeable target and don't have a meltdown over their insults, they miss out on the "Gotcha!"

- If you're targeted in public and embarrassed by the Bomber's remarks, respond immediately. "(Name), that's a very inappropriate remark." If the Bomber responds with an apology such as, "Oh, so sorry to have embarrassed you," leverage that apology as a touché: "Actually, I think you embarrassed yourself." Responding in public provides you with a positioning tactic since you're likely to get sympathy from others.

- If you're attacked about an idea at a meeting, encourage others to give their input to flush out your allies. Should the critical comments continue, use the group's collective energy to find a solution. For example:

Bomber: "Where did you get that stupid idea? What makes you think you could succeed when others have tried this 'brilliant' idea before? You're an idiot if you think that would work!"

You: "(Name), I understand that you've got the good of our company at heart and you're really working hard on mapping out a strategy to win the contract. I realize how critical this new plan is to you. However, there's no need to say insulting things since we all have creative ideas to share. I've been reassessing this project and think we might have a better chance of having it approved if we considered this alternative plan instead. Now, what do the rest of you think about this plan? Do you think it might work? I want us to do whatever is best for this project."

Bullies

Bullies play out their cruel games everywhere. No matter their size, shape, age, or where you find them, bullies are masters of manipulation. To gain control, they deliberately intimidate others and knowingly abuse their rights. They're not interested in getting along, cooperating, or creating win-win situations; they just want to control, win, and rule. Bullies reject reason and rational efforts. As a result, they diminish, demean, and dictate, all as part of their plan to dominate.

Bullies act superior, as reflected by their characteristic condescending attitude of arrogance. When something isn't up to their approval, they see others as inept and incompetent, and go on a rampage, snarling about how awful and stupid everyone is. They feel quite justified in their outrage, treating people with disdain and disrespect.

Bullies are blamers—blaming everyone else for what goes wrong. They want to have the last word, although they won't admit fault or apologize. To apologize means that they are taking responsibility for their actions. Since they don't see how something could actually be their fault, they don't apologize. In fact, they often demand to know why you are giving them such a hard time!

They wield their power with aggression, both verbal and physical. Bullies are experts in character assassination and take particular pleasure in aiming their viciousness at others' tender spots. When they perceive a weakness, they use it as a vulnerable point for entering your psyche to deliberately erode your confidence and self-esteem. Since Bullies are masters of blame and criticism, you may end up questioning your competence, wisdom, and worth, making you even more susceptible to the onslaught of Bully attacks.

In personal relationships, Bullies love to control every arena of your life, from how you spend your time to who you spend it with. As a result, they're excellent guilt-trippers, and possessive by nature; they often

become resentful when you're with other people or doing things you enjoy. Possessive by nature, they keep you isolated from other relationships, depriving you of the input, perspectives, and support of others. That makes it much easier for them to indoctrinate you with their erroneous and erratic thinking.

Bullies play mind games and deliberately contradict themselves to confuse their targets. They break promises and deny your criticisms, warping your sense of reality. This keeps you second-guessing and wondering if you've lost your mind. Feeling deflated, de-valued, and rattled by the ravages of a Bully's behavior, our inner critic senses shame and begins to accept the allegations and propaganda as our new reality. All this maneuvering messes with your head and heart and keeps you off balance, enabling the Bullies to keep you just where they want you— confused, vulnerable, and disempowered. Tyrants terrorize and their targets' world becomes topsy turvy and torn apart.

In line with their stereotype, Bullies use aggressive body language, pick fights, and are prone to physical violence. They also verbally pick on people who won't fight back, especially targeting "nice" people who like to get along and who tend to give up and give in rather than make a scene or escalate the problem. However, "nice pays a price" when it comes to Bullies. Bullies take advantage of people with big hearts or who refuse to be firm with them. As a result, Bullies get away with trampling over those who don't establish boundaries, which they interpret to mean that they've got free rein. Allowing Bullies to trespass on your needs and desires sends them a signal that it's OK to do so.

Bullies can be charming in public and even admired for their appealing natures, but still turn dastardly in private. Others may not witness their mean streak. They may criticize, condemn, and disgrace you, then try twisting themselves back into your accepting graces. They break promises and deny your criticisms, warping your sense of reality.

At its worst, Bully behavior can be caused by more deep-seated personality problems such as psychological, emotional, biological, or mental disorders. Bullies' brain biochemistry, coupled with environmental and psychological factors, can ignite their verbal volatility. They might be bipolar, with manic-depressive mood swings making them highly reactive and easily provoked, have drug or alcohol problems, or suffer from schizophrenia or other mental dysfunctions, and as a result, be unable to relate properly. While their behavior may be outrageous as well as unacceptable, filtering it through these factors as possible explanations may make it seem less personally directed. It doesn't excuse the behavior, just gives you some insights as to what might be causing it.

Being around Bullies is exhausting. Seeking professional intervention may be required and well-advised for handling the complexities of Bully behavior as well as for your own safety. Family members or loved ones should encourage or help Bullies to get therapeutic treatment for the benefit of all.

Tips for Handling Bullies

Adopt strategies that support your ability to stand up to them and stand your ground:

- Take an assertive approach early to prevent escalation. Bullies will likely continue to target you unless you establish and enforce your boundaries.

   Demonstrate that unacceptable behavior is unacceptable to you. Let them know they can't get away with it. Silence gives them the green light, so establish and maintain clear boundaries to ensure your needs and desires are respected. Speak your piece to keep your peace.

- Be forceful. When people don't respond to peaceful, reasonable approaches, it's appropriate to become more aggressive in dealing with them to equalize the balance of power. However, never resort to physical aggression. Bullies are out to win only what they want and try to dominate you in the process, which is an infringement of your rights. By showing them that you mean business in how you communicate, you're preserving your rights and they will likely back off. Keep your senses and act wisely.

- Hold Bullies accountable for their actions. Remember, they don't want to cooperate with you, just control you.

- Avoid giving them long explanations about your actions. The more reasons you give, the more they can manipulate and twist them around and fire them back at you. Be clear that certain things are non-negotiable and not open to debate.

- Don't get hooked by their taunts. If you're tempted to retort "That's not true!" drop it; instead, address them by name and tell them to stop: "(Name), stop!". Take command with some body language: extend your arm about shoulder-height with your palm facing toward them or use the universal "T" gesture for time-out.

- State your demands, using "you" statements. (Note: this is an exception to the recommendation for using "I" statements in more civil exchanges.) People acting aggressively often run roughshod over statements made from personal perspectives and are more likely to fling them right back at you. Tell them what you want in a firm way; it will get their attention: "You need to speak to me with courtesy and in a civil tone."

- Take the time you need to make decisions rather than be pressured by them. If they continue to put on the squeeze, hold your ground and freedom to choose when you're ready. Insist on fair treatment.

- Speak with authority and with a commanding presence. Any perceived weakness makes you susceptible to being bullied. For a discussion about cultivating your inner courage, see Key #1: Call on Your Courage: See Yourself as Brave.

- Recognize their attempts to make you feel bad when you don't give them what they want. Avoid making unacceptable compromises and refuse their unreasonable requests. Consider the potential consequences when dealing with them. Don't let their unacceptable behavior prompt you to take action that would be detrimental to your best interests.

A BEAST IN BUSINESS

One of my very dear friends, whose name for the bully protection program is Belinda, had several encounters with bullies over the past year, her latest being a building contractor who bullied his way through the entire construction of her sun room addition. Belinda has a reputation for transforming negative energy with her joyful presence. In fact, we've conducted many success seminars together and her radiance always brings out the best in our participants. Yet she was absolutely astounded how her normally outstanding conflict resolution and "people skills" tactics didn't work with him.

The sun room wasn't being constructed with the same quality Belinda and her husband expected. Belinda showed the contractor exactly where repairs were needed and diplomatically requested them. This is when he showed his true bully colors, launching into a tirade, called her demanding and unreasonable, and making other intimidating remarks. He unleashed his ABC nature in force (aggressive, belligerent, and cantankerous), and attempted to make the repairs she had requested.

In the end, his work was still not the quality they had expected and he had promised. Belinda said, "He had about 100 reasons why things were the way they were, projecting a defiant attitude of 'How dare you even question my ability or quality of work'!" Even worse, their new addition had become such an exasperating experience that it came to symbolize "the project from hell," robbing them of the desired pleasure from their sizable investment of resources.

(Continued on next page)

(Continued from last page)

When he showed up to collect the final payment, she firmly expressed her displeasure. He proceeded to twist her words and rattle her to such a degree that she just wanted the whole ugly mess to be over. She wrote him the check, knowing that without the incentive to make the repairs they wouldn't get done. Belinda said it was the price she paid to never have to see him again. On one hand, she admitted, it saved her from more emotional wear and tear. But on the other hand, she knew he had manipulated her, drained her, and gotten just what he wanted.

This incident strengthened her resolve to arm herself with strategies to not let another bully get the best of her. Watch out, world—Belinda's armed and ready as a 5'2" tower of power, never to yield to bully tactics again! —S.S.

- Offer them options instead of an ultimatum to help them save face. Mean what you say by standing firm and following through.

- Do the unexpected, such as retorting with humor, to break the mold of what they think will be your reaction. This throws them off balance.

- Name their game. When you detect manipulation, reveal their hand by saying "I see what you're doing." This tells them that you're on to their game and won't be a player. Proceed with determination that you won't be a pawn on their chessboard.

Don't tolerate intolerable situations. Take responsibility for constantly monitoring your needs and recognizing when they're not being honored. Seek support from health professionals, counselors, human resource departments, friends, family, and other sources of assistance. Chronic exposure to bully behavior puts your physical, emotional, and mental health at risk. Protect your health and well-being. Keep in touch with the truth—that you are wise, courageous, and worthy of respectful treatment.

Because many prickly personality behaviors overlap, review the other profiles for additional information.

Grumblies:
Whiners, Grumblers, and Grouches

The Grumblies forecast: Gloom and doom, with 100 percent chance of something going wrong or never being quite right.

There's nothing that drains the creative, productive, and buoyant environment of enthusiasm faster than the Grumblies, a family of killjoys that includes complainers, cynics, fault-finders, and other types of pessimists. When you're committed to sustaining a positive atmosphere, they're a formidable, negative force to reckon with.

These curmudgeons relish playing the "Ain't it awful!" game, grumbling, groaning, complaining, and whining about nearly everything—other people, situations, events that can't be changed, and life in general. In their book, nothing ever goes right. They're masters at fault-finding and blaming others for their mistakes.

Their cynical comments, such as "It's not going to work!" or "No one cares," spreads negativity like a highly contagious disease. Others often "catch" what they've got and start whining and griping as well. This infectious phenomenon is deadly everywhere. Because this malady is so contagious, it's wise to inoculate yourself against its draining effects. Anticipate situations and pull out positive strategies, powering up your positive self-talk statements ("I am enthusiastic about this new project!") to counter the negative ones that arise from Grumblers: "There you go again with another crazy, no-good idea!"

There's a big difference between legitimate complaints and nonstop whining or fault-finding. See Key # 7: Bridge Connection Chasms, for a detailed discussion. Grumblies are perpetual fault-finders. While they may feel justified in their complaints, they persistently play the role of victim. But they usually don't take any action to improve their condition—they're addicted to moaning and groaning about it. Some Grumblies simply "do life" with that pattern so firmly entrenched even presenting them with a compelling case for cultivating a good attitude won't change it.

Grumblies are not interested in solutions, because their attention comes from not having any solutions! Investing their time and energy in finding and working on solutions would reduce or eliminate their grumbling about the problem. Even while working on a solution, they may continue to poke holes and find fault with it. Grumblies are resistant to change, so talk to them about the benefits of an anticipated change: "This new system will dramatically improve the processing of paychecks."

Grumblies are particularly challenging for optimists. Avoid letting their pessimistic attitude squash your optimism. Demonstrate enthusiasm in what you say and how you communicate with them. Ask them to voice positive comments relating what might be good and valuable instead of always reporting doom and gloom—whether at meetings, family events, vacations, or anywhere negativity looms.

Tips for Handling Whiners, Grumblers, and Grouches

- Ask them to describe the problem and explain their judgments. Let them voice their concerns about the situation: Who's involved? What happened? Where's the problem? What results is it having? For a further discussion, see Pinpoint Problems on page 281 in Key #7: Bridge Connection Chasms.

- Acknowledge the nature of the complaint. Agree with what you can:

  - *I see how this could be affecting staff performance.*

  - *It sounds like the current procedures are causing a snag in getting everyone to cooperate.*

  - *You're probably right that it might not work; but I'm confident in our abilities.*

- Ask them for suggestions in finding solutions; use directed questions, as listed below. This makes Grumblies responsible for coming up with ways to alleviate things they believe aren't working well.

  - *What do you suggest?*

  - *What would you like to see happen?*

  - *What can I do to help you handle this situation?*

- *If you feel this isn't working (or won't work), can you suggest some ways it might work (or work better)?*

- Agree on an acceptable solution or offer your recommendations along with the specific actions that are required to get the desired results. If appropriate, set a time to follow-up to monitor the effectiveness of the action.

Rx for the Grumblies

> *"Blessed are the happiness makers. Blessed are they*
> *who know how to shine on one's gloom with their cheer."*
>
> Henry Ward Beecher

Sometimes it's useful for Grumblies to learn how their attitude isn't serving them. They may be so busy complaining that they don't notice how other people are responding to them and their comments. Describing the impact of their behavior can alert them to a new level of awareness and willingness to adjust their attitudes: "It's just my observation, (Name), but it may be in your own best interest to find a better way of expressing your views during meetings. Some staffers think your comments are hindering the goals of the project. It may work to your advantage to find more effective ways to express your concerns."

Another technique is for you take on the role of facilitator, providing the Grumbly with an opportunity to assess the impact of his or her negative attitude:

- *I'm not sure why you have such a gloomy picture of our operation.*

- *It's surprising that you're still working here when you keep finding so many things you dislike about our company.*

- *I wonder why you seem to delight in shooting holes into so many of our ideas.*

- *It seems like you do things on purpose to derail our goals.*

> *"When opportunity knocks, a grumbler complains about the noise."*
>
> Source unknown

GRUMBLIES BEWARE! FAULT-FINDING IS HAZARDOUS TO YOUR HAPPINESS

If you notice that you grumble, groan, and tend to "awfulize," you can be setting yourself up for more misery. Here are 10 good reasons to stop grumbling and groaning:

1. Makes people want to avoid you
2. Destroys respect people may have for you otherwise
3. Pollutes the atmosphere
4. Creates negative programming in your brain
5. Attracts negative people (misery loves company!)
6. Makes you feel worse and brings down others around you
7. Increases your stress level
8. Reinforces negative energy
9. Gives power to problems rather than solutions
10. Drains you of productive energy

People don't like Grumblies because hearing constant complaining gets on their nerves. They don't need any more problems to pile on top of their already overtaxed stress levels. Plus, they often stop listening and tune you out, even when you have valid complaints.

Whining doesn't serve your best interests. If you want to improve your chances of getting more of what you want, get all those awful thoughts out of your system. Gather up your "Ain't it awful!" attitude—all the reasons why life's unfair, how mistreated you feel, how others get all the lucky breaks, and how hopeless it all seems. Then, throw yourself a short-lived pity party, inviting all your negative thoughts to it. Wallow in them for a while, but when you've purged them, quit complaining! Don't allow chronic negativity to sap any more of your energy, or contaminate anyone else with it. Incessant fault-finding may also be a symptom associated with chronic depression, in which case therapeutic assistance is advised.

Invite thoughts of gratitude and appreciation as an antidote to all the awful, no-good, dirty, rotten ones. Think about some ways you're willing to improve your situation, and act on them. Focus on solutions, not sorrow; cultivate good connections, not toxic ones. Misery may love company, but who really loves to keep company with those who focus on finding fault?

Know-It-Alls

"It's what we learn after we know it all that counts."

A.C. Carlson

Their name says it all. They believe they have all the right answers and know what's best for everyone. The problem is that deep down, they know that they really don't know it all; their behavior is a cover-up for their feelings of inadequacy. They pretend to know everything; being right makes them feel validated, which temporarily eases their feelings of insecurity.

Know-It-Alls don't listen to the opinions of others and offer information or advice whether it's asked for or not. Their smug, superior attitude implies that others are stupid, weak, and inferior; they speak with a tone of authority, even when addressing issues outside their expertise. Know-It-Alls relish saying, "I told you so!" if you fail to follow their advice. They can't be right without making you wrong, so they persist at the know-it-all game in order to gain a feeling of power, albeit a false power.

Some Know-It-Alls are perfectionists by nature and have plenty of talent to offer; yet they can flaunt their intelligence and competence, turning people off in the process. They're sometimes so self-absorbed that they need a reality check. Depending on your role or relationship to them, you might open their eyes regarding how their behavior is getting in the way of their success or positive connections: "Chan, you have such tremendous talent and knowledge. I've noticed though, the way you treat people sometimes gets in the way of their accepting your brilliant ideas." This can send a well-intentioned message or open a much-needed conversation designed for improving a Know-It-All's connections.

When they're challenged, it exposes their raw feelings of inadequacy, the part they're so desperately trying to cover-up, so deal with them gently to give them the validation they seek.

Tips for Handling Know-It-Alls

- Give credit to them when they're right, but resist the temptation to rub it in when they're wrong.

- Don't discount, discredit, or disagree. Validate their ideas first and then introduce your own: "Justin, that's certainly a possibility. Here's what I thought."

- If they deliver information with a surly tone, tell them that while their advice is instructive, their tone is a turn-off.

- If you should be a recipient of their favorite line, "I told you so!" respond that such a statement isn't productive, focusing on the consequences of such a comment.

- If you have concerns about the validity of what they say, ask probing questions as well as verifying their information to keep them on their toes. Ask "what if" questions to put their logic to the test. Have them play out worst-case scenarios as a way of checking the legitimacy of their suggestions:

  Know-it-All: "Remember, the last time how well my plan worked with the ORI client? I know it would work just as well on this account. My plan is really the only way for us to handle this situation. After all, I've been working with the client the longest, and I know what's best because I know everything about ORI inside and out."

  You: "Okay, what would happen if we were to put that same plan into action? Let's project all possible outcomes."

Variation: One-Upper

In their hunger for attention, One-Uppers love upstaging the achievements of others, discounting their contributions or value by brazenly remarking, "Oh, that's nothing!" and then describing how their experience was better, faster, slicker, more powerful, or more efficient, in a nothing-surpasses-it way. Acknowledge their remarks, then move back to the more pressing issues of the moment.

Monopolizer Maniacs

Some people absolutely adore basking in the limelight by hogging the conversation and the floor. In the extreme, Monopolizer Maniacs are control freaks and seize control through their vocal chords. This prickly behavior is like playing verbal monopoly; it's a bored game for sure because they're all talk with little ability to listen.

When they're dominating a situation, take back control. More manageable Monopolizer Maniacs may relinquish the floor, if you break into their monologue with a specific question or wait for an appropriate pause. Acknowledge their comments; then, redirect the discussion. In a group setting, immediately turn your attention to someone else and ask for their insights:

- *That's a very interesting way of looking at it. Now, I'd like to hear (Other Person's) thoughts on the situation.*

- *We're here today to make some important decisions. While (Monopolizer) has shared some unique insights with us, let's get back to discussing ...*

Monopolizer Maniacs constantly seek attention by making frequent interruptions, all for grandstanding in their favorite style. They may butt into the middle of your thoughts or into a sentence. Tell them politely that you're not finished talking and would like to finish. Use their name followed by "I'm not through yet," and continue or try another variation such as "(Name), you interrupted me. I was saying ... " Each time you're interrupted, stop and repeat the same message, using a little louder voice so they hear you loud and clear. When you're alone with the Monopolizer, if they can't stop interrupting, excuse yourself so they're unable to play their favorite interrupting game, at least with you.

Slugs

While many variations of Prickly People are aggressive in nature, those who move at a snail-like speed can be equally irritating; they're just not as intense, vocal, or abusive. Like the slow-moving garden pest, Slugs plod along sluggishly. Fear keeps them moving at a snail's pace. Their prickles come in the form of passivity. Their inertia is the bane of those with big goals and plenty of initiative, because Slugs poke holes in progress with their pokey behavior! They are experts at putting the "pro" in "procrastinate."

They fear making decisions and expect you to take action and just work around them. Slugs don't want to be blamed for any failure or mistake; they need to be prodded along and encouraged to exhibit personal responsibility.

To activate some accountability, ask them if you can help them reach a decision or assist them in some way. Hold them accountable by getting their commitments for deadlines, and follow up with them as the deadline nears.

If they say "yes," make sure they mean it. They're known to give false hopes and disappoint trusting souls. If they've let you down in the past, explain to them that based on your past experience, you need to be certain they'll meet their responsibilities.

Tips for Handling Slugs

Prod Slugs with questions to get them moving in the desired direction and make sure they get to the finish line:

- *Would you like my help to get this in process?*
- *When can I expect this to be completed?*
- *Does 'yes' really mean 'yes'?*

Volcanoes

They are abrasive, loud, demanding, impatient, confrontational, and lousy listeners in their volcanic mode. They rant, rave, overreact, and spew lava-like language—hot and stinging. Volcanoes are aggressive by nature and take charge of situations by force. They typically target those who don't know how to manage their eruptive, aggressive behavior. Seeing this as weak, they pounce on and pound those they perceive as easy marks to exploit.

Tips for Handling Volcanoes When They're Hot, Hot, Hot!

- Don't laugh or criticize them (unless you want to see Mt. Vesuvius spew some volcanic verbiage!).

- Appear strong, firm, and calm. Fake it if you must. Your strength with them lies in showing that you're strong and you mean business. Avoid mirroring their out-of-control behavior. Respond with a centering statement: "I'm ready to talk about solutions as soon as you are."

- Let them know you disapprove of their aggressive behavior.

- Use "you" statements rather than "I" statements. They see "I" statements as your problem and will throw them back in your face. "You" statements make them accountable for their behavior.

- Address their concerns directly and ask for specifics:

  Volcano: "I can't believe this! What type of operation are you running? Is everyone in your department that incompetent? I just received a report from the home office and I demand some answers!"

  You: "Give me some specifics about exactly what's in that report and what it says about our department."

- Steer conversation toward solutions rather than letting the Volcano continue ranting:

  You: "This situation has obviously taken us all by surprise. Let's put our energy toward focusing on how we can work to correct it."

- Project an authoritative, powerful voice. When the Volcano screams, respond in a lower tone to bring down the decibel level.

- Let them run out of steam (or their volcanic lava) and regain some self-control. They won't hear anything you say until they do. Leave them alone if they continue to dish out abuse.

- Use their name at the beginning of a statement or when you want to take control. Repeat their name until you get their attention.

  As with Monopolizers, stop Volcanos from interrupting by using their name first followed by a statement such as "I'm not through yet," then continue speaking. Or try another variation such as "(Name), you interrupted me. I was saying... " or "Please hear me out with the same courtesy I've given you." Each time you're interrupted, stop and repeat the same message, turning up the volume so they hear you loud and clear.

- Ask questions that direct the discussion and show you're willing to talk and not interested in having a shouting match. Asking questions shifts the discussion away from blaming, raging, and other unproductive activity to one of seeking solutions.

- Look for common ground—literally. If you're sitting and the Volcano is standing, stand up. A person standing is perceived to be more dominant and conveys a more powerful body position than someone who is seated. Because sitting is less intimidating, you may want to invite the person to have a seat, as long as you sit, too. Either way, sit or stand at the same eye level so you have a better chance of literally seeing eye to eye and not have the person making a power move on you.

- When they're more able to listen, offer an evaluation of what's needed for handling the situation. Grab their attention with a positioning statement that demonstrates a solution:

  Volcano: "I can't tell you how shocked I am to see these sales figures. What an outrage! Here I thought you were on board with the company's new goals. Obviously, I was wrong. What in the world have you been doing?

  You: "(Name), this is what I plan to do to turn this around. "

THAR' HE BLOWS!

Years ago, I had on-the-job training for putting my people skills to the test when I took a position as Vice President of Marketing with a national trade association. After joining the staff, I realized that my boss had a volcanic nature; I couldn't help waiting for his inevitable spewing, even though I was uncertain when he might erupt.

A few weeks after coming on board, while I was presenting a staff briefing about some of my marketing ideas, my boss yelled, "That's ridiculous, that will never work!" While I wasn't totally surprised by his reaction, it was still unsettling and I responded to him saying, "I'm sorry you feel that way. What exactly do you find unworkable?"

He had an immediate knee-jerk reaction, dismissing and discounting the value of my recommendations rather than analyzing their merit. Even worse, my ideas would have helped to revitalize the organization and increase membership, which was bound to suffer without some fresh ideas.

Feeling strongly about the value of my suggestions, as well as the need to reduce the tension between us, I knew it was critical to clear the air. After the meeting, I knocked on my boss's door, asking if he had a few minutes to talk. I related my experience to him: "I was upset about how I was treated at the staff meeting today. Is there something I said or did that offended you?" I continued stating that my intention was to do my best for the association and offered some fresh ideas to increase membership. He saw my enthusiasm and sincerity and we talked about what would work better for both of us in the future. We decided to meet in advance of staff meetings to discuss new marketing ideas so he wouldn't be surprised.

Going head-to-head at the staff meeting would have jeopardized our working relationship. By meeting with him later to calmly discuss my concerns, as well as restore a tenuous connection, we were able to outline mutually agreeable ways to work together productively. —A.S.

- If the Volcano erupts on the phone, don't hang up. Calmly state, "(Name), I need to hang up right now and will call you back later." This will provide a cool-down period and protect you from the verbal volcanic ash spewing your way.

- Avoid accepting chronic apologies for their outbursts (if they have the courtesy to apologize). Suggest a meeting to discuss the negative impact of their behavior and obtain their commitment to end it: "I'd like to arrange a time for us to explore ways we can communicate better and work together with less stress."

ARE YOU A THORN STUCK IN THE PRICKLY PATCH?

If any of these prickly behaviors seem to describe you, make a commitment to stop them. They're neither serving you nor your reputation, nor are they creating quality connections. People won't respect or trust you if you continue to resort to these tactics. They needlessly ruin caring connections—vital for yourself, your loved ones, your colleagues, and others, as well as essential for your own health, well-being, success, and happiness. If you find yourself unable to put an end to your destructive behavior, seek professional support. Thorns hurt and you're also hurting your own chances for enjoying mutually satisfying relationships. Make every effort to get out of the Patch for good, for your own good.

Endurance Tests

The word "enduring" takes on new meaning when dealing with prickly behavior. Throughout this book, we've defined the word as "long-lasting and permanent," which is, of course, a much-desired characteristic of quality connections.

A second definition conjures up a different context, that of "long-suffering, to put up, tolerate, to bear pain." Relationships involving perennially prickly behaviors can indeed be all of these and more. They become endurance tests that beg the questions, "How long will I be able to put up with this? How long can I go on? How much longer will this last? Will he ever stop? Why must she always be so difficult? What can I do to protect myself against rude, irritating, or cruel behavior?"

Prickly People do indeed test us. Our stamina. Our ability to maintain self-control. Our effectiveness in managing their difficult behavior. Our confusion about whether to confront an unpleasant interaction or just let it go. Our decision not to let their behavior control our own.

Remember that you always have a choice regarding what you think and do when people don't treat you the way you want to be treated, or do what you want them to do. The best way to deal with difficult situations is to manage your reactions, and use assertive strategies to handle Pricklies with as much care and compassion as possible.

Recognize your feelings of irritation, annoyance, and anger as signals for dealing with challenging situations and the people who cause them. Don't hold others responsible for your reactions. Shift your thoughts away from blame and toward solutions. Dwell on the possibilities for creating a more cooperative environment rather than condemning the problems you face. Warning: the prickly behavior of others can provoke prickly behavior in us; keep a tight rein on your responses so they don't perpetuate or intensify prickly interactions.

SHIFT HAPPENS

Shift focus…

To see those who are difficult to deal with, as those who may be dealing with many difficulties.

To see those who do not smile, as those likely in need of one.

To see those who are in your face, as those who really want to have your ear.

To see those who have hurt you, as those who also hurt, often for reasons you cannot see.

To see those whose ideas cause conflict, as those whose different perspectives may offer perfect solutions.

To see those who upset you, as those who serve as the perfect teachers for opening your heart.

To see those with a strong need to be right, as those who have a strong need to feel validated.

To see those who hold grudges, as those who are choosing to invest their energy in hanging on rather than letting go; closed hearts cannot give or receive their intended gifts.

To see the desire for connection, even when the possibility appears remote.

To see how a hostile situation plagued with disconnection might be transformed into an opportunity for coming together.

To see eye-to-eye, rather than an eye for an eye. When not seeing eye-to-eye, to seeing heart-to-heart.

To see that you either choose to connect or choose something else; your actions either result in connection, or something else.

When you shift your focus, you enter interactions with a new perspective; this powerfully transforms difficult dynamics and makes a world of difference in how you respond and the experiences you create for yourself and others. It all depends on what you choose.

Life presents us with continuing opportunities to look beyond appearances. Remember that underneath that prickly armor is a person who wants the same things you want, but who is unable to secure them diplomatically, thoughtfully, with sensitivity, or in an empowered manner. Although their shield of prickles is a poor form of protection for their inadequacies, their coping mechanisms will continue challenging their connections as long as they keep on using them.

Prickly People constantly challenge us to keep our hearts open when they'd rather close, to seek understanding when we wish they would change, and to forgive them for the anguish and distress they cause. You may not think you're meeting the challenge, but if you're doing whatever you can to maintain your self-respect and honor legitimate needs, you are. You are passing the test.

Keep on Connecting!

"Happiness is when what you think, what you say, and what you do are in harmony."

Mahatma Gandhi

So there you have it—eight keys for creating enduring connections. Building successful, well-tended relationships is a crucial component for manifesting abundance, whether in the form of fortunes, friendships, family connectedness, or other personal treasures. Getting along skillfully with people colors your world with a vibrant network of connections, enriching your relationships with a never-ending collection of infinite rewards.

Cultivating enduring connections requires an unyielding commitment as a Conscious Connector in every interaction. The investment of your time, energy, and effort in doing so produces a priceless legacy—a combination of how well and how often you've listened, encouraged, and supported others; empowered them to express their best; recognized and appreciated their gifts, talents, and contributions; respected their feelings and honored their ideas and opinions; preserved their trust by keeping promises; acted with integrity; and valued them so they know their well-being is your priority.

Keep a vigilant eye on the quality of your connections, because the quality of your total life experience is directly linked to that network. Regularly assess your determination to infuse an enduring value into your relationships to make them thrive and flourish:

- Are you making good connections a daily priority?

- Do your words and actions usually prompt positive responses from others?

- When problems arise, do you seek solutions that hold the greatest possibility of satisfying mutual needs?

- Do you claim your fair share of mistakes, misunderstandings, or other misbehaviors and seek to repair them?

- Do you constantly monitor what's important to people in every arena of your influence and explore ways to honor those needs?

- Can people count on you? Do you keep your promises?

- Does every member of your family know how much you care and value them? If yes, how do you know for certain? If you're not sure, what might you do to demonstrate how much each family member is valued, appreciated, and treasured?

- Do your business associates, friends, and others realize how much you appreciate their talents, friendship, support, and investment of their personal energy? What are some ways you might acknowledge how much you value them and their contributions?

- Have you experienced a "falling out" with someone, resulting in unfinished business? If so, what might you do to repair, heal, or restore it?

- Are you holding a grudge or resentment toward anyone? If so, how is it serving your best interests? How long do you want to stay connected to that experience? What conditions make it difficult to forgive those involved and let it go?

- Is there any relationship that's not working as well as you'd like? What might you do to improve it?

- Do you have a special way of adding your personal signature of uniqueness to your working relationships—special things you do to create good feelings with your colleagues and customers? If not, how might you add your own special signature for creating an enduring impression? What might further fortify your unforgettable nature that reinforces your values?

- What legacies are you creating in your personal relationships that reflect and reinforce your character and your values? How do you want people to think of you, and are your actions supporting that perception?

Enduring connections are active in nature. They require the right actions and attitudes to make them last and withstand the forces that might break them apart—negative self-talk that can steer them off-course, judgments that can obstruct or sever the connections we desire, and negativity that blocks the expression of our personal best.

Even when it's difficult to do so, extend to others what you wish to receive and relish in your relationships. When people are unreasonable, judgmental, self-centered, irrational, or treat you carelessly, recklessly, thoughtlessly, or in any way that is less than you desire, remember your power of choice—to choose whether your words and actions are likely to generate experiences and outcomes with positive impact.

For relationships to last through thick and thin, tough times and turbulence, and all the moments that test our patience and perseverance along the way, we must guide each one with the wisdom of the heart. Enduring connections are actively cultivated; lethargy is lethal to them.

The Active Ingredients of Enduring Connections

Make people your passion

Be a Conscious Connector in building positive relationships

Boost good feelings in others

Communicate with care

Engage the interest of others by focusing on what interests them

Approach each interaction with positive intent

Take the initiative to reach out to others first

Project a positive presence

Be attentive

Express empathy

Build trust; mean what you say, and say what you mean

Adapt how you communicate to best serve what others need

Act in ways that make people feel valued

Give feedback tactfully and receive it willingly

Create a sense of safety and openness

Mend misunderstandings

Keep an open mind

Seek to understand how others see a situation

Acknowledge and honor the feelings of others

Monitor and master your emotions

Hear people out

Drop any need to "be right"

Let go of grudges

Manage difficult interactions with effective strategies

Greet people with a smile

Open your heart when it closes

Seek peace when others don't

Be responsive to what others want or need

Respect differences

Let words of caring and kindness work their magic

Don't take anyone for granted

Thank people for their help, their time, their service, their thoughtfulness, their caring, and their support

Act as a catalyst to help others get what they want

Praise positive behaviors

Energize the winning spirit

Make the right choices to create the desired outcomes

Give people credit for their ideas

Express a dazzling attitude, even when it's difficult

Resolve conflicts with diplomacy

Build bridges that join; remove walls that separate

Release negative labels (of yourself and others)

Speak your truth

Accept responsibility; avoid playing the blame game

Forgive others (and yourself) for flubs, faux pas, and foibles

Light the way with laughter

Project a cooperative spirit

Express enthusiasm

Encourage the expression of gifts, talents, and personal excellence

Model the behaviors you want others to express

Handle every connection with care and keep them in good repair

Enduring connections are fostered by giving people what they desire most from their experiences with us and what we want as well. These flourish best in harmony with HEART wisdom, which whisks us faster into the Connection Zone and keeps us there:

To be **H**eard, offer a listening, compassionate ear

To be **E**ncouraged, extend support and optimism

To be **A**ppreciated, express gratitude and an attitude of caring

To be **R**espected, act with honor and personal excellence

To be **T**rusted, build and preserve a reputation of integrity

We hope you'll take to heart the people-connecting attitudes and actions we've shared for crafting positive, powerful, and productive relationships in every realm of your connections. We wish you much happiness, harmony, and success in creating a legacy of enduring connections and a lifetime of getting along. Happy connecting!

> *"To put the world right in order, we must first put the nation in order, to put the nation in order, we must first put the family in order, to put the family in order, we must first cultivate our personal life; we must first set our hearts right."*
>
> Confucius

The Magic of Connection

A beaming smile
An encouraging word
A gesture of appreciation
These are such simple gifts
for making enduring connections.

Choose to listen with open ears,
An open heart and mind
And you will gain the best from others
For being the caring kind.

Make a habit to value others
For all they are and do.
This creates golden connections
That shine right back on you.

Connection magic simply grows
From all you say and do
Because expressing your best
Very simply reveals
The connection champion in you!

About the Authors

Arnold Sanow

Arnold Sanow focuses on developing strategies for attracting customers, keeping them, and getting enthusiastic referrals. He is the author of Marketing Boot Camp, Entrepreneur Boot Camp, Nobody to Somebody in 63 Days or Less, You Can Start Your Own Business, and Speaking for Dollars.

Arnold has written more than 200 articles, writes a biweekly Internet newsletter, is quoted in publications including USA Today, Time, and the Wall Street Journal, and periodically appears on radio and television programs including CBS Evening News with Dan Rather, WorldNet, Financial News Network, Business Radio Network, and CNN.

Arnold has delivered more than 2,500 presentations and holds the prestigious designation of Certified Speaking Professional, an honor awarded to fewer than 300 people in the world. He speaks on topics such as marketing, communication, and customer service to companies and organizations worldwide. He has served as a national spokesperson for AT&T and Intuit and is an adjunct professor at Georgetown University. Arnold holds an MBA from Southeastern University in Washington, D.C.

For more information about his presentations, programs, or materials contact Arnold@arnoldsanow.com, or visit www.ArnoldSanow.com, or www.GetAlongWithAnyone.com.

Sandra Strauss

Sandra Strauss is a communications strategist who helps people to communicate, cooperate, and connect for building positive, powerful, and productive relationships. Sandy has promoted everything from appliances to zucchini and brings her expertise in image positioning and product promotion to her communications programs.

Her work focuses on how to best position individuals and organizations for quality connections in all their circles of influence. She presents programs highlighting the attitudes and actions that bring out the best in people and their performance for corporations, associations, nonprofits, government agencies, and youth organizations.

Sandy is the founder of Success Champions℠, interactive seminars designed to energize excellence, and is the author of Building a Successful Life, a training manual for teaching the habits of success to teens and adults. She also publishes the Success Champions℠ electronic newsletter featuring the attitudes and actions of excellence.

For more information about her presentations, programs, and training materials, contact success@SandraStrauss.com, or visit www.SandraStrauss.com, or www.GetAlongWithAnyone.com.

Also by Sanow and Strauss: *Charisma Cards—50 Irresistible Ways to Energize Your Personal Magnetism*, designed to activate enduring connections.

Bibliography and Recommended Reading

Alessandra, Tony, Ph.D.
Charisma. Warner Books, New York, NY, 1998.

Axtell, Roger E. Gestures:
The Do's and Taboos of Body Language Around the World.
John Wiley & Sons, Inc., New York, NY, 1998.

Baber, Anne and Lynne Waymon.
**Great Connections—Small Talk and Networking for
Businesspeople,** Impact Publications, Manassas Park, VA, 1992.

Bolton, Robert, Ph.D.
People Skills. Simon & Schuster, New York, NY, 1979.

Boothman, Nicholas.
How to Make People Like You in 90 Seconds or Less.
Workman Publishing, New York, NY, 2000.

Charlesworth, Edward A., Ph.D. and Ronald G. Nathan, Ph.D.
Stress Management. Ballantine Books, New York, NY, 1984.

Crowe, Sandra. A., MA.
Since Strangling Isn't an Option.
The Berkley Publishing Group, New York, NY, 1997.

Crum, Thomas F.
The Magic of Conflict. Simon & Schuster, Inc., New York, NY, 1987.

Dimitrius, Jo-Ellan, Ph.D.
Reading People. Random House, New York, NY, 1998.

DuBrin, Andrew.
Personal Magnetism.
AMACOM, American Management Association, New York, NY, 1997.

Elgin, Suzette Haden, PhD.
The Gentle Art of Verbal Self-Defense at Work.
Prentice-Hall Press, Paramus, NJ, 2000.

Fishbein, Martin and Icek Ajzen.
Belief, Attitude, Intention, and Behavior.
Addison-Wesley Publishing, Co., 1975.

Gabor, Don.
Speaking Your Mind in 101 Difficult Situations.
Fireside Books, New York, NY, 1994.

Gabor, Don.
Talking with Confidence for the Painfully Shy.
Three Rivers Press, New York, NY, 1997.

Glass, Lillian, Ph.D.
The Complete Idiot's Guide to Verbal Self-Defense.
Alpha Books, New York, NY, 1999.

Gray, John, Ph.D.
Mars and Venus in the Workplace.
HarperCollins Publishers, New York, NY, 2002.

Helmstetter, Shad.
Choices. Pocket Books, New York, NY, 1989.

Horn, Sam.
Tongue Fu! How to Deflect, Disarm, and Defuse any Verbal Conflict. St. Martin's Press, New York, NY, 1996.

Horn, Sam.
Take the Bully by the Horns.
St. Martin's Press, New York, NY, 2002.

Kummerow, Jean M.; Nancy J. Barger; and Linda K. Kirby.
Work Types. Warner Books, New York, NY, 1997.

Lavington, Camille.
You've Only Got Three Seconds. Doubleday, New York, NY, 1997.

McKay, Matthew, Ph.D. and Patrick Fannino.
Self-Esteem. St. Martin's Books, New York, NY, 1987.

McKay, Matthew, Ph.D.; Peter D. Rogers, Ph.D.; and Judith McKay, R.N. When
Anger Hurts: Quieting the Storm Within.
New Harbinger Publications, Oakland, CA, 1989.

Namie, Gary, Ph.D. and Ruth Namie, Ph.D.
The Bully at Work: What You Can Do to Stop the Hurt and Reclaim Your Dignity on the Job. Sourcebooks, 2000.

Phillips, Bob.
The Delicate Art of Dancing with Porcupines,
GL Regal Books, Ventura, CA, 1989.

Reardon, Kathleen Kelley, Ph.D.
They Don't Get It, Do They? Little, Brown and Company, Boston, MA; New York, NY; and Toronto, Canada, 1993.

Shafir, Rebecca Z., MA.
The Zen of Listening.
The Theosophical Publishing House, Wheaton, IL 2000.

Simmons, Gary.
The I of the Storm. Unity House, Unity Village, MO, 2001.

Swets, Paul W.
The Art of Talking So That People Will Listen.
Prentice-Hall, Englewood Cliffs, NJ, 1983.

Trout, Susan S, Ph.D.
To See Differently. Three Roses Press, Washington, DC, 1990.

Wainwright, Gordon R.
Body Language. NTC Contemporary Publishing, Chicago, IL, 1999.

Weisinger, Hendrie, Ph.D.
Emotional Intelligence at Work.
Jossey-Bass Publishers, San Francisco, CA, 1998.

Printed in the United States
211527BV00003B/2/A

9 781600 372193